SOULS

— *from* —

MERCURY

Raju Ramanathan

ISBN: 978-1-64314-595-2 (Paperback)
       978-1-64314-596-9 (Hardback)
       978-1-64314-594-5 (Ebook)

Readers with any illness should not take any action or inaction solely on the contents of this publication. Keep in mind that no book can replace the diagnostic expertise of a trusted physician who is familiar with your situation.

AuthorsPress
California, USA
www.authorspress.com

Contents

· · · · · · · · · · · · · · · ·

What do "The Souls from Mercury" really
look like?

The connection between Mars, Venus,
and Mercury

Mercury and Earth-based spirituality

What are chakras?

How are chakras related to becoming Souls
from Mercury?

Where are the chakras located?

What is the difference between higher and
lower chakras?

Is there a difference between the ways we
awaken the higher and lower chakras?

What happens when the chakras come to
bloom and blossom?

How do I know if I am transcending one
chakra and moving onto the next?

Can we measure chakras and their status
scientifically?

What is the link between chakras and the five
elements in nature?

Is there any connection between chakras
and colors?

Is it possible to use colors during meditation?

Can you give more tools on healing, colors,
and light?

Can we use sounds to awaken and work with
the chakras?

What is the connection between musical
instruments and chakras?

Can you give some examples of musical
masterpieces that one can use for their spiritual
development?

Chakras and Spirituality

What is the connection between chakras and
spirituality?

What lifestyle preparations are required before
seriously practicing chakra purification and
awakening?

Were great Masters aware of chakras?

What is the connection between breathing
and chakras?

How does a Soul from Mercury view money,
wealth, and abundance?

Ancient Wisdom About the Eight
Forms of Wealth

Daily Gratitude Exercise for Abundance

Answer the following questions and abundance
will come your way:

Exercise to do a self-evaluation on abundance:

Why do so many people get stuck in this
unconscious state?

How does a Soul from Mercury manage
sexual energy?

When does transformation and transmutation
of sexual energies begin to shift into love?

What is the difference between the love of an
ordinary human being and Soul from Mercury?

Does it mean that when you break one
commandment you break all of them?

Can you bring purity into the body?

What is a meditation process by which the
sexual energy is transformed?

How is sex energy related to other energies
such as anger?

Are we violating the law of nature by ignoring
the sexual force?

What is the connection between love
and prayer?

Are there levels of love center as well?

Can you explain the difference between
emotions and feelings if any? Is there a creative
way to deal with them?

Can you tell us a practical way how we can
recover soon when someone pushes our
hot button?

How do you personally develop self-love and
become a master at it?

How do you develop spiritual relationship?
What is the connection between normal and
spiritual relationships?

What is the easy way to be happy and
live in love?

How do you deal with fear and guilt?

Can meditation help with suicidal thoughts
and feelings?

What solutions can you offer to someone
feeling suicidal?

The Opposite of Depression is Expression

What do you think is the perfect relationship?

How can we always have fun in our
relationships?

How do you live in love?

What guidance have you received from the
scriptures regarding living in love?

Section 1- Religion and Spirituality

What is the connection between religion and
spirituality?

How can we develop our religiousness as a Soul
from Mercury?

What are the outer signs of someone reaching
perfections in spirituality and religiousness?

Can you elaborate on the uniqueness of your
purification process?

Section 2- Purification Process

What is the speciality of your breathing
techniques?

How do you work with your breath?

Why are some people so afraid to meditate?

What is unique about your system of
meditation?

Can you give us some tips for deeper
meditation?

Why do you never give any instructions on
meditation initially?

Section 1 - The Ten Commandments

Can you elaborate on the psychological
importance of the Ten Commandments?

Who is the God in reference and who are the
other Gods?

How did the other scriptures make reference to
this important commandment?

What was the meaning behind the word graven
images or icons used in the Bible?

Do the graven images or icons spoken in the
commandment have any relevance in the
Kingdom of God?

Why do the Hindus make images and
worship them?

Can you elaborate on the psychological
importance of the name of the Lord?

Can the Sabbath day be any day of the week?

What else can we do to deepen the practice and
discipline of the Sabbath day?

Why does this commandment refer only to
the parents?

Can you explain how this is referred in other
traditions?

How does it refer to the two sides of our
personality?

Is it possible to have no violence in us so that we fulfill this commandment always?

Will there not be some violence in connection with the body?

Tell us some deeper levels where killing and violence goes on in a human being?

How do you interpret the commandment thou shall not commit adultery in the Bible?

What does it mean to be a right witness then?

Will following all the commandments enlighten someone?

Prayer: Souls from Mercury Talking to God

How are the chakras related to the Lord's Prayer in the Bible?

Meditation: Souls from Mercury Listening to God

Is total silence needed to experience deep meditation?

How do you attain authentic silence?

How can we meditate better or become a Soul from Mercury?

Why is a Master or a teacher so important?

How does meditation provide healing or prevention from diseases?

What is the source of tension in human beings?

How do you as a teacher manage to remain without tension and joyous all the time?

In any spiritual practice, what is the highest level?

Is it not necessary to be a monk and renunciate to practice meditation?

What is in short the Samadhi meditation that you teach?

What is enlightenment in its essence?

From your teachings, sometimes I feel that you are against knowledge?

Are you against the mind and mental powers?

What is the master key to deepen our meditation practice?

What is the difference between thought and consciousness?

What is the main reason that we are not able to get to the state of true meditation?

Please explain your polarity meditation?

Is there a connection between meditation and the sound "OM?"

How do you bring the meditative awareness into daily life?

Can the thoughts be a creative force as well?

Does prayer have a place in meditation?

Does meditation help you to become a leader, a man from Mercury?

Can you explain the inner self and the outer self, the terms you often use?

In what sense do you use the word "God?"

What do you see as the future for mankind?

Conclusion

This book is dedicated at the feet of Sri Sri
Sri Ganapathy Sacchidananda of Avadhiootha
Dattapeetham, Mysore, India.

Acknowledgements

· · · · · · · · · · · · · · · ·

I bow down in boundless gratitude to the Creator of this beautiful world, solar system, and the universe who is the intelligence behind all that exists.

I bow down to the cosmic energy that gave rise to the sun, moon, stars, and all of nature. I bow down to Cosmic Consciousness who manifests as "Souls from Mercury."

I bow down to all the five elements and the resulting five types of life force and vital airs in me without which I will not be here.

I bow down to all my ancestors and parents (my first Gurus) who blessed me with this healthy body and who gave me beautiful DNA and "samskaras" (i.e., good aptitudes) to be proud of.

I bow down in love and reverence to all the spiritual masters (whom I refer to as "Souls from Mercury" herein) from the past, present, and future on whose shoulders I stood and spoke or wrote these words contained within this book. Special mention should be made to His Holiness Sri Sri Ganapathy Sachchidananda of Avadhootha Datta Peetham in Mysore, India, who as the Adi Guru Dattatreya, embodies all other teachers and Masters whose names are numerous. (I better not start this list or I will never finish).

I am so grateful to all my family, relatives, and friends who contributed with commitment and continue to help me in my physical, mental, and spiritual life.

I am also grateful to all the people that lived, are living, and will live in the future for whose needs this book was created. Special mention should be made to my dearest son Arvind Bharathi and his wife Tagrid Akl. They were the ones who requested that I summarize and share what I have been teaching all these years. Kudos to my son and his beautiful wife who contributed all the photographs—captured by them during their globe-trotting over the years— seen in this book.

I am grateful to Jack Pauley who wrote down my speeches in the nineties, Mona Nivose who compiled and edited them in the last decade, and Christina Theophilos who reviewed and commented on my work during the final review. This book would not have seen the light of day without their initiatives, drive, and even sometimes, the courage to push me to its completion.

Last but not least, I would like to thank all my students and my teachers (those out of the millions) which I divide into three categories: Those who taught me 1) what to do, what not to do, 2) what qualities to have and not have, 3) and what to be and not to be. Without these friends, I would not be what I am today.

And to the readers who are still my students, I say to you "Feel and Grow Rich," contrary to what Napoleon Hill said, "Think and Grow Rich."

About The Author

· · · · · · · · · · · · · · · · ·

Mr. Raju Ramanathan, also known as Datta Yogi Raja, is a scientist of both the *inner* and the *outer* worlds. He is sought after by major corporations to be their pioneer and champion for continuous improvements, and sought after by individuals in great positions of authority to be their *life coach*.

At the age of thirteen, Mr. Datta Yogi Raja started teaching meditation to his school teachers and priest in his native village in India, near Kanya Kumari. While in college, he began teaching mediation, under the guidance of Swami Chinmayananda and Sivananda, to his fellow students in engineering and in other temples and spiritual communities. After completing his doctoral work in Space Sciences, Raju came to work for the major space contractor for NASA, Rockwell and Honeywell, and continued sharing his passion for meditation to those in the corporate world. Honeywell noted Raju as their "teacher, mentor, and guru with cherished friendships across many of their companies."

For more than twenty years, Mr. Yogi Raja has been empowering seekers in Europe, Asia, USA, and Canada. His unique approach brings life transforming spiritual message to people of all religious paths and cultural backgrounds. Mr. Yogi Raja re-introduces the lessons of ancient masters to the Western modern community. All those who are concerned about the well being of today's world will find Mr. Yogi Raja's teachings enlightening and inspirational. Each seminar or a retreat with this highly educated and very articulate Master is a truly unique experience. Whether it is your first, or one hundred and first encounter with Mr. Yogi Raja, whether you are just a beginner, or an experienced yoga practitioner, each time you will find a new insight to meditation, and your understanding of Yoga will deepen.

Mr. Ganapathi Sachidananda Swamijiof Mysore Datta Peetham gave initiation to Raju Ramanathan in the year 2002 during the Datta Jayanti in Mysore and renamed him as Datta Yogi Raja. Mr. Datta Yogi Raja recently visited India twice to study the operation of a 90-bed hospital using music therapy established in Mysore, India by Mr. Swami mentioned above. Mr. Datta Yogi Raja has given several radio and TV programs in Canada on these subjects.

Mr. Datta Yogi Raja hails from the family of famous South Indian poet Subramania Bharathi, a great friend of Mr. Aurobindo. Mr. Datta Yogi Raja has learned to uniquely synthesize science and religion and unite the extrovert and the introvert.

Mr. Datta Yogi Raja has spent the last thirty years teaching and coaching professionals in the art and science of relaxation using new ways of breathing and meditating with music in the advanced retreats that he conducts. Many participants have reported the healing effects of this approach. The unique approach of Mr. Datta Yogi Raja has been his lucid style of explanation that appeals to the modern scientific community.

Many psychiatrists and doctors have learned advanced relaxation techniques. Recent lectures include the ones delivered to 100 doctors of the Indian Medical Association in Chicago, 100 doctors of Southern Illinois School of Medicine in Springfield, IL, and the Psychology Department of University of Chicago to name a few. He has also given talks to hundreds of doctors to create awareness of cures for chronic diseases, like cancer. Mr. Datta Yogi Raja is also a certified yoga teacher from Yoga Bliss Institute, and trained by Dr. Madan Bali, who is recognized for his contributions to complementary medicine.

Further Contribution to the Business World:

- Mr. Datta Yogi Raja was the first one to come up with an ECG Amplifier designed for the Indian Market.

- Mr. Datta Yogi Raja was part of the Canadian team that introduced the first X-ray machine that today uses a hundredth of radiation dosage used twenty-five years ago.

- Mr. Datta Yogi Raja has assisted in the early development of the first ISO 9001 series of quality standards and still works with the US advisory group.

- Mr. Datta Yogi Raja was part of the Montreal Protocol that eliminated the production of Halon gas for fire protection, which damages the ozone layer.

- Mr. Datta Yogi Raja served in the fire protection industry since 1989, and retired in 2014 in order to teach yoga and meditation on a full time basis to students of all ages.

To find out more about Mr. Datta Yogi Raja, please visit his website: www. dattayogiraja.com

My Voyage Through Life in a Nutshell

. . . .

I was born during the tenth precious day of the sacred Navarathri ten-day festival in India known as "Vijaya Dashami" (meaning victory to Divine Mother). This happens in the month of October and celebrated all over India. There was already one older sister in the family by the name of Sita who is a great musician, has sung as a Class A artist in All India Radio and lives in India. My parents performed many spiritual rituals in order to be blessed with the birth of a great divine soul in their family, and when the baby boy was born the entire family rejoiced. My parents gave me the name Raja Ram and later added my grandfather's name Ramanathan, which means "Guru of Lord Ram." that is Lord Shiva himself. But everyone in the village of Krishnapuram called the new baby Raja Ram from which "Raju" is derived. Krishnapuram is a village near the Tirunelveli district, in Tamilnadu, South India. This is in the Kanyakumari or Cap Comorin area.

My father, Anantha Subramanian, and my mother, Lakshmi, were a very religious couple. My father went on a pilgrimage to a famous place in Ceylon—present day Sri-Lanka—to pray for a child of divine merits. During this time, he visited the temple of Lord Shanmuga or Subramania in a place called Kathirkamam in Sri Lanka where a miracle happened. The chief priest working at the temple experienced a spiritual vision of the Lord. He heard in his dream the commandment from the Lord that the special Vel ornament in his hand should be given to this person with the name Subramanian who has come from Tamil Nadu, the land of sage Agastya. He added that his prayers would be answered. Ten months after the father visited this shrine of Lord Shanmuga, the baby was born. It is to be mentioned that the Mahavatar Babaji of the Himalayas was born in the same town before he left for Himalayas. My parents consulted the famous Nadi astrology scriptures and learned that I was a disciple of Mahavatar in the last birth and lived with him in the same town. For the parents, it was a blessing, and his arrival brought great happiness to their lives. My grandparents and my father's sister, Subbu-Lakshmi, brought me up. My grandparents were strict disciplinarians and when they were too hard on me, my auntie was always my savior.

Here is what my father wrote about me:

"My son was very affectionate towards my parents and the villagers. As a student, he was a very bright boy. He always ranked first in the class and was the teacher's favorite. He was very popular among his classmates due to his soft, humble, kind, and gentle nature, which touched the hearts of his comrades. He earned the Presidency Merit Scholarship to pursue higher studies. When Raju was a child, I discerned in my boy the seeds of greatness. When he was a student, he foresaw a period of upheaval and revolutionary change, and believed that he was destined to play a part in it. For this he started a movement called SAIGAGIA that means "see all in God and God in all."

To his fellow students, he was a friend, helper, teacher, and guide. At a young age, his consciousness awakened to the call from the Lord which encouraged him to spread love in the mortal world, bringing peace and happiness. He was a voracious reader. As a teen, he was able to obtain books from Somalia University in Hyderabad. He read books of all kinds but always had a particular interest in spiritual books. His other favorite interests were yoga, pooja, and playing chess.

When it comes to food, he is partial to South Indian cuisine such as Idly, Dhal, rice, and vegetable Curry dishes. He rejected roasted and oily food. He also preferred cow's milk over buffalo's milk because he considered the former to be a purer animal (satwic).

He acquired his spiritual knowledge through long hours of study and great devotion and sadhana. This allowed him the opportunity to meet a number of great sages of India, namely: Swami Sivananda from Rishikesh, Jagadguru Shankaracharya Sri Sri Abhinava Vidya Tirtha of Sringeri, Paramacharya Jagadguru Sri Chandrasekharendra Saraswathi of Kanchi, Sri Vimarsanandanatha of Bhaskara Prakasha Ashram of Chenna,i and many other enlightened people. Sri Vidyayanandanatha of the Sringeri tradition initiated him into the practice of Sri Vidya and Sri Chakra pooja and named him: Athmanandanatha. Mr. Prabhu R. Venkatarama Iyer of Swamimalai guided him on an all aspects of Hinduism."

As a "Mercurian," I was a searcher since childhood into mysteries and could learn almost anything even without a teacher. As mentioned by my father, spirituality has been my main interest for very long time, and I started giving spiritual teachings at a very young age. Several villagers, including my grandfather, used to gather to listen to me at the age of twelve. Even back then, I was open to all faiths. I went to Hindu temples, Muslim mosques and Christian churches to listen to all the Scriptures. It was a way of preparing me to address the different audiences I would meet over the course of my future. Sometimes I wondered: "How do I know all this?" I told my grandfather that I had acquired this knowledge in a different way than simply listening to Scriptures. This aspect will be covered in another chapter.

I lived with my grandparents until the age of thirteen. After that, I joined the rest of the family in Hyderabad in the state of Andhra Pradesh now called Telangana. There, I completed my Master's Degree in Electronic Instrumentation specializing in Biomedical and Aerospace Engineering.

Growing up as a teen, I learned to uniquely synthesize Zorba the Greek and Gautam the Buddha, meaning combining one's zest for life and science with religion, thereby uniting the extrovert and the introvert. I spent the past thirty years teaching and coaching people from all walks of life in the arts and sciences of relaxation and of enlightened leadership. My unique approach is couched in my lucid style of explanation that appeals to the modern scientific community. With academic background in Biomedical Engineering, I had also carried out research in the science of the outer 'material world' that is important to us all.

Case in point, I was the first to come up with an ECG Amplifier design for the Indian market. I was also part of the Canadian team that introduced the first X-ray machine in 1975, which used a 100th of the radiation dosage for twenty-five years. I participated in the drafting of the Montreal Protocol that eliminated the production of Halon gas for protection against fire, which damages the ozone layer. Since 1989, I continued to serve in the industry of fire protection and gas sensors. In addition, I have assisted in the early development of the first ISO 9000 series of Quality Standards in 1985 and I continue to serve on the US advisory group for technical committees of ISO (International Standardization Organization).

When it comes to the field of science of the 'inner world,' my long list of accomplishments includes the following:

- I assisted Rishi Prabhakar, a disciple of Maharishi Mahesh Yogi in the teacher training for the Siddha Samadhi Yoga program that has been taught to hundreds of thousands of people in India. Examples of people who took this program include the families of some important political figures in India, and even the management teams of international corporations in India.

- I traveled in the USA, Canada, and Europe almost every month for the past twenty years to disseminate this knowledge to thousands of people. Many psychiatrists and doctors have learned advanced relaxation techniques from me. Some of my most recent lectures include ones delivered to 100 doctors of the Indian Medical Association in Chicago, 100 doctors of Southern Illinois School of Medicine in Springfield, IL, and the Psychology Department of University of Chicago and Rush Medical Center Chicago where I have given talks.

- Furthermore, my lectures have been recorded and are part of the curricula at Bangalore University, San Jose State University, and Carleton University in Canada.

- In July 2003, I went to Venezuela, South America to teach meditation techniques to a group of sixty people. Amongst the group were some highly regarded representatives of the medical field and the government as well. Similar sessions were conducted in parts of Germany, China, Korea, and Japan.

All of these achievements followed personal consultations with many influential spiritual leaders in India with their blessings. I was blessed with a special and private mantra initiation by both Sri Sathya Sai Baba and Sri Ganapathy Sachchidananda Swamiji in 1993. Sri Swamiji Ganapathi Sachidananda of Mysore, India initiated Raju and bestowed on me the title of "Datta Yogi Raja" on December 19, 2002. I have enjoyed close spiritual affection and coaching from the following spiritual leaders: Shri Chinmayanand Ji of Chinmaya mission in Bombay, Sri Sivananda of Rishikesh, Sri Rishi Prabhakar of RSVK in Bangalore, Bhagwan Rajneesh in Pune later known as Osho, Sri Sri Ravi Shankar of the Art Of Living movement, Sri Yogi Amrit Desai of Kripalu Yoga movement, Sri Guru matha Amma of Sridhara Sri Gudda in Bangalore and many others. The list is very long indeed! Their teaching has come through this work in many profound ways.

I also had personal connection with great men who started personal coaching sessions for millions of people in the west in early 70s and 80s. Examples are

Werner Ehrhardt of The EST Erhard Seminar training programs and DMA by Robert Fritz and many others.

I also lead a full personal life. I pursued a career in the field of quality standards in life safety for a major Fortune 500 corporation. I am always supported and loved by my family especially my son, Arvind, regardless of which part of the world he lives or which part of the world I live. Arvind has nicely incorporated my mission, vision, and values in his corporate life. He has taken his company working culture to such admirable level that Montreal Gazette newspaper voted his company as the best company to work for in the year 2013. In parallel to my work and family responsibilities, I continue to share my wisdom and love with whoever crosses my path anywhere in the world. I have hundreds of friends and students who love to spend time with me or have teaching sessions arranged for their families and friends especially all over North America.

My meetings with all the remarkable leaders mentioned above will be published in the future as a separate book by itself.

[1] Pooja is a religious ceremony conducted in adoration of God.

Testimonials

· · · · · · · · · · · · · · · ·

Raju Datta Yogi Raja has touched thousands of lives across the globe. Here are a few snaps from some of those who have been privileged to have their lives transformed by him.

In my opinion, Master Raju is the embodiment of love and compassion. I have come to see this through the time he has spent teaching me many life altering lessons where I learned about forgiveness, non-judgment, acceptance, and detachment. He demonstrates to all of us how to open our hearts in the most challenging trials of our lives, and come out of these experiences with tremendous growth, poise, and grace. This generates joy and peace in our entire beings, no matter what we are going through or where we all are in our respective paths or stage of evolution. - Christina Theophilos M.Ed. (President of the Glory of Education, The Glory of Yoga, and published author in the field of behavioral psychology)

On my spiritual journey, I learned from many masters and remain eternally eternal to many of them, including Raju Ji. - Sunder S. Arora M.D. (Author of *Ushering in Heaven: A Psychologist's Prescriptions for Healing, Joy, and Spiritual Awakening*)

I would say that Master Raju is a very special kind of man. He lives as we do in the world, but in a very special way! I think he reminds others and me in a very subtle way of the purpose and the importance of life. He reminds me that there is more to life than living like flies. He reminds me that it's not just about money, food, and sex, but that there is this thing called enlightenment. There are also the fundamental questions of "Who am I?" and "Who one really is?" So coming into contact with him reminds us of all that. By sitting around him, we are reminded that work is important, but in the context of Sadhana, it has to be done in the context of awakening. - Basil (Corporate VP)

I would say that if you were looking for God in person and were wondering what God looks like, he would look like Master Raju. His depth of character and affectionate personality always leaves a lasting impression on all who know him. He is a beloved friend to countless people in North America. - Shilpa (Marketing Manager)

I would introduce Master Raju to people as a genuine article. He is just real, he is not false. He is authentic and you don't doubt anything that he says. When he says "I love you," there is no way you question it, you just believe it. He is also truly kind and very gentle. He talks a lot about children and in some ways he has completed the circle; he has come back to that. He is child-like, he is innocent, he lets himself go and he sees the world in such a better way than so many do, as through the eyes of a child.
- Vani (Financial expert)

I want to mention something very special about Master Raju: that is simplicity. He is a man without ego! One time we were out at a friend's place where he taught. Master Raju reminds me of a child. He can be like a child. I have seen him playing soccer with the kids. A man of that much knowledge, yet the way he takes life in such a simple format and I wish we all could be like that—the way I see him. I remember his answers on the first day of the program. We were all sitting there, and during the introduction he asked everybody "what are you here for?" The majority of people answered, "To learn this thing, to learn that thing, etc. He simply laughed and said "I am sorry you are at the wrong place, I have nothing to teach you!" That came as a shock. Now I understand what he meant. As we go through life, we learn bad habits; he is there to correct them. What he is saying is "I am here to de-program you!
- Karunesh (Author of *Ayurveda to the Rescue*)

I would say "Master Raju is child-like, living in the present moment all the time, as a child does." A child does not think of the past or the future; they live in the present moment. Raju is in the present, here and now. I wish that I could be like him too; not worrying about the future or thinking about the past. He is always there in the present, in this moment, at this time. Only a child is like that! - Vyas M.D. (Dean of Radiology)

Master Raju is Love and Spiritual Energy!
- Padmaja (Biochemistry expert)

When I think of describing Master Raju, the first word that hits me is "graciousness." I also think that he is a man who has lived a normal life like all the rest of us, and has been able to live it consciously from the start. He enjoys each moment, in spite of trials and error, and he gives all of that right back to everyone he encounters in society.
- Neha (Psychology of Religion Specialist)

If I had to introduce Master Raju, I would say: "Here is Divinity; here is the path to Divinity! Don't miss the boat!" - Valerie (Airline pilot)

If I have to present Master Raju to the world I would say: "He is love incarnate." - Shoba (Financing expert)

To present Raju, I would probably say he is a teacher. I would say "This is my inner teacher." What I consider to be an honor. Someone else would have said he is not a teacher. It's too difficult to be explained, so I would just say "He is an inner teacher and a very nice person. "I would also add that he is a fighter. Usually fighters engage in destruction. But that is the opposite for him. He is a fighter that creates, he does not destroy. He is more or less putting things or building something new, something new instead of going against the old. He is setting the example, so other people can see — Oh okay! I don't want to live my life that way. He is the example of how to fight. I think it's really subtle. You can't really notice it if you don't see him teach or talk, and you probably would not think that something like that exists in him. Once you get in touch with him you basically think: "Even my life can count, everybody does not need to know about me for me to make a difference," and he can make such a big impact. He just goes along, knowing that "I can create a small difference and that can give hope to everybody." He does not think "Here I am; I am going to show off."
- Bojana (Corporate Engineering Manager)

Master Raju is a remarkable person who can make you realize your dreams and can help you or contribute to your growth or awakening. He can help you have wisdom and all the things you long for. He can help you have character, and anything you can dream up, whatever is worthwhile. It's not about granting wishes, it's not about him giving to you; it's about supporting you in realizing these things on your own. And that is possible for everyone if you just allow him to show you the way if you trust him. - Anand (Corporate Project Manager)

Master Raju has a special impact on the people he meets. He is also special in the way in which he touches others: the way a child would, because of the very nature of how children approach life—constantly connected to divinity, in the here and now. - Mona

Raju has a beaming smile and infectious laugh that draws people in. His intellect is unmatched and his huge heart endears him to all who know him. - Valerie

A Message from the Author

· · · · · · · · · · · · · · · ·

My foundational message is that enlightenment is a piece of cake. But to be in *discipleship* is all it takes to understand this foundational statement. Only then one will see what it takes to be in that state of enlightenment.

Once you are in a state of *discipleship*, you are in a boundless state. So when you have no boundaries and you don't know who you are, you are in enlightenment. But many do not have the ability, readiness, and willingness to stay in that state. This is why enlightenment appears to be difficult. However, for one who understands discipleship, the commitment, humility, and sacrifice of your own personal identity comes about naturally.

What do I mean by discipleship? The very word disciple comes from *discipline*. As Jesus says, "Blessed be the meek, for they shall inherit the earth." I would like to rephrase this statement as, "The right brain will eventually rule the world," as someone once said because the right brain is more submissive, integrative, creative, and filled with positive emotions. Humility and living in the right brain comes naturally to a disciple. When these two are present, it is easy to see how simple the process is and what it takes to be enlightened.

To be a disciple to a certain person is only the beginning. But to be a disciple of the entire cosmic energy is another story! This state of discipleship is attainable to anyone who is committed to live in the state of enlightenment. Discipleship offers a tremendous opening to the energy field of a master, which can be Jesus, Buddha, or anyone. In this process, they learn the state of attunement, which is to live in the energy field of the Master.

Most people try to get to enlightenment, but that will get you nowhere. You must be 100% committed to the cause of your own life working, and anything less than that will not due. What I mean by commitment is to take daily actions such as practicing yoga, meditation, pranayama and self-inquiry. There is a quote by W.N. Murray of The Scottish Himalayan Expedition that reinforces this message:

"Until one is committed, there is hesitance, the chance to draw back, always ineffectiveness. Concerning all acts of initiative, there is one elementary truth, the ignorance of which kills countless ideas and splendid plans: That the moment one definitely commits oneself, then providence (God) moves too."

This book will give you an introduction to what kind of practices are available on the path to enlightenment, and also answer most questions that arise in the mind of a seeker as they become more dedicated to their practice. As many people already know, I am not a conventional guru or spiritual master. Most of the gurus found in the spiritual masters' tradition do this kind of work as a full-time activity with the support of an organization. I am unconventional in that sense. My Ashram is the companies where I work; my disciples are the clients I meet, my colleagues, and anyone who is open to letting me assist him or her to create the life that they want. The main focus of my life is to share my wisdom and provoke spiritual transformation in their lives. I do all of this with simplicity, humbleness, and through a personalized relationship with each willing individual.

What is this book about and how is it organized?

. . . .

This book is like a ladder with seven steps. All the topics of common interest to any reader have been presented in a graded fashion so that each chapter becomes a preparatory section to the next. Each chapter becomes a platform standing on which the "higher level" truths are revealed. Therefore, I have decided to use chakras as a way to guide you through the book and into the glory of what lies ahead.

This is a book about spiritual insights supported by actual experiences and science.

After reading this book, you will be able to:

- Achieve unity of mundane and spiritual world;

- Understand chakras and their connection with ancient and modern thinking;

- Realize that you are a conscious evolving soul with mysterious powers to be unlocked and not a stereotyped man/woman;

- Discover that you too could become a Soul from Mercury;

- Fathom the inner vastness of your being and learn the pathway to Samadhi[1] (i.e., enlightenment or "Mercury space") within yourself, which is no longer an airy fairy state.

---

1   Samadhi is considered to be the final stage in the eightfold path of yoga by Patanjali.

Who are the Souls from Mercury?

What I mean by becoming a "Soul from Mercury" is an *individual* who is growing beyond classifications and compartments and religious bigotry, which inherently creates certain limitations about our identity and abilities. "Souls from Mercury" are, in other words, the "emerging human beings" and homo sapiens still in the making and not a finished product of the creator as some of us believe.

I have always appreciated the insights from John Gray, the author of the national number one best-selling book *Men Are from Mars, Women Are from Venus.* This has been very helpful to me to understand human relationships. But personally, I saw that this clear distinction and focusing on the differences between men and women had been the greatest limitation for humanity to grow into a new possibility. In these times of growing chaos around the world, more than ever before, we have to create souls that think and feel that they are from Mercury, which means neither from Mars nor from Venus and will be a fine balance. As men, we have to develop our heart-based qualities such as caring, sharing, and intuitive understanding. As women we have to be more action oriented in the world to be able to create a world that works for everyone. When men awaken their feminine, they honor the feminine more and vice versa. They will come to appreciate how wonderful and valuable women are and vice versa.

What do "The Souls from Mercury" really look like?

1. **They are balanced**

   If Mars represents "the scientist," Venus "the artist," and Mercury "the searcher and mystic," then a total human being (i.e., a Soul from Mercury) is one in whom both the left and right brain are equally active. For instance, the left-brain activities relate to logic, reasoning, mathematics and the like, while the right-brain activities relate to art forms, music, dance, and emotions. Therefore it is very important to develop the right side of your brain by doing pranayama (i.e., breathing exercises), yoga, and the development of consciousness through the purification of chakras.

   Humanity has been progressing in a lopsided manner with the left and right-brain activities being mutually exclusive to either side, which should not be the case. Everyone, including "the scientist" needs the "artist" and heartfelt feeling for others, to understand the impact of their work on the rest of humanity.

2. **They are fully evolved**

   The new age groups are actually creating Souls from Mercury and further evolution of man. Even if one believes in the evolution, I ask why nature should stop with the evolution of man from the monkey?

   Most of the spiritual masters were Souls from Mercury, and never accepted external authority. They went through an "inward revolution" that *removed* all life-negative thinking in them. Thus, they brought out a life-affirming impulse into the existing religious traditions. Similarly, Souls from Mercury will not look for external sources for spiritual authority, but will find it only within themselves through intense inner practices.

   If you have a well-developed scientific and artistic mind, and you are a psychic as well, you can call yourself a Soul from Mercury. If you are not sure, but practice "spirituality" (i.e., true religiousness) and work on the purification and opening of the chakras along the lines suggested in this book, you could become a Soul from Mercury and a powerful human being, really.

3. **They are the creators of the future**
   As Heraclites, the Greek philosopher said, "The truth is contained in neither this nor that." We need to rise above being introverted or extroverted in personality. We have to learn to grow beyond all polarities. The future of mankind belongs to *these* people who can naturally be this way. I call such people supermen and superwomen. They will become the creators of our future.

4. **They understand true religiousness**
   The Souls from Mercury will also understand true religiousness, which is there in every human heart. They will never become a fundamentalist in any one religion. They will be able to appreciate the basic truths common to all religions. They will have tolerance and even appreciation and respect for the different practices and rituals of other religions.

The connection between Mars, Venus, and Mercury

Let us investigate why I chose Mercury as the balance between Mars and Venus. Before I do that, let me explain why historically and astrologically Mars is associated with manly qualities and Venus is associated with feminine ones. Mars is a red planet visible in the sky at times and seen very well with a telescope. Mars is a planet of outgoing impulse, courage, bravery, combativeness, and anger. The military men were even called "Martials."

In contrast, mythological Venus was the Latin love goddess. Venus is the bright evening star seen mostly after sunset. She is called a feminine planet because she governs the gentler and more refined attributes. She signifies the emotions and affections especially those arising out of love, aesthetic sense, the appreciation of beauty, comfort, and pleasure.

I chose Mercury as the golden mean between Mars and Venus because it symbolizes wisdom in the astrological tradition. Mercury became synonymous with the Greek god Hermes. He is the son of Jupiter and a friend of Apollo. He represents wit, wisdom, and agility. Astrologically, he rules over the solar plexus and the nervous system. Those who are born under the influence of Mercury are highly intelligent and ingenious.

Mercury and Earth-based spirituality

To me, Mercury presents a more complete picture of the human being and also supports the new psychological movement of "reawakening the goddess" and the Tantra (i.e., body of knowledge similar to yoga) from the Eastern tradition. The goddess represents an image of empowerment for modern women. I am sure that the emerging "earth-based spirituality" will heal the "split" between spirit and matter, above and below, which has been created by early religious imagination. The Souls from Mercury who stand for and manifest the "earth-based spirituality" will also synthesize science and religion. They also synthesize the introvert and the extrovert in man.

"The five values of Truth, Right Action, Peace, Love, and Non-Violence are really the five life breaths of man according to Sathya Sai Baba, a great spiritual leader in India. One who considers human values as his life breath is a true human being. These five values are the fundamental powers of human life. Forgetting these powers, man relies wrongly on worldly power. All the awakened ones like Jesus, Buddha, Guru Nanak, and many others throughout history realized that these five values are meant for the peace and prosperity of the world. One cannot understand "humanness" at all without understanding the significance of these values.

Human values are not something that you need to acquire and renew. They are born with you and innate in you. Within man's body lie these valuable jewels as if they are hidden in an iron safe. They are covered by the door of the heart. You must earn the key of love for it. When the safe vault of the heart is opened by the key of love, the valuable qualities of the five human values emerge naturally." (Sri Sathya Sai Baba, Sai Discourse Values Education, September 2000).

What are chakras?

The term chakra literally means a wheel in Sanskrit. They are vortexes of energy and information within the quantum mechanical entity that we are as human beings. The very process of human manifestation from the unmanifest happens through the blueprint coded in the DNA of each cell. From one cell only, we came, and became many. In the sixth week of a baby's formation the first thing that forms is the pineal gland, second, the spinal cord, and then the rest of the body. Note that your spiritual foundation came first and then the rest of your structures. So chakras and their status define who you are today and who you will be tomorrow.

We have to learn to unfold that which is right in front of our eyes, but which seems to be hidden. The way to go about this is to understand what the chakras are in the subtle world and how to work with them.

Here is a story to illustrate this:

An airplane got stranded in a remote island, and the native local inhabitants had never seen an airplane before. So they investigated it carefully. One person managed to open the doors and they said to each other, "This is a good storage space to keep our grains!" After a few days, another kid meddled with the controls and the engines, and lo and behold, the plane moved! Weeks later, another guy managed to maneuver it as well. They thought that this is better than a bullock cart and they were very happy. Then, one fine morning, a young teenage boy found the courage and skills to drive the plane to almost 300 miles an hour and wow; the plane took off in the air to their great surprise. They said this "voyage" was a gift from the gods and used it carefully for the use of their Chief alone.

In the same way as the boy explored the plane, it is up to us how we explore the great wonder of our body, its life force, and subtle centers we call chakras. We can either deny that they do not exist, or learn to understand, work, and awaken them in order to live a more fulfilling life on planet earth. We can be static, or we can move towards a higher goal and eventually soar into the portals of heaven! The choice is ours. I am sure that the future scientists will try to elevate themselves and reach up. The code, the key, and the information are all printed within us. As the Scriptures say, "*We are created in the image of God.*" What is the meaning of this? Let us go back to the formation of the universe and the human body. God said in Genesis "Let there be light," and there was light. When the human creation started in the pineal gland to the endocrine system, light was the "stuff" of which the subtle body was made. Then from the subtle body, came the physical body. The subtlest body is consciousness bliss, which is so much akin to God's very nature.

How are chakras related to becoming Souls from Mercury?

Chakras are the pathways through which consciousness evolves and continuous to create the next level of the human being and the next prototype for the next model of the human being. Nature is already doing this work, which is to create "Souls from Mercury."

The term "chakra" has become somewhat of an *exotic* concept for most Western people. They are beginning to understand more than the biology related to our seven endocrine glands: 1) adrenals, 2) the gonads, 3) the spleen, 4) the pancreatic islet cells, 5) the thymus, 6) the thyroid, and 7) the pituitary. Throughout this chapter, one discovers the correlation of these glands and our energy centers, called chakras, which maintain *balance* and health of "the body-mind complex." We not only discuss the role they play in relation to our emotions and health, but also how this powerful energy field, is *directly* linked to … God.

Our goal on earth as humans is to transform the way we think and feel in a more positive way. And our glands play a vital role in this. The current limiting beliefs in the medical world makes many to believe that we can simply give a pill to heal the negative thinking in people without due research conducted on the long-term effects of such pills. In my opinion, the answer lies in the effectiveness with which our endocrine glands are operating, and the way they operate, in turn, are dictated by the normality or abnormality of the chakras. For example, an underactive chakra can create insufficient amount of glandular secretions, while an overactive solar plexus chakra will give you adrenaline and create cortisol, which is a toxin in the body. So the very way you think and feel today in your current level of consciousness depends upon your understanding, and the way you work with your own chakras, which will be described in this book.

Here are the common terms used in the West to simplify each of the seven chakras:

Lower chakras:

1. Base/root chakra
2. Navel chakra
3. Solar plexus chakra

Higher chakras:

1. Heart chakra
2. Throat chakra
3. Brow/third eye chakra
4. Crown chakra

The Man from Mercury lives and operates from the higher chakras rather than the lower chakras. The reason for this is because the lower chakras are of low vibration and are disempowering, whereas the higher ones will elevate, ennoble, and enrich the human being.

Where are the chakras located?

First and foremost, you need to get clear about the fact that we have a quantum mechanical body. Let me simplify quantum mechanics and the findings of neuroscientists in this regard so that you can understand the placement of chakras easily.

Chakras are located in the subtle world inside the physical body. This is why doctors and surgeons cannot see chakras when they dissect the body. You are comprised of five bodies or "layers," called "pancha-koshas" in Sanskrit, one within the other, all the way leading to the innermost center of ourselves. One being physical and the others being subtle bodies. These bodies can be imagined as five concentric circles, one within the other.

The five bodies are the following:

1. The "*physical body*" that can be seen and touched;
2. The "*prana body*" where the life force is working, also known as "*bioenergy body;*"
3. The "*manas*" is a layer where mental energy resides;
4. The "*consciousness body*" is where the intellect and higher mind operates;
5. The "innermost body" or the "*body of bliss,*" which is the *bridge* that links us to the entire macrocosm.

People try to locate chakras along the spine, however, in reality, you cannot localize something with is non-local, so the question itself is wrong. This is analogous to the presence of air all around us. We cannot see it, but we can feel it is there through movement, just like the wind.

There are two levels of prana:

1. The *prana* that is our life force that is felt in the physical body which vibrates and moves muscles, internal organs, managing etc.
2. The *psychic prana*, also known as "Kundalini energy," moves along the spine from the pelvic plexus to the top of your head. Kundalini energy travels through all the chakras along this axis, only when they are open and balanced.

What is the difference between higher and lower chakras?

Let us now discuss the higher and lower chakras separately, so that the self-realization process will become much clearer. The four higher chakras form the very foundation of our spiritual being. We are all spirits having a human experience, not the other way around. A great saint in South India by the name of Sathya Sai Baba described the four basic pillars of life as: Truth (Satya), Righteousness (Dharma), Peace (Shanti), and Love (Prema), which correspond to the four higher chakras (Heart, Throat, Brow, and Crown). In other words, if one "leg" is missing, the chair will collapse, similarly, if one pillar of life is missing, a whole life collapses.

Let us look at the *higher chakras* in a descending path (7–4):

Truth is that which does not change with time and space. This relates to a master's everlasting love, which is called "True or Divine Love." When you go beyond the localization of yourself in space and time, you realize that Truth resides in the highest crown chakra. This is located on top of the head and in the space a few inches above. The feeling is akin to oneness and intimacy with *all* that exists, which can be experienced through as OM chanting or other forms of *deep* prayer. "I am sustained by the love of God," is the feeling at this center. The effect is also felt inside the head, also at the pineal gland and pituitary gland, where one gets a feeling as if there are a thousand lotus petals fully blossomed. This has been mentioned by great people like Jesus, Buddha, Shankara, and Patanjali. That is the experience of Truth and the Oneness of life. The very essence of living is to recognize this Oneness of Life: *That we are all one.* This principle of "Non-Duality of Existence" was referred to as "advaita" by the great Indian teacher Shankara. This non-duality propels us towards Universal Love. The upper four chakras are opened one by one as this realization grows within us.

Righteousness (Dharma) is that which holds everything together in this coherent universe. Dharma arises from the vision emanating from the third eye, which is located inside the center of the forehead and is part of the transcendental vision. We all have three eyes but one has become inactive. This is why we are not always in touch with our own mission, vision, and values in life. The third eye sees way beyond the visible spectrum. Your "Dharma" will become very clear to you when the third eye is "open." Understanding right from wrong becomes your second nature, which helps you to have clarity and less confusion about your life orientation, such as, "Do I have the right job, appearance, partner, spiritual beliefs, etc.?" Meditation will help open the third eye, and is the art of moving the energy and merging it with consciousness at this center. Here and now, everything is right, or made right ... that is righteousness.

Peace (Shanti) is stillness of mind and purity of the heart, known as "Vishuddhi chakra" located in the Throat Chakra. There is no more conflict or agony at this level. One experiences peace with oneself and all living beings. Truthful communication and full self-expression opens this chakra, whereas thought, speech, and action become one. What you think, you say, because you have a beautiful mind with pure thoughts. And what you say, you will do in life, because it comes from a deep place of commitment. Only when there is this sense of peace, you can clearly see.

Love (Prema) is of many kinds: Personal love (including loving oneself and others), compassionate love, and universal love. The heart is always inclusive and integrative in its nature, while the mind always excludes and differentiates. In other words, when you operate from the heart, then you See God in All and All in God (i.e., SAIGAGIA). Love emanates from the heart chakra, and is the connecting link between the higher and lower chakras.

The state of the seven chakras within us dictates our life and the way we are experiencing it. If we learn to experience life from the higher chakras, life will be nothing but blissful. You can be sick and still blissful, and not convert the pain into misery. Pain is mandatory for living beings and misery is optional.

Now let us look at the *lower chakras*, from an ascending path (1–3):

As Krishna says, "Life is like an inverted tree with roots above and branches below. The real roots are in the higher chakras, which form the pillars and foundation of life." The first chakra is located at the bottom of the spinal column and it is called the base/root (Muladhara) chakra. It is associated with the security and survival of the individual. This chakra cannot be ignored because no higher work can be done if a person feels sick, financially unstable, and insecure physically. When you feel rooted and connected to the earth and the abundance in the nature, these issues will disappear. Eating natural organic foods will eliminate sickness, seeing the abundance in nature will bring in financial stability, and feeling rooted to the earth will solve insecure feelings. Most asanas (i.e., yoga postures) will work at this level and help awaken this chakra.

The second or navel chakra (Swadhisthana) is below the navel and drives family relationships, sex, and defense. This chakra too cannot be ignored since relationships play a significant role in our lives. Ways in which we can activate this chakra is by sublimating or transmuting the sex drive by engaging in artistic and spiritual pursuits. The following sections will elaborate on this methodology and give you tools to fully activate and heal this chakra.

The third, solar plexus chakra is located in the navel and a little above it in the stomach area. It is the seat of power, and spoils all relationships when it is imbalanced or blocked. *Forgiveness* and *acceptance* of self, others, and perhaps even God, will help heal this chakra and bring it to normalcy. Regrettably, many individuals live around and cater to the urges created by these three lower chakras their entire lives. This is the source of the spiritual crisis in the world today, which in turn, is creating other crises such as social and political that we are so familiar with. There is a "tide in the affairs of men," Shakespeare said. Therefore, to bring about an inward revolution in this tide and create a different upward spiral in humanity, the most important step will be the awakening of the *higher chakras* in human beings.

Is there a difference between the ways we awaken the higher and lower chakras?

Absolutely. This is the point that has been forgotten or not known in most of the current available literature. We need to de-emphasize the workings and urges of the lower chakras. We need not open the lower chakras since they are *already* open. People are predominantly living in the lower chakras, so there is no need to awaken them. All that is required then, is to "purify" them. When we talk about purifying lower chakras, what we really mean is to understand this "inner lab" and figure out the way these chakras are whirling; either clockwise or counterclockwise. Some chakras are currently overactive, while others are underactive, and this needs to be properly addressed by the coaches and masters, so that one can learn how to reduce "the noise" of the lower chakras.

People try to do so much work on their lower chakras, but this will not lead to transformation or evolution as higher beings. For instance, special breathing exercises to open specific lower chakras are risky and may lead to health issues. As the ancient Yogic text indicates, these breathing exercises should be only learned from a qualified and/or realized master, and not from a book. Visualization exercises are harmless and useful as part of self-exploration. The only benefit I see in any of this work is that people become more aware and sensitive to what is happening within themselves. This is known as "Pratiyahara" in the Hata Yoga system in the East. It is a Sanskrit word meaning "to look within," which will help align and tune ourselves, so we can hear "the still small voice" of the Indweller (i.e., God).

We cannot really talk about God or spirituality; we can only *experience* it. Talking about God is not *experiencing* His presence. Talking about chakras is not *experiencing* chakras. And talking about meditation is not *experiencing* meditation.

What happens when the chakras come to bloom and blossom?

In ancient Yogic literature, chakras were depicted as lotus flowers with a certain number of petals, so the awakening creates a feeling like they are blooming and blossoming. Just like when a lotus flower opens and responds to the early morning rising sun.

I want to remind you that each chakra has a specific effect when it is open and balanced, which results in some of the feelings described below:

1. Base/root chakra (**Muladhara**): You become rooted to the Earth (centering/sense of stability). All sense of insecurity about life and future disappears, regardless of what is happening in one's life. Abundance shows up naturally and spontaneously. Even if a person has a million dollars, they may still feel insecure. Whereas when this chakra is blooming you feel secure and courageous, as the word "Muladhara" means. For more detailed information on this chakra, refer to the chapter on "Creating Abundance."

2. Sacral chakra (**Svadhisthana**): You become more aware of your "gut brain's workings" and how you have become a slave of it. Oftentimes, we carry most of our past and present pain in this region, especially related to our sexuality and in some cases sexual trauma. The pain we feel is actually caused by the natural and creative energies that are blocked, which become destructive to the self and others. However, when we learn to "really let go, *'forgive* others and ourselves, then you will feel gentleness and clarity, and self-expression, instead of guilt, shame, and anger. Sexuality can be a creative energy, so learn to respect it. As the

Sanskrit word "Swadhisthana" indicates, you will become a "master of yourself," a great creator of all art forms, such as music, dance, and spirituality.

3. Solar plexus chakra (**Manipura**): When this chakra is *not* in balance, one feels like controlling, dominating, and manipulating everyone around. But when *balanced*, you are in touch with a new sense of energy and power within you. You become the "master of the house," just like a baby who becomes the center of attraction for the whole household. And as the Sanskrit word "Manipura" describes, you will feel as though you are living in a "city of jewels" and have no one to conquer and nothing to conquer, where true surrender happens. Conquering the mind is greater than conquering the world, because you discover a power within yourself that can make everything perfect.

4. Heart chakra (**Anahata**): The first higher chakra *links* you with the higher level of the inner world. This is the first chakra where the word "activation of a chakra" becomes valid because it is normally open. If it is activated, one will be always living in love. The solar plexus chakra deals with "How can I get more power and be better than everyone?" This heart chakra, on the other hand, deals with the question: "How can I truly be myself?" Once you are able to do this, you start moving from the "downward-pull, to the upward-pull." The downward-pull is all about the "love of power" and the upward-pull of about the "power of love." As the Sanskrit word "Anahata" means, "Un-stuck sound," you are living in entrainment, where you are tuned with the cosmic rhythm that is moving everything into an order and harmony. Some call this sound Om, while others Amen.

5. Throat chakra (**Vishuddha**): "Vishuddha" means purity of communication and gives energy of lucidity and transparency of one's self-expression. Once this chakra is activated, wisdom pours out from everything one says. In other words, "what" you are saying is not as important as "where" you are saying it from. So when you become the purest essence of purity, whatever you say becomes true, and that is the power of Vishuddha. This is why there is validity in receiving blessings from an enlightened person.

6. Brow/third eye chakra (**Ajna**): Ajna means "command" in Sanskrit, and is related to the master gland (i.e., pituitary gland). This chakra is the foundation of our "psychic powers" and is related to how we can see

and get an insight into the future. You could be lost in the visions and powers arising from your enhanced perception of a whole new world. Therefore, one can become enchanted and too attached to these "powers" and addicted to what they can bring to one's life, such as money and fame. You will feel as though you are rising in the sky of consciousness. However, the potential for falling is also high at this stage because the higher you rise, the steeper you fall.

You need to be watchful of the ego at this stage more than ever, since it has not dissolved yet. This can only happen when you move into cosmic consciousness, which is experienced at the crown chakra level. When this chakra blooms completely, you need to just watch it, be a witness to it (without judging), and do nothing. Miracles can happen, when they do manifest, don't get stuck to them, just let them happen, and keep meditating.

7. Crown chakra (**Sahasrara**): This chakra is not even a chakra really, since nothing is whirling like a wheel. You will feel for the first time that all the dualistic and materialistic desires are gone and total peace dawns upon The Inner Being. The blooming process is now complete as if a thousand petals lotus has bloomed, hence the name "Sahasrara." True religion is also born at this level. In fact, all religions were born in the hearts of spiritual masters at this level. This is known in the Sanskrit language as "Soham." This is similar to the declaration of God coming to Moses saying, "I Am That I Am."

Love is no more an emotion but simply "unity consciousness," where you can experience everyone as a part of yourself. As famous writer and teacher J. Krishna Murthi said, "The observer becomes the observed." The experience is one of cosmic consciousness where the individual identity is completely merged with the cosmos. Individual consciousness is localized thinking such as "I am here." In contrast, cosmic consciousness is all-pervasive and is the same for all. As some masters have said, "I am mute in the core of the sun, I am the sun, moon, stars, and ultimately, I am the universe."

How do I know if I am transcending one chakra and moving onto the next?

You will know you are stuck in a particular chakra when the energy is not flowing through that chakra to the next level. Here are some tips on the feelings at each chakra level when you transcend that level to the next one.

1. Base/root chakra (**Muladhara**) – If you reach the feeling of "I am not the body" and "I am truly secure in my inner self," then you are transcending Muladhara. Fasting is a good spiritual practice because you are letting your body know that you are the master and the body is just an instrument. So when you honor the body, the body also honors you in return.

2. Sacral chakra (**Svadhisthana**) – Relationships take on different contexts bigger than sex and possessiveness. At this stage, you have a feeling of truly honoring *others*, and you know that you are transcending your second chakra. So when you honor others, others will honor you in return.

3. Solar plexus chakra (**Manipura**) – When you feel that you are truly and naturally honoring *yourself*, then you are transcending the Manipura chakra. You go beyond the level of superiority over others and controlling them, and here your emotions are purified. So when you honor yourself, you are actually honoring your Higher Self, and now love is ready to be born.

4. Heart chakra (**Anahata**) – Here you get a feeling that love is a Divine Power. This is the first of the chakras, which gives you that loving feeling. This loving feeling indicates that you are getting closer to understanding God and all spiritual matters. So when you start living in love, love becomes a milieu around you.

5. Throat chakra (**Vishuddha**) – Here the feeling is that you are able to communicate love and the love of God *effortlessly* to others. Also, you tune-into the "vibration of God" more easily. So when you start to practice the presence of God, you will also begin to get visions of higher spiritual dimensions.

6. Brow/third eye chakra (**Ajna**) –This is where meditation really begins. It is where you go beyond the ego awareness, egocentric mind, and games. You move from *having* things and *doing* things, to pure *being*

and consciousness. You move from simply feeling good to feeling great and in touch with you who really are. That is when you know you are transcending at the level of Anja, and moving beyond. At this level, you will love Truth, and nothing else.

7. Crown chakra (**Sahasrara**) – Here you have the feeling that All is One. You live in the present moment and in the orbit of the Power of Universal Love and Absolute Peace. Jesus refers to this as "Peace that passeth all understanding." In my opinion, Universal Love and Absolute Peace mean the same. "Absolute" does not have an opposite or feverishness. All the other chakras have "pairs of opposites" such as: "I like this or I don't like it," "This is less and this is more," "This feels good but this feels bad," "This is wrong and this is right." Even some philosophers will not be able to experience such a state of Absolute Peace because they are stuck in the rightness of a particular philosophy. Whereas at this chakra level, you go beyond the pairs of opposites, a sense of abiding peace and benediction is available now. As Sri Chinmoy, a teacher at the United Nations indicated in his poetry, "The final end of nature's dance, I am It whom I have sought."

Can we measure chakras and their status scientifically?

There is an application of electronics to holistic medicine, which became popular in England in the 1970s, called Radionics. This system essentially involves taking seven pieces of your hair and placing it them into different compartments of electromagnetic fields created by a Radionics machine. This machine measures some variables, which indicate the percentage of health associated with each chakra. You might be wondering where you can access such a fine machine, unfortunately I do not know at this time. However, I had a direct experience with this machine many years ago, used by a friend, which indicated the level of health from all my chakras. It helped me understand what additional work was necessary before being able to follow my true path as a successful teacher.

What is the link between chakras and the five elements in nature?

The body is comprised of the five major elements that correspond to our five chakras. Our "human experiences" through the five sense organs are also connected to the five elements, which the following chart describes:

The Five Elements	The Five Major Chakras	The Five Human Experiences
1) Earth	Base/root chakra	Smell
2) Water	Navel chakra	Taste
3) Fire	Solar plexus chakra	Sight
4) Air	Heart chakra	Touch
5) Ether or Space	Throat chakra	Sound

The reason why the two highest chakras are not listed in this chart is because they are above and beyond the five elements. In other words, the third eye chakra creates the *vision* of God and the crown chakra creates the *experience* of God, referred to as Pure Consciousness. These two chakras are the mystical and supernatural part of ourselves, not nature. Hereby we notice that God, the invisible is living at the very source of the visible and makes these wonderful human experiences possible!

Here is a snapshot of the process of creation (i.e., Genesis) according to "the perfected beings," known as the Siddhas:

> In the Beginning … there was Ether, and with Ether there was Sound, the primordial sound Aum (OM), Amin, Amen. From Ether came Air, with the attribute of Touch. Now Air has both Touch and Sound. From Air came Fire, with the attribute of Sight (form). Fire now has Sight, Touch, and Sound. From Fire came Water, with the attribute of Taste. Water now has Taste, Sight, Touch, and Sound. From Water came Earth, with the Attribute of Smell. Earth now has Smell, Taste, Sight, Touch, and Sound.

Sathya Sai Baba described the process of creation in the following manner. He says that transformation is actually a process of becoming lighter and lighter. If you look at nature, earth is dense and heavy. Water is lighter than earth, so it has the capacity to flow and move. Fire is lighter than water and so has the capacity to rise and spread in all directions. Air is lighter than fire, and more pervasive than fire. Ether is the ultimate lightness and so unrestrained in its capacity to pervade among all other elements. Where does Ether exist in this case? It exists everywhere because sound pervades the entire creation.

As for the creation of each individual being, the pineal gland is the first thing that forms in a baby in the mother's womb. The other endocrine glands were formed thereafter. Then the spine was formed soon after this. All the other organs in the human body were created under the direction of these glands, which have their origin in the corresponding chakra systems.

Is there any connection between chakras and colors?

Contrary to what most people think, chakras are energy vortexes, so they do not have an inherent color per se, nor do they emit colors constantly as shown in most diagrams in the literature. It is possible to use colors during meditation by focusing on various chakras and visualizing the colors corresponding to those chakras as noted above in order to help balance or open them.

The connection between chakras and colors is studied through the *human aura*, which is a mysterious luminescence around the body, with constant color emanations. The aura is defined as a "magnetic force-field of the human body." "The combined manifestation of body, soul, and mind creates certain emanations around the spinal column and the medulla oblongata." (Djwal Kul & Kuthumi, 1996). It therefore appears that aura stem from the inside out. Auras can be verified through the well-known "Kirlian Photography of The Human Aura." Some clairvoyants have also confirmed the way colors are assigned to the chakras through their inner vision and sensitivity to the vibrations. The aura and the color emanations are transmitted from moment to moment. There will be differences in the color of the auras depending on one's current stress level, thoughts, and emotions. For example, if a person is anxious or angry, their aura colors will be red or orange, which corresponds to the lower chakras. When the person becomes more relaxed, on the other hand, their aura will change to yellow, green, or blue, corresponding to the higher chakras.

Here are the colors corresponding to the various energy centers or chakras:

Muladhara: red
Swadhisthana: orange
Manipura: yellow
Anahata: green
Vishuddha: blue
Ajna: mauve or violet
Sahasrara: white

A shift in color can be seen much more rapidly in the Kirlian photography during meditation, which I personally verified. When I personally had the opportunity to try this photography, my colors were red to orange before meditation and move up the spectrum corresponding to the higher chakra colors. During deep meditation, auras were blue or violet. However during Samadhi state of meditation, all my colors were merged into white. So when you align the chakras through meditation and they are balanced and open, then the noise and shift in colors stops. Now there is only one color that remains, white, where all colors come from and the purity of heart that is talked about by all the Masters.

Is it possible to use colors during meditation?

There are lots of books devoted to the subject of using colors and chakra visualization and healing. However, it is important not to *assume* or *force* the color. Let the color come to you. For example, on a given day when you are going through certain agitation in the mind and forcing the color red or orange corresponding to your lower chakras, you will make your condition even worse and leave you with little spiritual benefit of such visualization. A lot more personal coaching may be required by an expert teacher to work with chakras and their healing. In this case, in may be helpful to use colors corresponding to the heart chakra and above. The following chart will assist you in choosing the colors you could use to meditate on when you have particular issues on a "bad day."

Chakras	Colors to Use on a "Good Day"	Key Words to Use	Colors to Use on a "Bad Day"
Lower chakras:			
Base/root chakra (Muladhara)	Red	Energy	White
Navel chakra (Swadhishtana)	Orange	Joy	Mauve or Violet
Solar plexus chakra (Manipura)	Yellow	Detachment	Blue
Higher chakras:			
Heart chakra (Anahata)	Light Green	Balance & Immunity	Dark Green (Turquoise)
Throat chakra (Vishuddha)	Blue	Relaxation	Sky blue

Brow/third eye chakra (Ajna)	Mauve or Violet	Dignity	Indigo (Magenta)
Crown chakra (sahasrara)	White	Universal Love	Transcendental

The healing colors are those related to the higher chakras. In other words, you cannot use red orange or yellow for healing emotions in particular. You can use turquoise, turquoise blue, blue, violet, or magenta instead. White does not directly heal in general, nor does it heal emotions in particular, but it can give you an energy field of protection from the negative emotions of others.

It is important to be cautious about how long you use the colors in the visualization. Three to seven minutes is the maximum time period to meditate on a given chakra. Also note that what will work for one person may not work for another because of their association with that color. Therefore, you need to *study* your own body and its anatomy before you can embark on the journey of the "anatomy of the spirit." Keep in mind what my Master once said, "The human body is the greatest book that you will ever read on health and wellness." Unfortunately, some people do not make time to study, know themselves, and attain spiritual growth. They would rather read a book for eight hours about chakras than meditate for fifteen minutes.

Can you give more tools on healing, colors, and light?

When you use colors and light for healing, the forms and shapes are as important as the colors themselves. For example, in color therapy, therapists take a specially made colored glass such as blue filled with water overnight. Furthermore, they can also take a blue colored light and focus it on the water. Once the water has completely absorbed the color, the patient will be asked to drink the water. In some cases, the effect will be further enhanced if the patients sit in relaxation in a room where the walls are either painted blue or the lights are blue in color. In this case, therapists are only using the "form" of the color blue all around the patient. However, in the case of internal meditation, the shapes also come into play. For example, the same blue color imagined in the shape of a rectangle will produce much less healing energy compared to the petals of a lotus or rose of the same color. This is because the corresponding chakra automatically receives the healing energy when the color is contained within the shape of the lotus or rose flower.

Chakras	Mandalam
Lower chakras:	
Base/root chakra (Muladhara)	Square
Navel chakra (Swadhishtana)	Crescent moon
Solar plexus chakra (Manipura)	Triangle
Higher chakras:	
Heart chakra (Anahata)	Hexagon (Two interlaced triangles)
Throat chakra (Vishuddha)	Circle
Brow/third eye chakra (Ajna)	Bindu (dot or point)
Crown chakra (Sahasrara)	Beyond time and space

If you want more or long-lasting healing, you may want to pay attention to the color of your clothes and/or the colors of the walls in your home, which have a deep impact on the psyche. These colors worn or around you becomes your automatic color visualization because it is surrounding you so much.

Foods are another critical area to focus on when wanting to cleanse and heal. The color of the foods you ingest may work on the areas on the chakras as well. So it is important to include green leaves and green sprouts as well as orange and yellow vegetables/fruits in our daily diet to have an immediate impact on the lower three chakras. Ironically, foods that are white in color are not good for the body. Foods such as white rice, white sugar, white bread, milk, and white fat, when consumed in large quantities, are considered to be unhealthy by most nutrition experts. In a spiritual sense, such foods create a "big load" on the lower three chakras and obstruct the flow of energy.

Can we use sounds to awaken and work with the chakras?

Sounds are a great help to "protect" you from negative thoughts and feelings while creating greater awareness in meditation. The sounds used in meditation are traditionally called mantras. But the master key to inner peace is in how to use the sound or mantra, which will help deepen your meditation to a higher level. When you combine the effect of color with the sound related to that chakra, a permanent healing process can occur. For example, there are two types of meditation you can do when healing chakras. One is called chakra breathing (which we will cover elsewhere), and the other is called *chakra sounds* described below:

Chakras	Sound
Lower chakras:	
Base/root chakra (Muladhara)	Lum
Navel chakra (Swadhishtana)	Vum
Solar plexus chakra (Manipura)	Rum
Higher chakras:	
Heart chakra (Anahata)	Yum
Throat chakra (Vishuddha)	Hum
Brow/third eye chakra (Ajna)	Om/Amen
Crown chakra (Sahasrara)	Silence

When we combine the chanting of the sounds with breathing exercises, the impact on the chakra becomes more powerful. Focus on your experience while chanting these sounds, and do not worry about what the words mean. These are primordial sounds. The great seers and sages in India who sang the Vedas, which are the Hindu Holy Scriptures, saw in their vision that these sounds originated in creation. Therefore one should not look for any intellectual meaning of these sounds. These sounds are considered to be seed letters for the element of nature that they represent. For example, Lum is the seed letter for the earth, and represents the earth element. Vum for water, and Rum for fire, and so on. Some texts may refer to these sounds with different spellings like "Lam," "Vam," etc. This could be misleading. Keep in mind however that the actual pronunciation of these sounds is very similar to the alcoholic drink "rum." The repetition of the sounds can also reinforce the healing process.

Here are some strategies on how to practice using these sounds:

1. Sit up straight in a comfortable meditative position.
2. Feel free to play any chakra sound music of your choice in the background.
3. Relax your body and your breath by completing some deep breathing techniques.
4. Inhale slowly and deeply through the nostrils, and exhale slowly and with control.
5. Begin to chant and extend the end of the sound "Lum" and focus on your first (base/root) chakra (Muladhara). Repeat this sound three times.

6. Move to your second (navel) chakra and intonate the sound "Vum." Repeat this sound three times.
7. Then move up to your third (solar plexus) chakra and chant "Rum." Repeat this sound three times.
8. Next, move to the fourth (heart) chakra and repeat "Yum" three times.
9. Move to the fifth (throat) chakra and repeat "Hum" three times.
10. Then to the sixth (third eye) chakra and repeat "Om/Aum" and repeat this three or more times
11. Finally, stay in silence focusing on the top of the head and let the body be surrounded by white light.
12. After several days of practice, you can repeat this cycle five times. Each time starting with the first to the seventh chakra.

Sounds specific to each chakras can be used through chanting or repeated mentally. The chanting particularly creates a mental imprint. Each chakra can be worked in three different ways: we can activate it, balance it or cleanse it. The purification can be done through breathing, meditation, and repetition of the sounds. An ounce of practicing is more precious than tons of theory, and what makes this knowledge penetrate to your inner being. One becomes wise, receives cosmic love, and develops all divine virtues. My Master used to say, "This practice is like the celestial wish healing tree Kalpataru."

Depending on where you are in your life, you can find your own meditation that works the best for you. You have to listen to your body and you can evaluate. For God, every soul is precious and he has a different path for everyone. We cannot go through the same process as somebody else. What we can do is accommodate different methods and make them work for us. I am not here to teach you every step of the way through a book. I am here to give you guidelines on how to become Your Own Masters.

What is the connection between musical instruments and chakras?

I have heard my musical and spiritual Master say the following, "Whatever may be the form of music, its key constituents are always rhythm and tone. Let us look at the human organism. The pulse rate, the beating of heart and brain, the circulation of blood and the inward, outward movement of breath: all of this is related to the system of rhythm and tone in the human body. Music can change the body chemistry, and raise or lower the positive energy of a person. The mysticism of music in the context of meditation and healing lies essentially in the quality of sound vibration emanating from the rhythm and tone of music. It is through their fusion of the rhythm and tone that different vibrations get created and thus the soul is tuned. This can raise one above the depression and despair of everyday life."

I suggest if you are feeling stressed or depressed in your life, you may want to use the energy or instruments related to the higher chakras to heal the lower ones. For example, by listening to the piano or violin for a considerable period of time, you will be slowed down and operate at a higher chakra level. However, by listening to flute music all day, you will be spaced out very soon, which is okay if you want to remain in a meditative state. It is important to note that the person or musician playing the instrument should be taken into consideration as a key component.

Here is a wonderful classification of musical instruments shown in accordance with the chakras that they impact:

- The first chakra (Muladhara) is affected by drums, percussions, and trumpets, formerly signifying the beginning of a war. The drums and "base sounds" are generally used in bars, pubs, and clubs to give people energy. But if overused, can influence the triggering of base sexual and aggressive behaviors and the "fight or flight response" in people. So if you listen to the beat of drums all day, you will be operating from a lower chakra level, however, you should not listen to them during meditation or when purifying a chakra.

- The second chakra (Svadhisthana) influenced by piano, violin, and synthesizer is related to the relaxation response. In other words, when you are relaxed, you can also have a healthy sexual relationship. You can also notice these instruments in movies during intense, romantic or even sad scenes.

- The third chakra (Manipura) is touched by pipe instruments such as the clarinet, bagpipes, organ, etc. This is why the clarinet is used in all the marriages in India since it awakens the positive emotions and brings people together.

- The fourth chakra (Anahata) is opened by string instruments such as the guitar, harp, sitar, cello, accordion, veena (a popular Indian instrument), etc. You can hear these string instruments in many of the Indian movies since it makes people feel more poetic while allowing the opening of the heart.

- The fifth chakra (Vishuddha) is activated by all kinds of flutes and awakens the compassion and better communication in people. So if teachers want to encourage these values, they can use background flute music in their classroom.

- The sixth chakra (Ajna) is awakened by cymbals and bells especially those used in temples and churches. In other words, when you hear a temple or church bell ring, it's actually a reminder from the Creator that it is now "prayer time."

- The seventh chakra (Sahasrara), also known as "the spiritual heart," can be opened by the conch shell sound. The conch shell is often used in South Indian Hindu temples and held by Krishna depicted in many pictures of the Mahabharata War. Its sound is similar to the primordial sound in creation and promotes universal consciousness. This sound and particular vibration can help us tune into cosmic energy. As a cautionary note in the use of playing the conch, it should only be played a few times (i.e., 2-5 times) in order to avoid mental "feverishness" or a headache.

The impact of music is tremendous. In his book *The Secret Power of Music*, David Tame makes the following statement: "Music influences virtually every physical intellectual and emotional process. Harmonious music makes plants grow faster while dissonant music stunts and kills the plants. This fact was proven by J.C. Bose who was given a Nobel Prize for his discovery that plants have feelings too.

Music can create a balance within us, elevate us, or pull us down. So we must be aware of the kind of music that we feed ourselves with. I have heard that a Chinese emperor would go around in disguise just listening to the music of the masses in each province in order to see their level of evolution and to determine the help and guidance they needed! So the reader must consider his or her own self-evolution and determine what type of music will enable you to higher consciousness.

Can you give some examples of musical masterpieces that one can use for their spiritual development?

My spiritual guide, world-renowned musician Dr. Sri Ganapathy Sachchidananda (addressed as Sri Swamiji) has developed music for meditation and healing, also known as "Raga Ragini Vidya" in India. Swamiji has designed a synthesizer, which incorporates many of these instruments into one. One of his many CDs published is called "Inner Healing." He has also travelled around the globe conducting over 100 concerts of "Music for Meditation and Healing." His ongoing mission includes music therapy in a hospital setting in Mysore, India providing music and traditional medicine to various patients. The doctors recommend specific songs and instruments related to different types of diseases. For further information on music therapy, the reader can make reference to *Music Therapy, A New Anthology* compiled by Lionel Stebbing.

The music by *Deuter*, a German group, can also be used as support to meditate on the chakras. Two CDs are worthy of mention, one called "Chakra Sounds" and the other "Chakra Breathing" both published by Osho Foundation. Stephen Halpern is another great New Age musician who has released an album called "The Chakra Suite." I have played these albums to corporate workers who attended my classes throughout a whole year and witnessed a great shift in the corporate culture. All the albums mentioned provide a specific kind of music in which the sounds move systematically from each chakra to the next, starting with Muladhara and going all the way back to the same Chakra. The music systematically changes covering each chakra one by one. You can feel the vibrations changing and shifting to the next chakra and completing one whole cycle (starting and ending in first chakra).

Musical instruments and the types of sounds they create can create a profound impact on different chakras. You can also Google or YouTube "chakra healing music" or a certain musical instrument for additional resources. Be mindful of your music selection and use your intuition. If certain music does not suit you, stop it and simply choose another. Once you select music that you feel comfortable with, sit down with it somewhere with little distractions, close your eyes (for at least 15 minutes), and be with the music alone, in order to reap the benefits of true healing.

Chakras and Spirituality

There are well known seven wonders of the world. There are seven wonders in the human body namely the ability to see, taste, touch, smell, and hear and also the ability to laugh and love. These wonders connect us to the world. There is really no such thing as independence. We are intertwined with all we come to contact with. We see the impact of our interaction or first contacts have on others; the entire world is connected—from family ties to the community in ever expanding ripples to the town, the state, the nation, and the world. We are really one entity, but we show ourselves as being separate. This, to me, is the essence of spirituality refined, redefined, and reimagined for a new age.

Spirituality begins by trusting and believing that your inner force is unfolding your life the way it should. Accept what is flowing in your life right now. Love yourself and others, meditate, and start to fill your spiritual life each day with this new understanding. Actually all are spiritual because they are a spirit in essence. To be spiritual is to see that all are spiritual.

The most profound reason for man to be on Earth is to take the spiritual path or the inner journey to a higher purpose. The spiritual path is for those who have made available to their conscious mind the lessons that their evolving "self" chose to learn in this life. The profound reason for all suffering in the world is to create that perfect human being in spirituality. There is bioenergy in man that is unconsciously moving you to this.

Spiritual people know how to cooperate with others, and how to play and be joyful in what they do. They love themselves unconditionally, and are aware of the lesson of caring for people. They have recognized and trust that there is a benevolent and supporting intelligence that cares about them and their well-being, and with whom they have a personal relationship. They know how to raise a family, and how to assist the Earth through this challenging time in its evolution. Discovering your higher purpose in life automatically brings joy and happiness.

What is the connection between chakras and spirituality?

In the famous book entitled *The Anatomy of The Spirit,* Dr. Caroline Myss discusses the seven stages of power and healing. She has summarized seven sacred truths of the body and spirit in relation to the seven chakras:

1. All is one.
2. Honor one another.
3. Honor oneself.
4. Love is divine power.
5. Surrender personal will to divine will.
6. Seek only the truth.
7. Live in the present moment.

She goes on to say that these seven statements will help us to focus our body, mind, and spirit back to a contact point with divine awareness whenever we lose it. These truths are like reference points. We can retrieve our spirit by recognizing which truth we are not honoring. For example, if you lose connection to the heart chakra or physical problems in this area, a simple repetition of this sacred truth will bring us back to balance.

What lifestyle preparations are required before seriously practicing chakra purification and awakening?

Anybody who practices yoga or meditation should integrate in their life the following Yamas (basic restraints) and the Niyamas (spiritual practices). These lifestyle preparations are similar to the Ten Commandments. However, these have become the "forgotten foundation of yoga." As much as one will try to reach enlightenment through yoga or meditation, they will not have success without naturally embodying the following observances translated from the Patanjali Yoga Sutras, the classic treatise on yoga.

The Yamas (or basic restraints) are:

1. *Non-injury/harmlessness:* To have reverence to all living beings at all times through our thoughts, words, and deeds.
2. *Truthfulness:* To speak truth at all times and for the benefit of all beings.
3. *No Stealing:* To have respect for other people's property.
4. *Divine Conduct:* To have "appropriate" behavior at all times by honoring the Light in others, traditionally called "celibacy" or "sexual purity," by having full control over our sexual drive.
5. *Acceptance:* To be totally content with what we have or don't have.

The Niyamas (or basic spiritual practices) are:

1. *Physical and Mental Cleanliness:* To abstain from internal and external substances such as food or drugs that may harm the body.
2. *Contentment:* To be grateful for what we have.
3. *Austerity or Penance:* To have tolerance for the pairs of opposites, such as heat and cold, pleasure and pain.
4. *Study Scriptures:* To learn more about oneself and one's divine nature.
5. *Full Aspiration for God:* To surrender to Him in our every action.

   1. Patience
   2. Compassion
   3. Honesty
   4. Moderate appetite
   5. Purity
   6. Giving
   7. Faith
   8. Worshiping of the Lord
   9. Reading Scriptures
   10. Cognition
   11. Repetition of God's name

Ultimately, the motivation that will enable you to follow these restraints and practices are the result of your commitment to a disciplined life. When you come from a limited commitment for these practices, you have limited power. When you declare that there will be total commitment then you will have unlimited power.

"Yamas and niyamas control the yogi's passions and emotions and keep him in harmony with his fellow men. The practice of asanas without the backing of yama and niyama is mere acrobatics. Success in fulfilling the yama and niyamas provided the stability in our life and is a requirement for sustained success in meditation." For a more in depth understanding of these important teachings, I suggest you read *Yoga's Forgotten Foundation* by Satguru Sivaya Subramuniyaswami of Himalayan Academy, Kapaa, Hawaii.

Were great Masters aware of chakras?

Yes. Great masters were aware of the chakras in their own way, but did not call them chakras.

Jesus once mentioned, "In my master's house there are many mansions," and I can see that. He was actually referring to our chakras and the subtle parts of our inner life. We tend to keep busy and spend most of our time in the lower mansions (i.e., lower dimensions such as food, sex, and power trips, which linkto our root, sacral and solar plexus regions of the body) and keep our upper mansions locked. When in reality, long-lasting joy and real power both come from the upper dimensions of the body, which are uncared for and undernourished generally. So Jesus said, "Seek ye first the kingdom of God, and all these will be added unto you." Jesus used cryptic language to give confidential and special messages to his disciples. Jesus referred to the higher chakras as the kingdom of God.

Furthermore, there is also a mention in the Revelations chapter of the Bible about "the seven churches," which calls for serious study and research to see the parallels between these seven churches and the seven chakras. Many saints in the Christian tradition experienced the blossoming of the chakras and referred to it as part of the "Holy Spirit." It is only a different nomenclature. That is all.

A great Sufi mystic Mansoor Al Hilal exclaimed during a crown chakra awakening "Anal Haq," which means "I Am That, I Am God." He was punished for this as this was considered blasphemy. He did not say Mansoor, the man, is God. He exclaimed very much like Jesus who said, "I and my Father are one." This is exactly the experience for anyone at the level of the highest crown chakra called in Sanskrit as "Sahasrara." At the crown level one feels as if the Creator and the creation are merged into one. God is felt everywhere, and we can feel a miniature universe within us.

Masters like Buddha, Patanjali, Krishna, and many more had similar understanding of the chakras, which came from their perception and a sense of "immortality," which is beyond the five senses. They had the courage to state their experiences openly and were willing to face the consequences because of this sense of immortality and knowing *they were one with God.*

What is the connection between breathing and chakras?

Before we work on chakras we need to investigate and understand how we misuse our body and our breath. We subconsciously let the negative aspects of our emotions dictate our breathing, and this blocks the movement of energy through the chakras. For most people, even under normal circumstances our breathing system is in "emergency mode," also termed as "fight or flight response." This is breathing from the upper chest rather than the relaxing diaphragmatic breathing. When you learn to breathe the natural way like a baby, the breath will revert to a calm breathing from the diaphragm. Through meditation the psychic energy travels from the base of the spine to the highest point. As you grow deeper in your meditation, a point comes where breathing may even stop, and now you know you are at the crown chakra level. As Jesus said, "Man does not live by bread alone, but every word that proceedeth from the mouth of God." I believe that what he meant by the "bread" is the "breath." And what He meant by the "mouth" of God is the crown chakra and *the prana*, which is your life force emanating from it.

Chakra One: Creating Security and Abundance

. . . .

"Muladhara Chakra" located at the base of the spine.

Our first chakra is all about stability, safety, survival, stillness, and grounding. These are some fundamental principles, which everyone is naturally seeking. It is natural to associate money with stability and safety, but it is unnatural to use money as a symbol, rather than a reality. It is even more unnatural to use money as a substitute for life! Just as when the 1920 stock market crashed, half of the brokers died of a heart attack, while others committed suicide. This shows that there is a lack of understanding of the true context for abundance in their hearts.

Just like the casino effect, if you win a million dollars today and then it is taken away from you a month later, such people will be the most miserable on Earth. Therefore, we need *eternal wealth* at all times. Where do we get this? From the inside! Howard Hughes was one of the richest men in America and was once asked, "If there was one thing you could keep for the rest of your life, what would it be?" He said, "It would be my courage in life and the ability to recreate everything from scratch, not my money." So if you do what you truly love to do, it will no longer be a hard task, but a privilege and an honor to be involved in that task. This is the true art of living.

How does a Soul from Mercury view money, wealth, and abundance?

We are the main instruments in creating abundance in our lives. For a Soul from Mercury, abundance starts from the inside out. Abundance operates from the nucleus level inside man. And whatever he appreciates and give thanks for will automatically increase in his or her life. When you have sincere gratitude, you literally send out a call to the universe to give you more by your inner vibrations. The expression of gratitude starts these vibrations, which will magnetize towards you the things that you want. Do you presently appreciate what you already have? The universe claims that if you truly appreciate what you have in your life and focus on the good of the world, then the rest will follow. Because gratitude heals the emotions, you will now attract positive things and people.

Consider money as a form of pure energy and not as a thing. Look at it as a value to be exchanged; this balance of value is a must. Money is certainly unlimited, and the limit put on the abundance of money in the world today is a myth created and perpetuated by man. It is this myth that is the source of misery for the world. Instead of only focusing on money, focus on the value you can produce for others with that money. The wealthy people who produce value for themselves and for others are to be considered honest and the best and the cream of society. However, wealthy people who produce value only for themselves and not for others should be considered to belong to a lower class. This is the true way of looking at the caste system that exists in some parts of the world.

As I was listening to one of my old talks, I came across this question: "Which country is richer, Japan or India? Japan just had an earthquake and so did India around the same time. When this happened, the local Japanese municipality asked for help but not much happened. The municipality then went on to ask the provincial government and the provincial asked the federal government. And the federal said, they would discuss with the emperor and get back to them. The emperor then reached out to the neighboring countries. It took weeks before real tangible help arrived. Whereas when it happened in Western India, the news spread and the provincial chief minister went to visit them. He was pleasantly surprised to see that everything was already handled and all that was required was some funding to rebuild the homes and infrastructures. What happened here was that the people took responsibility for each other and showed their caring for each other as well despite their religious differences. The volunteer force is so strong in India that you can get 100,000 people on the streets for a good cause. Another reason why the difficulty arose in the case of Japan, even being one of the richest countries in the world, is because that town was not living up to Buddha's noble teachings and truths.

So which is the richer country? India. While walking in the streets of India, you will see cheerful faces despite living in very poor conditions. One can also notice less personal boundaries, which results from connecting at the soul level. Even though they may not have as many resources, they have more of a living connection with the soul and spiritual teachings, which emerges truthfully in times of need. So true abundance is an offshoot of the "inner riches," which resides within and gets evoked in a moment's notice. When you produce value for others, you may not necessarily create money, but you will be full, filled, and fulfilled.

When you learn not to focus or worry about money, money will come. This may seem challenging because of the way we have been cultured and conditioned. Most of us equate money with abundance. But this is a limiting belief and a mental block to actually manifesting abundance. Abundance is like all manifestations, a showing-up phenomenon. If you believe that you do not have enough money, then you have developed a consciousness of lack and poverty. Therefore, your subconscious mind is always listening to the word and the feeling of lack. As a result, it will manifest more lack. So my first advice to you is to never carry limited and lacking beliefs about money and remember that abundance is a natural characteristic of the inner self.

All the virtues, which are all inherent in the Inner Being, can be called inner riches. Enthusiasm, playfulness, patience, and perseverance are a few examples of inner riches. Outer riches only grow as an expression of these inner riches. Your attitude, inner riches, and spiritual strength will expand also when you help others through the use of money. It is impossible for you to have low self-esteem when you help others to produce value in their lives. Share with others what you have and obtain mutual trust and respect, and then you will automatically realize true wealth.

Ancient Wisdom About the Eight Forms of Wealth

There are eight forms of wealth in the Eastern tradition. My Guru has composed prayers for all the eight "goddesses" who represent these forms.

I bow to the Goddess of Lakshmi (i.e., wealth) using the following eight forms of life. I would like to honor:

1. The *goddess of grain* who provides the essential nutrients for all human beings.
2. The *goddess of cattle* who helps in the production of grains, provides milk, nourishment, and other forms of support.
3. The *goddess of the five elements* in the human body, (i.e., space, air, fire, water, earth) who controls our health and inner well-being.
4. The *goddess of courage* who helps us to face ourselves, speaks truth, and lives in trust. Living in total trust is courage, because when you have courage, you will not have jealousy, anger or envy.
5. The *goddess of victory* who is in the form of all powers and perfections within us, where we gain victory over our lower selves and lower chakras.
6. The *goddess of wisdom* who bestows unique knowledge that creates liberation from the ego and purifies the intellect, helping us make better choices for others and ourselves.
7. The *goddess of progeny* who assumes the form of a good son, grandson or student who comes to help you.
8. The *goddess of goodness* who is a combination of graciousness, good mind, and excellent disposition. Even if all other forms of wealth be there, in the absence of goodness, everything amounts to nothing.

Daily Gratitude Exercise for Abundance

Answer the following questions and abundance will come your way:

1. Name all the things you are grateful for? (Write these down daily. This should be related to health, wealth, relationships, career, and so on.)
2. Write all the wow moments in your day.
3. Write all the random acts of kindness that you received today.
4. What are the good things that you have created from the past? Have you ever changed your behavior based on a past event? Has this change helped you to develop a new personality trait, or did it lead you to new relationships with other people?

5. What is happening in your life now that is really working for you and that you feel good about?
6. Finally, what would you like to receive from the universe today?
7. Say *"thank you, thank you, thank you,"* several times throughout the day, even though your wishes have not yet manifested.

These questions should be answered honestly and periodically as a method to evaluate your relationship with the universe. The daily connection with this gratitude process will clear some of the basic belief systems we have about abundance in general and money in particular.

This is a question to be asked in order to have a connection with the soul level and for the alignment to happen. Why am I doing what I am doing right now and at any moment of my life? While cooking, reading, walking to a destination, or even while reading this book, ask yourself this question: Why am I doing what I'm doing? If your response is that I am doing this or walking there to get some money for my own survival, comfort or habit, then you are on the wrong track. Whereas if you shift your intention and attention to serving others or if you ask how this action will help you towards your spiritual growth and connection to God, then you are on the right track. As the renowned Rev. Michael Beckwith said, "Behind every problem, there is a question trying to ask itself. Behind every question there is an answer trying to reveal itself. Behind every answer there is an action trying to take place. And behind every action there is a way of life trying to be born."

Exercise to do a self-evaluation on abundance:

1. Do you agree that money is good and not bad? What do you think of the statement that "money is good versus less money is good?" How do you feel about the scarcity and the abundance of money; is it good or bad? The two most common beliefs about money are the lack of it or the fear of scarcity, and that you are not good or capable enough to have or deserve it, which is the denial of your creative potential. Both of these beliefs are listed under the heading "Poverty Consciousness." The opposite to these beliefs is "Prosperity Consciousness," which insists that there is, indeed, a universe of abundance, and that you have every right and the ability to fully partake in money and wealth.

2. Do you focus your attention on the lack of money throughout the day? If you do, you will reinforce the lack. For a person without a job, I would

like to say, you are not unemployed, you are simply free and available for something greater than a "menial" job. Do not mentally dwell on poverty because that is what will be nourished by the energy of your thoughts. When you are emotionally and psychologically prepared for poverty, it will come straight to you. However, prosperity will be attracted to you if you are emotionally and intelligently ready to expect it, to accept it, and to enjoy it. Whatever you direct your mental attention to, will be created.

3. Can you look carefully and honestly at the role money plays in your life? Sift through the various beliefs that you have been exposed to from your parents, peers, religion, and society; and when you do, pay particular attention to the programming and conditioning that you received relative to the impact of having or not having lot of money.

4. Can you see that money is not a thing but pure energy?

A Poem by Kalidasa

Look to this day!
For it is life, the very life of life.
In its brief course
Lie all the verities and realities of your existence.
The bliss of growth,
The glory of action,
The splendour of achievement
Are but experiences of time.

For yesterday is but a dream
And tomorrow is only a vision;
And today well-lived, makes
Yesterday a dream of happiness
And every tomorrow a vision of hope.
Look well therefore to this day;
Such is the salutation to the ever-new dawn!

Chakra Two: Uniting the Trilogy of Sex, Love, and Divinity

· · · · · · · · · · · · · · · · ·

"Swadhisthana Chakra" located at the sacrum area of the body.

Within each human being, there is only one energy that manifests in three different forms: sex, love, and divinity. At the lower level, it manifests as sex. At a slightly higher level, it manifests as love, and at the highest level it manifests as divinity. So when you are in prayer and experiencing your own divinity, you will automatically not operate as a sexual being at that time. You will you will be just one organic unity within and that makes you a true master of your own life.

For example, when you are "running" after someone else (either romantically or sexually), you are in a struggle and miserable state of frustration. Sex is based on division, whereas when one is in divinity, one sees oneself as a unity and present everywhere. What you are seeking during sexual acts and intimacy is unity, when in fact, it never delivers what it promises. You still remain two separate beings. So what you were really seeking was not even achieved. After sex, you might think you are in bliss, but that is an illusion and only lasts for a while before the fight and struggle begins again.

Lovers all over the world are fighting. Why? They have become intimate enemies (with the exception of the honeymoon phase). So why are they still unhappy? Because they feel cheated. What you and others desired was unity that lasts and that was never delivered. The soul wants permanency in all things: happiness, satisfaction in food, comfort, safety, everything. But permanency is not in the very nature of things. Flowers fade, leaves wither away, the body gets sick and ages, and feelings change.

This chakra will only give you grief if not properly controlled and directed. With the exceptions of sexual pleasure, conception, and childbirth, this chakra cannot even give love. Love comes from the higher being and higher chakra. It is through the heart chakra that a mother loves the child. It is through the heart chakra that you love others—despite their age, gender, ability and so on—because it is coming from a soul level. When you are in a state of divinity, which I will express more in detail later on, there is no need to hold onto or possess another man or woman. Even animals have a tendency to possess each other. It is nature. They will fight with other animals to gain the right to possess others. But in divine love, you free the other person, which is where The Man from Mercury lives.

If God choose to possess us, all the world's problems of today would be solved within a split second. But God has chosen not to be possessive and give man the utter freedom to be who he is, and to evolve the way he is evolving. He wants you to be good, generous, peaceful, and honest of your own choice. Just look and see how much respect God has paid to you as a unique being.

Why do so many people get stuck in this unconscious state?

There is a natural low level vibration and keeps you fastened to the unconsciousness. You are not aware of the inner vibrations but only aware of your thoughts.

This sexual energy is dissolved once we get united with the soul. There will be no spiritual growth inside you unless you comprehend this change in energy. What many people fail to see is this great adventure in life, and that sexuality is larger than sex and the energy involved in sexuality is more powerful.

Spiritual experience is only for the strong and courageous, and not for the weak. You will be moving against the current continuously. This is the reason many saints said that lust is somewhat like the dark side of the soul, and when you are held up by your thoughts, you are living, not as a soul, but as a body. You are just yielding to inner gravitational force. When you build up a spiritual structure, a new force will start operating that will be in opposition to the force that wants to pull you down like gravity. This I call as "The Law of Grace" and this will manifest. And the surge to reach for the sun and the stars will begin to operate in you.

How does a Soul from Mercury manage sexual energy?

Man, by nature, is a bundle of energy. You do many things to accumulate more energy, and now you have the option of using it creatively or wasting it. Masturbation is the last resort. When you eat, drink, etc., you accumulate energy because the food is converted into inner resource.

The outer part of the food becomes calorific energy that supplies fuel to the muscles. Then there is also a subtle part of the food itself, that you cannot see, which is psychic in nature and works with the chakras. So when you eat food that is high in prana or life force, your chakras are nourished and function in harmony and peace. So when for example, you eat a pig, you essentially become a pig, think like a pig and feel like a pig. So become a vegetarian if you care for spiritual growth and activation of higher chakras. When you are lazy and doing mechanical work only, the only outlet left is sexual activity. Whereas if you find other means of creativity and self expressions such as music, arts, sports, dance and prayer, you will less bothered by the pressure of the sexual drive.

Look at all the monks, nuns, and saints. How did they manage their sexual energy? They did this by being so engrossed in prayer and connection to God that there was no time and focus given to physical attraction and lust. Some people may think this process is a cop-out or seen as a repression of natural urges, but in reality, there no longer exist a need for these intimate expressions.

A Soul from Mercury is not a nun or a monk. "They live in the world but not of it," as Jesus explained. For example, they live in a relationship with either their partner or spouse, and treat them compassionately as a best friend and as divine goddesses to begin with. Out of this living realization, natural love arises for the other, where they also care for their feelings. Once this love is present, the body naturally follows that inner feeling of love.

Whereas, when humans try to create love and union first out of the sexual contact, (i.e., "He will love me more if I give him sex") they will only create frustration and disappointment because love is missing. Let me explain this better with an analogy. Think of a funnel. At the top of the funnel is the energy of compassion. In the center is natural love. And at the bottom of the funnel is sex. So the top of the funnel is your spirit, and the middle of the funnel is your mind and heart. And the bottom of the funnel is body.

According to science, energy cannot be destroyed. In the same way, sex energies cannot be destroyed, they can only be transmuted into other forms of energy. The ancient Ayurveda system of medicine believes that sex energy, when channeled inward, can be transmuted into energy called Ojas (which means vigor and vitality). Ojas then converts itself into Tejas, (which means divine light) by special meditative techniques.

Managing your sex energy becomes easy when you meditate, practice pranayama, contribute to others, and pray. This way, your mind will be focused on God and serving others rather than what you are getting and your own pleasure. Sex and sexual energy are parts of nature, and like breathing, you cannot stop it. So instead of thinking about how to control your sex energy, think in terms of *transmutation* of sex energy, which is a change or conversion of energy from one form into another.

When does transformation and transmutation of sexual energies begin to shift into love?

Transformation begins when you ask yourself this question: Is there something higher than this lowest center? Spirituality will begin when you say to yourself: "There must be something more than this." Devotion to God will overcome this lowest level of living. You also need energy from food, sleep, etc. to grow spiritually. Most people allow the energy they get from food and sleep, etc. to dissipate downward to the lowest level. The flow of energy that shifts downward is called lust and the current of energy that moves up to a higher level is love. You as a human being will only have meaning when you are no longer stuck at the lowest level. This meaning comes from beyond. And when you discover God, you will see and learn what was intended by the Lord your Father. When lust is born from true love, then even lust has meaning and you gain energy. When a higher meaning is brought into your life, no energy will be lost. This is happening inside you continually, and the energy is always there. The energy for the process of evolution is part of the soul, and not the body.

What is the difference between the love of an ordinary human being and Soul from Mercury?

A Soul from Mercury lives in love, while the ordinary man or woman is focused on sex and lust. There is an ocean of difference between love and lust. Love is not only the last expression of energy, but also the highest. It is centered inside you. With love, you give yourself, thus it is also creative and unlimited. However, with lust, you come from taking and it is destructive, possessive, and limiting. Lust is the lowest form and expression of energy and it is the result of a conditioned mind.

In love, you are conscious, and in lust you are unconscious. Love is coolness, is giving, and has no attachments. Lust is hot and has attachments. As an evolved being and as a Soul from Mercury, you will live in love and live as a *nobody*. By living in lust, only "you" will exist. By living in love, only the other exists. And when you have total devotion and surrender to God, both lust and love, as you know it, will disappear into Divine Love and One Universal Love.

Does it mean that when you break one commandment you break all of them?

When you break one of the Ten Commandments, you break them all, but if you keep the Commandments, you will be free. Pursue all you need to know to have a vision of the Divine within you and to know God, and then when you experience the temptation of lust, it will disappear or not bother you because you would have learned not to act on that thought. Create high level awareness by conscious breathing, meditation, and prayer. They are the means to climb to the highest level of energy and the transformer is your consciousness. You will automatically move into meditation within a short period of time once you begin to concentrate on awareness. Divine Grace, which is a gift of God, will help you to reach for Him and His love, and will help you to let go of temptations. When you operate under the law of Grace, coolness and love will manifest in you. Be aware of a tingling sensation within you as the spiritual lightness begins. The effect of lust is similar to the law of gravity; it pulls you down to the lower level whereas divine grace pulls you up to higher levels of awareness. The Ten Commandments were not given to saints. They were given to ordinary man like you and me. So the moment you say that you cannot follow all the Ten Commandments, you have already ruled out the possibility of ever achieving this.

Can you bring purity into the body?

Many religious people believe that the body is born in sin and lives in sin, and that there is no such thing as sexual purity. This is far from truth. You can bring purity into the body, but it requires a level of transformation within your own self to bring purity into something that is impure. There is a pure being inside you and you are not conscious of it.

There are some ways that you can bring purity to the body. Some examples are by doing certain rituals that purify the body called *poojas* in the Hindu community. For example, one can bring certain rituals into their daily practices such as burning incense, blessing the food, and lighting the candles/oil lamps. This way, your body is awakening the five senses in a spiritual way. Doing these rituals once a week, or even once a year, will not give you the ability to bring the purity of the Pure Being into the body.

Some people think that priests or bishops are the only ones who can do rituals for the blessings of the body or family. However, one can certainly perform their own daily powerful rituals of some sort as long as the devotion and prayer comes from the heart center. Even though you may not be having the purest of thoughts during these daily practices, it's okay in the beginning. Let them be. As the practices deepen, these thoughts will slowly give way to the pure vibrations of the chants or positive affirmations, which are called mantras in the Hindu tradition.

Here are some simple phrases that you can use:

> *"Dear God my heart is open to you. Please come and stay in my heart.*
> *Dear God, bless this body and make it into a channel for your divine energy*
> *and instrument to do your work in this world.*
> *Dear God, let noble thoughts come to me from all sides and awaken me.*
> *Thank you, thank you, thank you."*

What is a meditation process by which the sexual energy is transformed?

The process by which energy is transformed is the most important. For example, the way to transfer lust, and also anger into love is through conscious fast breathing and special meditation such as the ones taught here:

Just witness and become aware of the thought process, but do not focus on them in your mind. When you sense the energy, move down to the center within yourself and watch it, but do not name it. Do not take action on a thought, or resist it. Close your eyes and do not contemplate on the thought. This is the principle of the "Middle Path" by Buddha and consists of just watching it like a witness with no judgment. You close your eyes; move down with your consciousness to the lowest point of the spine until you notice a slight vibration. Watch and witness the sensation, but do not judge it as something weird. Watch it, but do not resist it or name it.

You become separated from the body when you watch it. The ability to watch and understand this process is a great power to have. You are not the body, you are not the thoughts and you are not the sensations. Now you can rise in consciousness and do not care what happens to the body, because you know you are not that, you are the spirit. You learn how to let go and become an independent of other beliefs you have about yourself.

Now you have learned to surrender to God. There is only one you, no other, and you are with the universe. Love is only a step toward God, and in pure aloneness you will feel God. In meditation, this love is like the bud of a thousand-petal lotus flower opening up.

How is sex energy related to other energies such as anger?

Lust only continues as long as violence is present and vice versa. Is greed more violent than lust? Will one desire overcome another such as killing lust with lust? Move to a higher plane, which is compassion. How will you sense change in your body as you move to a higher level of energy? Sexuality began with a flame and the sun is fire, which is heat. However, the moon represents coolness and you will feel this coolness inside you as the spiritual structure develops.

The phases of sexual transformation, which a man can go through, include sensual sexuality, which is sex for the sake of sex, the emotional sexuality, and the rational sexuality, which defines what is right and what is wrong. The next stage is called love, and to live in this phase is so important and is almost a matter of life and death.

Live during the first stage of life as a student by questioning, understanding and then training. Are you going to create a new pattern of living by regulating your life? The path is simple when you work to support your spirituality and apply yourself. Time is of the essence in the early years of your development.

Sex is not a lion, it is just a mouse, and you have made it into a lion. You cannot conquer it; you can only see the role it is playing in your life. So instead of seeing it as a predominant force in your life, see it as a submissive one and use it wisely.

Are we violating the law of nature by ignoring the sexual force?

According to the Law of Nature, man will always seek communion between two bodies. Nature cannot depend on man. There is death and nature wants to create other bodies. It is natural for man to seek intercourse with other bodies, but man abuses the instinct; other creatures do not. Lust is so strong it has become an obsession. When death disappears, lust as a desire, will also disappear. Seek this permanence and experience something inside you that is beyond death. It will take a lot of practice for growth and understanding to acquire the higher levels of meditation for this permanence. According to Yoga, death is fiction, the real you is ever born and never dies.

What is the connection between love and prayer?

Love is communion between two saintly souls, and prayer is a kind of spiritual intimacy or intercourse between you and the universe. Learn by prayer to feel that you are with God and hence you will have the vision of God. Jesus said, "My Father exists in me. Under every stone is the Lord." True longing is for God only, and the goal of man, in fact, is to reach the state of being one with God and feel him in every fiber of your being. When you offer your lust energy to God, you are offering your spiritual love to God. When you do this, you will grow in the higher dimension of communion. Energy always flows as bliss and for higher bliss. It will only flow also in one direction.

Are there levels of love center as well?

For the spiral of "oneness" or communion, there are a number of levels of love centers. For example, you and the things that lead to "oneness" is the source. The power that you gain from dominating others is operating at the unconscious level. The next level is the man to woman differences, which include the communion of the soul and the body, and the interaction of polarities where jealousy may show up. The highest level of love emanates from your own being, which arrives like the sound of the universe and happens on its own. It is the goal of man and has no polarities; it is the meeting place of God and animal, and the animal is still there but purified. The more purified energy is at the throat level. This is the touching point, the ability to relate without holding the glimpse of the Divine, and the love relative to others in order to teach. The command center, which is from God, is the level that includes the fulfillment of the Ten Commandments and the third eye. Finally, the energies from God to man, which are opened to the purified mind, after the fulfillment of the Ten Commandments, will include knowledge, desire, action, and the first level of love.

Chakra Three: Self-Love and Self-Esteem

· · · · · · · · · · · · · · · ·

Chakra three, or what some people call "the limbic brain" is made up of our feelings and emotions which we need to integrate into a single whole, so that it can support the blossoming of the heart (chakra four).

Most people live in two extremes. One is poor self-image, and the other one is arrogance, which is overly high self-image. Both of these are not in touch with the reality of who you are. Self-respect is right in the middle and seems to be the hardest to maintain. It is hard because self-image by itself is a temporary phenomenon. As Mooji said, "Your self-image is as ephemeral as the play of play dancing on the surface of the water." We hold onto that self-image as a permanent phenomenon and somehow want to keep it in place the way it has always been. We think that our world will crumble if some self-image is not kept. Just as an individual tries to hold on to their worldview, the same way we hold onto our "self-view." The identification with this self-view is part of the identity crisis in the human being. So once a certain identity is in place, the function of the intellect is to protect what you consider yourself to be. And the *thoughts* that result from such an intellect will all be in support of this train of thought which are mostly negative. It takes a revolution (not evolution) to recognize that you are really a nobody, and every identity we assume, such as "I am an engineer, Republican..." is a limitation on our being and will block us from feeling and realization our inner core.

Bliss cannot be maintained because it is your very nature. So it is your responsibility to create it moment to moment. The secret is in being a "nobody" and attain "nobody-ness," which is the core of my teaching.

You cannot control the external circumstances of your life but you can control your reactions to them. Change is the only constant in your life, and things will definitely change. Even during illness, believe that you are healthy, because optimal health is the product of physical and mental factors. Your beliefs are powerful, and to escape from stress, fear and doubt, you must confront them directly, and see them for what they are. Emotions fall into the two broad categories of fear and love. When you learn to accept yourself and practice forgiveness by letting go of the past, you will always stay open to life's teachings. It is impossible to be right all the time. Be patient with yourself, be happy, and experience a level of peace. Being patient with yourself is an act of awareness. There is a strong connection between proper breathing and your body functions. You can control your emotions by regulating your breathing. Before responding to an emotionally charged event in your life, go back to your breathing and then decide if it is worth it to jump into the ring. You will stop yourself from doing many regrettable mistakes. You cannot handle emotions by affirmations alone but more easily by slowing down the breath.

Can you explain the difference between emotions and feelings if any? Is there a creative way to deal with them?

The difference between feeling and emotion can be understood by meditation. Emotion is as the word purports itself—energy in motion! Feelings arise first and the level deeper than thought, and then when you add energy to it, it becomes emotion. The ability to express emotion is missing in many people. You will have to validate your emotions for what they are to be able to feel and express your feelings in a healthy way. Be aware that the natural response to any feeling is humanity speaking to you. Listen to your feelings and emotions, and feel anger and joy when they happen.

Discover a creative way to express feeling, and have the courage to communicate this emotion even to you. If you find it hard, or impossible to do, then go out. When you change the beliefs that cause emotional upsets, you will be able to change the response to the feelings. Recognize that only you can make the choice to let go of such feelings, and to clear out the negative emotions that you carry from the past and to heal yourself. The hurts that you have suffered in the past can be released in either a short time, or you can choose to let them go wherever you are able and willing to do so.

Can you tell us a practical way how we can recover soon when someone pushes our hot button?

Most of our reactions and emotions manifest themselves like a tape recorder. You have to identify the undesired response to the feeling to really know what the emotion is. When something is said or done that "pushes your hot button," use the power of your emotional upset to trace the core beliefs that keep recurring. Root out your inner conversations from within yourself, and make the connection with the core beliefs that support them, and identify the old "record" which is now playing in your mind. Create a new "record," and the visualization that relates to it. Develop a pause function that will allow you the time to change the "record" before you respond to the emotion. Pause by taking a deep breath, count to three, visualize a red "stop sign," and if necessary, walk away. By mentally rehearsing this technique each day, the process may help you to identify the source of the inner conversation and the core belief that supports it.

How do you personally develop self-love and become a master at it?

Be yourself and become aware of both your masculine and feminine sides. The feminine side will always look for a solution to a problem with tolerance, trust and allowance for the differences in opinions, without violence. However, the masculine side of you will manifest that you are better, faster, stronger, and smarter than anyone else to handle a situation. Your relationship with your mother or father as an infant will always be in your subconscious and it may impact your actual relationship with the world. The easiest way to clear it is to develop a relationship with God, the Divine mother/father as the case may be.

How do you develop spiritual relationship? What is the connection between normal and spiritual relationships?

You must accept everything and do nothing. In meditation, you will witness everything go on and will accept it without reacting. Once you master this you will then be on your way to accept events and people in life, not before that! You have to be willing to give everything and take nothing back to reach prosperity spiritually. In a spiritual relationship service is the dominance.

Ask the following questions all the time.

1. What lesson will you learn if you accept everything from another person?

2. Will it help you to become aware that this is a part of the higher good in your life you have to reach?

3. Will it help you to recognize that suffering will only become an important fact when you believe that spiritual growth can only come through pain and suffering? Look at the whole picture of your existence, and see the higher perspective of life.

4. If self-love is essential towards spiritual development, then any form of negative feelings about you must certainly indicate a lack of self-love. Develop a creative approach and let go of something, or leave someone, until you love what you dislike and it will support you to be able to release the past. The more you love, the freer you become, and the more you hate, the stronger the attachment will be to what you hate. Can you develop a positive understanding by loving the past? In other words, accepting it and moving on with your life. Recognize the good you have done in the past, and create a new approach to life from this experience. So in light of this, can you reframe the past to yourself?

5. If you really feel negative about yourself, could it be that you have made a major change in your life? Is it possible that the impact of this change has an important connection with a person or a group? Whatever the change or contact was, it may have helped you to develop a new personality trait, or an inner feeling expressing your desire not to repeat a certain activity. Listen to your inner feelings and thoughts, and see the valuable lessons they have for your spiritual growth.

What is the easy way to be happy and live in love?

When you want to understand and experience love and happiness in your life, go beyond logic. Learn to drop logic and tune into people and events. Being happy is natural, so those who postpone happiness are anti-religious. There is no particular time or space for happiness; it is life. Happiness won't be found when you pursue it. When you think that you have to do something to be happy, you are setting conditions for happiness. When you build up a desire for something and it arrives, are you happy? Why? Do you think that happiness is related to a desire? When what you want is similar to what you have, it is equal to happiness. The unsettled mind is the cause of all unhappiness. When you have a settled mind, and are calm and steady in your thoughts, you will discover happiness. Celebrate everything when it happens, because like meditation, happiness only accepts what exists at the present moment.

How do you deal with fear and guilt?

The source of disease is fear. Clear yourself totally from fear. When you have fear, your mind will become brittle. Fear and guilt can also destroy you like an enemy. The more you resist the more they persist. Like in martial arts, do not resist them, observe your opponent's strength and use it to your benefit to win over them.

Always focus on the positive events and things in your life, and do not react to negative issues. Resolve to stick to your vision throughout the inevitable ups and downs that can occur. Discipline and daily dedication, as the effect of your commitment, will support your vision to manifest itself. A support system exists for you and it includes friends and relationships, which are dedicated to help you grow. The intuition within you is your inner guidance. Listen to it and obtain the answers to the questions that are fundamental to you. Approaching life with a good sense of humor, patience, and a light spirit is a great support. Love everything in the world, and develop a loving openness to all of your experiences. Discover your own truth, which is the principal guiding force for you to create your life, as you want it to be.

Can meditation help with suicidal thoughts and feelings?

Yes. People want to commit suicide because of three core beliefs they have within themselves:

1. Now I know nobody truly loves me.
2. There is no more meaning and purpose in my life.
3. Life has become such a struggle and uphill task that I want to give up.

Let us see how we can address each one of these core beliefs.

1. **Now I know nobody truly loves me.**
   "For whom shall I live and for what purpose do I live when there is none." This becomes the inner self-talk of the people who feel this way. If they only knew that there is at least one person who loves them unconditionally, they would change their decision to end their life. In addition, if they only knew that the existential purpose of life is to know and contact its creator, then they would not end this precious life and know that God loves them very much.

2. **There is no more meaning and purpose in my life.**
   Most people live as a question mark subconsciously thinking, "What about me? What will happen to me when, if ..." which is the perfect formula for creating misery, agony, and depression, which leads to suicide. The way to end this question mark is to be *engaged* in the question, "How can I use this life to share, serve, and help others?" This service has to be a direct service where your entire being is involved, which can be towards lovingly feeding your kitten or dog. You will then come out of this question mark and mind-trap "what about me?" Service about yourself is the final answer to most of life's problems.

3. **Life has become such a struggle and uphill task that I want to give up.**
   There are some people who feel that many people love them and who feel that they do meaningful work. Still they feel the results of their actions are not commensurate with the level of effort they put in. The thing is, there is only one solution to this uphill struggle stuff.

   They feel that since their efforts failed then they are a failure. This is a false conclusion of the mind. Their efforts failing only mean that there was a problem with the direction or intensity. You think I am the doer and I am all alone in this. However you are not the doer, only an instrument of God. God helps those who help themselves.

There are only two kinds of people in my opinion who are capable of committing suicide: Those without a master or those without faith in God. Friends and family might wonder what happened in many cases in spite of them being around. "I thought I gave her love and support," say friends and family. But then it's too late.

What solutions can you offer to someone feeling suicidal?

"The master's touch" gives you the impermanent nature using the "this too shall pass" mantra. It gives you the knowledge that you have strengths and skills. So whatever failure might have occurred is only in one area of your life. Awareness of this will help you see that you can do more with this precious life. In order not to punish oneself from your wrongdoings, you must know that it is past karma that is acting up, which you cannot do anything about right away. Let the time and karma work its way out. Your friends, family and God is there, but the biggest network of help is a master. He adds a third force that always balances out the other two.

A master sees you as a "family and a friend," but he is more than this. Family may fight about finances or disrespect and may no longer want to see each other again. And friends may also turn away if you don't fulfill their expectations at times. Whereas a master's love is guaranteed. Whether you are accomplished or not, have money or not, or continue to prove yourself or not. This is why the "fourth leg" is so important as the foundation of our life. Jesus, Buddha, Krishna and all masters said around these lines that "I am the gate and no man can cometh unto the father except through me." Basically egotistical people can't attain enlightenment, because they have to surrender to existence. "Most people say "I don't need a teacher, I have myself, I am my own teacher, etc." Whereas, the other polarity are those who have blind faith, which also doesn't help them. Somewhere between these two extremes is the way, and that way always leads to authentic surrender. You can say "I surrender, I surrender!" but it has to be authentic, which always leads to realization of self or God. So a master is like a mirror who helps you see your own self. How else can you see your face except through a mirror?

The longest distance to cross is the space from the eyebrow chakra to the crown chakra, which is one inch! From here to the moon is easier to reach than this space. (Coming from a guy who worked on NASA and space projects since college.)

You can read as many spiritual books as you want, and practice yoga as much as you want, but only a master can open that. A master's touch helps take the karma away. Because a master's hand, is God's own hand, at least from time to time, when he or she is possessed by God.

The Opposite of Depression is Expression

Journaling is a good way to dump all your feelings. However this is not total self-expression. Total expression happens when you let go of everything including your inhibitions. So I encourage you to play, dance, and cook. Playing to have fun, not win.

Chakra Four: Opening The Heart Center

Chakra four is known as the heart center or (Anahata). Opening the heart center is all about developing the ability to accept, moment to moment, whatever is happening to you. Understand this form of acceptance and learn to make it a transforming instrument by offering no resistance to the flow of events. Recognize that this understanding and acceptance is only an example for you to follow, and accept people as they are.

Are you aware that love is your nature and that hate is cultivated? When you love people, there is a commitment by you to hold to a higher vision of the other even though that person is not honoring this higher vision at the present moment. By focusing on bringing out the goodness in people, you will see their beauty and you will be able to express it to them. It is a very effective way to solve your relationship problems. When you work directly on relationships and the higher version of others, be aware of power struggle problems between you and them; do not fall in the trap.

What do you think is the perfect relationship?

The two polarities, which are the man and woman within each person, meet, and you are love. The perfect relationship that you can experience is with you, and your authentic self in silence. When you know who you are then you will reach enlightenment, which is the "oneness" with all that exists. This is the clear understanding of God and the Ten Commandments.

You will need to purify your thinking, physically and mentally, to clarify the mind and emotions and unify it in its totality. This path needs discipline, observation, compassion, love, sharing, friendship, humility, the praise of others, and thankfulness. The rest, meaning the Grace of God, will follow.

There is a difference between a lifemate and a soulmate. You can have many soulmates, but a lifemate is forever. And you are the luckiest in life if you can turn a lifemate into a soulmate. It is not easy, but it is easier than trying to convert a soulmate into a lifemate. And if you can do that, then you are the luckiest.

They are fighting because their love has become a big effort. For instance, "I'm married now to this person, so I have to love them." This is a lower state of being because it will keep you stuck there. Whereas, if you say to yourself, "I really love this person. I want to take care of this person. No one needs to tell me." This is being in love effortlessly. And this is what Jesus meant by agape love, which has nothing to do with sexual or physical attraction.

We can do the same in relation to our relationship with God. "I want to think about God. I want to connect with Him. I want to do His work, which is being clearly assigned to me. I want to serve and love Him no matter what. This is being in love with God effortlessly. This is called true devotion and "bhakti" in Sanskrit.

How can we always have fun in our relationships?

Firstly you have to recognize that your first love relationship is with the "Self." Create a higher version of this relationship beyond the daily joys and struggles. As a form of commitment to communicating with your heart center, speak honestly of your concerns and feelings, and gracefully let go of the hurts and resentments by silencing the internal chatter in meditation. Confront the desire to win over another person by thought, word or deed, which is simply a power issue on your part. Is it necessary for you to create a point to be debating endlessly with a person with whom you are closely related? Find a solution where both of you can win, and if you are unable to, then humbly request assistance from someone else. Do you want to be happy or do you want to be right? Make your choice.

How do you live in love?

Honor the continuous process of change in a relationship, and review your respect for each other as the changes take place. Create space and time for each other, and have fun in the relationship. In any personal connection it is also important to let others know your goal as the basis for a good relationship. Embrace the paradox of love/hate in a normal relationship, understand it but do not solve it, because there is no solution. Embrace also the paradox of love, relative to a relationship, by integrating the female and male sides within you. Relax and balance with your female side when there is too much action on the male side. If emotions take the upper hand, tell yourself "times up!" and go back to meditation.

Don't expect one person in your life to fulfill all the roles that you need, such as a romantic partner, spiritual coach, handyman, fashion consultant, someone to do sports with, cook with, etc. By doing this, you will not negate them and always feel they are not fulfilling your need. You are creating a problem without there actually being one. One person cannot be all these roles. He or she would crumble, and that is why people are unhappy. Two or three generations ago, people were not as discontent or demanding with each other because they appreciated their spouse's role as either the homemaker or the provider. They did not demand more. The mother's role is to develop her own esteem, of her spouse, and see him as the perfect spouse, so the child will automatically see him as the perfect father.

What guidance have you received from the scriptures regarding living in love?

For the development of your soul as a soul from Mercury please read the Sermon on the Mount from the Gospels about Jesus to understand the Beatitudes. Meditate on it everyday. You will develop the very same human characteristics and the "Be – Attitudes" that they stand for. Jesus used the word "blessed" in the context of happiness. Which actually means blissed." Therefore, the secret of how to find true happiness resides in the understanding of the Beatitudes. I developed a theme of selected passages:

"Blessed Are The Poor In Spirit; For Theirs Is The Kingdom Of Heaven." To be poor in spirit simply means not to be rich in pride and has nothing to do with worldly riches. When you are proud of any possession including health, duty, name, etc., and you cling to possessions solely for your satisfaction, you are not poor in spirit. Until you understand the poverty of spirit, you cannot possibly take the first step in spiritual development. You will not be poor in spirit and obtain bliss if you have preconceived ideas on what values should be, spiritual pride, intellectual pride, and established attachment to possessions of importance. You will feel very uncomfortable when you first let go of these possessions. When you are aware that it is all right to be wrong, you will create a new beginning by becoming spiritually a "Nobody." In front of God, what can you claim and take pride in? Keep in mind that "empty vessels shall be filled," and to do nothing and be nothing leads you closer to God. Let go and admit, in front of God, that you have failed and perhaps spiritually bankrupt, and you will be full and filled and fulfilled. It is significant to note that this is the only passage where the reward is immediate and so the word "is" was used instated of "shall" as in the remaining passages. Kingdom of Heaven refers to the state of deep meditation and connectedness to God.

"Blessed Are They That Mourn; For They Shall Be Comforted." Do not stand in front of God and shed tears for what is happening in your daily life. Look and see your spiritual loneliness, and cry for that. "I want a vision of God but cannot see Him." Weep for a vision of God and deep meditation; have grief for the right things. Be concerned for the problems of the world and do something about them, that's the right approach. The path of love, devotion, and surrender are the easiest way to reach God, and the beauty of this route is that you will be comforted, if you truly weep for God.

"Blessed Are the Meek; For They Shall Inherit The Earth." The earth as referred to does not mean our terrestrial globe, but the spiritual earth, or the revelations of all that is in your domain of experience, and Kingdom of Heaven is the inner basis for this knowledge to occur. To own the earth is to have dominion over this experience, and when you do, you will alter the outer manifestations. When you understand meekness, you will have the power inside you to make the changes. That will be the disclosure of your own consciousness. Meekness is not weakness, covetous, indolence, and it is certainly not acting as a doormat. Meekness is to have the correct balance and amount of inner energy. You can

be passive in your vigor, and aggressive in anger with meekness as the balance by a trust in God. Moses had meekness. At times, having a bit of energy and a small amount of anger, when you deal with people, is part of meekness as it comes from compassion. Even a small quantity of ambition and desire can be meekness, but you must look for the inner power to provide balance between inner peace and the energy from ambition. The inner power is to have this delicate balance. A certain degree of everything is meekness, but to replace what energy you will lose by ambition, you will need inner power. Meekness preserves this energy, and with understanding, you will find the power to change your life and develop spiritual awareness. You will also have dominion over your experiences as you know more and that is the meaning of inheriting the earth.

"Blessed Are The Righteous; For They Shall Be Filled." To be righteous means to have the right and balanced thoughts, to be full of fun, to have purity of heart, and peace-making abilities. Whatever you complete, in the state of awareness, is correct. In spiritual awareness, only good thoughts will come to you. Meditation and silence will increase your awareness to let go of your preconceived ideas. Let go of the known and become playful by discovering something new. When you hunger and thirst for righteousness, ask God for the right thought and be fulfilled.

"Blessed Are The Merciful; For They Shall Obtain Mercy." To obtain mercy you need to qualify by forgiving and showing kindness to others, and then you will obtain mercy from God. There is a reference here to a sentence in the Lord's Prayer, " As we forgive those who trespass against us, the Lord forgives our trespasses."

"Blessed Are The Pure In Heart; For They Shall See God." You have a natural restricted range of perceptions and because you think that you are limited, you cannot see God. "What I have not seen does not exist," is a common philosophy adopted by a majority of people today. It is a source of pain when you feel that you are limited, and when you accept the fact that you are limited, you will feel uncomfortable. When you consider the possibility that God exists and you lead your life accordingly, then righteousness will follow. The unseen reality that you want to experience will be your faith in God, which is purity of heart, and your non-judgmental and non-limiting emotions will add more and more to this purity. Such purity will lead you to unity and divinity. Look from the golden middle or the center, and discover the balance between what is not right and what is not wrong. To accept yourself and others as they are

is purity of heart. What is real and what is unreal? To know the real from the imaginary is a form of discrimination, but it will certainly indicate to you the way to go. Focus on the purity of other people, their strengths, and good qualities. To work with the best in each person is to be a leader, and if you are a good example, others will adjust their actions accordingly. Constantly work to strengthen the strength of others and weaken the weakness of others. Make real peace within yourself, and be a peacemaker and a child of God. If you have conflict inside you, go deeper into meditation to understand this struggle. A reflection of others' actions and feelings based on your own peace within, relating with joy, harmony, purity, compassion, and mercy, is purity of heart. When that is present, it is easy to see all in God and God in all.

"Blessed are the peacemakers; for they shall be called the children of God."
Generally the term peacemaker is used for someone who mediates between two quarreling persons or groups. It is easy to understand that they are children of God. To understand this beatitude, one has to go deeper than this. Jesus is actually referring to the inner serenity and peace that comes from meditation. He always referred to the state of mind in all his teachings, as he knew that the outer actions flow from that state.

When some disciples asked Jesus, "Master, who will be with you in the kingdom of God?" Jesus turned them inward rather than address such a superficial question. He just walked and reached out to a lady holding a child in her arms and said, "Unless you are like this little child, you will not enter the Kingdom of God." What he meant was that one cannot learn meditation unless one is like a little child in all the innocence and trust that the child depicts. This is the reason that there are many disciples of teachers of meditation today but only a small percentage of them really get what it is to meditate. They cannot do it unless they have the empathy with the teacher and get a glimpse into his inner state. Then like the chemical process called osmosis, the meditative state of the teacher can flow into the student.

When one is in deep meditation called Samadhi, then in the presence of that person, other people drop their quarrels automatically as if by magic. I bear witness to this in my life. I have seen this even in my corporate life in managerial meetings. I have joined organizations where there was total chaos and brought peace and friendliness among the fellow workers in an amazing way. The small division in which I worked and influenced the culture was rated as the best among the 100 other organizations of that major Fortune 100 Company. My son applies these biblical principles and heads up an organization that was voted by a major independent study as the best company to work for in the province of Quebec in Canada in the year 2012. He does not read the bible every day but he embodies these principles. Peacemakers have to be peaceful in themselves and that is not always the case in some world leaders, and is the true reason for all delays in the peace process!

"Blessed are they, which are persecuted for righteousness sake for theirs is the kingdom of heaven." At the outset, this statement seems to endorse martyrdom. But when you read this along with the fact that the will of God for his children is peace, joy and, harmony this will appear to be a very startling and surprising statement and a contradiction. The contradiction will disappear when we realize that all persecution starts from within. When one goes against current thought and belief system and makes declarations to open the eyes of others, others are upset to begin with. Jesus said, "Thou shall know the truth and the truth shall make thee free." What he did not say but implied, "Yes. The truth shall make thee free but it shall first upset you!" Facing the truth is painful unless one wakes up from the slumber and sleep that one is in. Eyes being open do not mean that the metaphysical sleep has already left. When one truly wakes up, then it is easy to see and chuckle at others when they get upset at your words coming out of righteousness and Dharma as you are fully awake. You can even smile when "they revile you, and shall say all manner of evil against you falsely." When you love the enemies sufficiently, and ask for their forgiveness, the persecutors will change their heart too. Have we not seen this in the lives of Martin Luther King and Mahatma Gandhi? They spoke the truth for which the time has come. They won eventually!

This is what Jesus did all his life and at the cross. I refer the reader to the section on chakras where the lower three chakras refer to the small limited self and the higher three chakras refer to the higher authentic self. Every deep meditation and prayer involves initially a tussle with our own self. The lower self tries to persecute but surrenders at the end when higher chakras and centers awaken in all their fullness. Jesus was not a martyr but made a demonstration that someone can be a model for triumph over death and be resurrected. *"I am life itself and I open my heart with all of nature." "Hello Krishna or Christ, my heart is open to you. Come and stay in my heart."*

For further reading on the Sermon on the Mount, I refer the reader to the book *The Sermon on the Mount: The Key to Success in Life* by Emmet Fox, published by Harper & Row Publishers, San Francisco. Copyright© 1966.

Chakra Five: Communicating with Self, the World, and God

· · · · · · · · · · · · · · · · ·

The throat chakra, also called **Vishuddha,** is the feeling that you are able to communicate love and the love of God *effortlessly* to others. Also, you tune in to the "vibration of God" more easily. So when you start to practice in the presence of God, you will also begin to get visions of higher spiritual dimensions.

There are three levels in communication: The first level is the communication with the self, the second level is the communication with the world, and the third level is your communication with God directly. Every morning, one should remember these three levels of communication and create a strong intention to purify oneself and one's relationship with the world throughout the day, and keep God in the background as well. Throughout this chapter, we talk about different approaches to doing this using prayer, religious practices, and meditation.

Section 1- Religion and Spirituality

What is the connection between religion and spirituality?

It is high time that we redefine and refine religion. Religion for some people is only a thought, not a reality. This is why there is so much pain and suffering in the world. Enough is enough! A sense of mystery is nurtured within you when you admit that you do not know what true religion is. The confirmation that you know something gives you an intellectual satisfaction, but for the things that are unknown, or unknowable, your intellect is puzzled and surprised. The worship of God, or gods, is a subject that will always be a mystery to many people, whether it is considered a myth, or a belief. God will always provide a channel to Him, to clear up this mystery, but you have to walk the path alone. This openness to God is similar to a clearing in the forest that is inside you, where this understanding will take place; this process of clarification will be in a form of transformation. This is called religiousness and is found in everyone regardless of their adherence to a religious organization, however, this has to be nurtured.

When you appreciate beauty or peace of mind, which is second nature to children, you will experience beauty, love, and compassion at a higher level. That is the essence of religiousness. The greatest gift that you can give to others is to help them to succeed in life. It is not the aim of life itself, but the process that leads you to the purpose, which is important. Indeed, the very energy to do the work is more significant than the purpose. Life is like an empty canvas. You can paint anything you want to on the canvas, but by itself, it is meaningless unless you give it meaning by a higher purpose. Your higher intention should not conflict with the cosmic energy. What really matters is the process by which you reach your higher purpose.

How can we develop our religiousness as a Soul from Mercury?

The Souls from Mercury will understand true religiousness, which is there in every human heart. They will never become a fundamentalist in any one religion. They will be able to appreciate the basic truths common to all religions. They will have tolerance and even appreciation and respect for the different practices and rituals of other religions.

Speak distinctly of your love to God, and be aware of the divine mystery within you; after all, you are a witness of the show of your life. Honor your own energy by allowing its power to transform you and uplift you to a higher purpose, and accept it with minimum resistance. By using this energy that is always inside you, you can create. Have respect for your own uniqueness. Know the highest intention of life, understand God's love, have true devotion, and recognize that Divine Love is always available to you.

What are the outer signs of someone reaching perfections in spirituality and religiousness?

You will be living in creative mode and living life magically. Before you reach perfection, you realize that you are living by reacting or at best responding to anything and everything, which is the reactive mode. When you go through life in a reactive mode, you act like a machine that has to be satisfied. You will show a positive reaction when you are satisfied and a negative one when you are not.

The alternative mode to this way of living is the creative mode, which should be the only way to live. To live in creative mode is to be truly human and truly alive. But the question of whether you are being satisfied will never arise in the creative mode because the decision to react or not to react will come from within you, and will not be based on the outer world. In the creative mode, you are empowered.

Operating from the creative mode is operating from God's love, and this is a Divine law. Love is the beacon of life and the source of power. You may live in a reactive environment, but you can always be in creative mode whatever your situation may be. You will grow in a creative manner quickly by loving and being connected to God. The Souls from Mercury would have developed an all around purity in their life which is characterized by the word Vishuddhi, in Sanskrit, hence the name of the fifth chakra.

Can you elaborate on the uniqueness of your purification process?

Traditionally many teachers have been teaching meditation to people whose bioenergetic systems will not even allow their mind to settle down. So I refuse to teach meditation to anyone who has not understood and transformed their breathing process, which has become chaotic, and unnatural, and they don't even know it. This purification happens through the energy interchange between teacher and student, which cannot even happen through electronic communications. This is the uniqueness of my (and many other yogic masters) teachings, who focus on breathwork as a preliminary prerequisite for their own deepening.

Section 2- Purification Process

What is the speciality of your breathing techniques?

As you meditate, focus on your breathing by watching how the breathing is happening. Notice that when you breathe in, you do not do it consciously, but when you breathe out, it is conscious. A bridge is thus formed, and there is an expansion of awareness or consciousness. The moment you become aware of something, the ability to know and realize it increases. It is said that "The slower you breathe, the longer you will live." My breathing techniques include methods on how we can direct life force into any part of the body.

How do you work with your breath?

You will know how exactly to work with your breath, when you think about the time when you were living in your mother's womb. At that time, you were directly connected to your mother's prana all along. This prana flowed through your umbilical cord, which was a transmission line for pranic energy. When the umbilical cord was cut, the connection to your mother's prana was no longer there. Now you had to take the prana from your breath and the outside air.

When babies take their first breath in, some muscles in the lungs move up. Most doctors and scientists don't know why or how this happens. There is not even a term for this. It is more than nature. The muscles move up because of what I would call as "the love of God." What is sustaining you now is the same magical energy. Not your food or your money!

The breath or this "life force" is also known as "prana." This term means "continuous movement" in Sanskrit, and the mother of all forces and energies in the universe. It is a complex multidimensional energy consisting of a combination of electrical magnetic, electromagnetic, photonic, thermal, and mental energies. The word prana is used as a generic term as well, to indicate the energy associated with the breath. This is the main current that works through the breath to keep you alive. What keeps you alive is more than oxygen. Oxygen is only a carrier of prana. That is why one cannot live in a cylinder of oxygen alone, because oxygen is not enough.

To understand more about the breath, you need to understand prana and the five sub-pranas: 1) prana, 2) apana, 3) udana, 4) samana, 5) vyana.[1]

1. *Prana:* The place of movement for prana is from the upper surface of the diaphragm to the throat, and the direction is upwards. The related organs are the heart and lungs. This controls the breath, respiratory functions, swallowing, and blood circulation.

2. *Apana:* The place of movement is from the navel to the anus, and the direction of the movement is downwards. The related organs are the kidneys, bladder, excretory, and reproductive organs. Apana expels the waste gases, bile, urine excretion, and also moves the baby from the time of birth.

3. *Udana:* The place of movement is our hands, head, legs, and above the throat. The direction of movement is downwards in the head, in the hands, and legs. The related organs are sensory organs, hands, and legs. This controls the activities of the sympathetic and parasympathetic nervous functioning.

4. *Samana:* The place of movement is between our navel and diaphragm. The direction of movement is sideways. The related organs are small and large intestines, stomach, and liver. It controls the activity of the digestive juices and the ovary functions and movement of sperms.

5. *Vyana:* The place of movement is all over the body. The direction of movement is also all over the body. The related organs are the muscles. This controls activities of touch, movement of muscles, and also balances and supports the other four sub-pranas. This is like the working of God in the human body!

During inhalation, the inhaled air consists of oxygen (20%), nitrogen (79%), carbon dioxide (0.04%), and other gases (0.96%). During exhalation, the exhaled air consists of oxygen (16%), nitrogen (79%), and carbon dioxide (4.04%). Generally we breathe in and out for a total of fifteen times per minute. As we practice more pranayama and other hatha yoga exercises, and learn to breathe in consciously, then this breathing rate comes down to ten breaths per minute. This is the scientific proof that the person has learned the art of naturally living in relaxation.

Prana is the inflow and the apana is elimination or outflow. We need balance between the two. There is a gap in between the prana and the apana. As you progress, you become aware of this gap and the upward energy flow or prana flow. The same way an acupuncturist recognizes the nerve meridians; there are also thousands of astral meridians called nadis, which are known in oga.

Relaxation and purification are the two wings of the upward movement in spirituality. The goal is a balance of life. Another book by the Theosophical Society, *The Human Aura,* is a deep inward journey to find God, but not suited for the layperson who needs to continue to function in society. Even though an "Inner view" is always so much more revealing than the "outlook."

It follows the three steps of *Awareness, Acceptance,* and *Adjustment.*

Awareness: Become aware of your posture, breath, and body as it is.
Acceptance: Accept your body and breath as it is, and become fully present to them.
Adjustment: Adjust your body to new levels of bending, or the change of frequency in your breathing per minute. There are two ways to work with awareness: pranayama and meditation.

The first method is through *Pranayama,* or breath control. This is the way to work with our life force or prana. The word ayama means "expansion of breath" in Sanskrit. Pranayama is the only way to change the flight or fight response into a relation response. Hatha yoga exercises (i.e., yoga postures, asanas) govern the movement of prana in the physical and the vital sheath. The movement of prana in the astral body is through the chakra system.

The second method is improving through meditation. As this happens, we feel tingling in the spine, which may spread to other parts of the body. Through Hatha yoga you can improve the physical, and with pranayama we improve the vital, and through meditation we improve the mental and the psychic. It is the Kundalini and chakra awakening that leads you to the Ultimate.

When you meditate, you move from the field of "no" experience to the world of experience. Sometimes you move from the world of experience to :no" experience. All other experience is meaningless unless this knowledge is gained, which is already inside you, meaning known already. The meaning of life is born from within you, and it is this meaning that you bring to life, not the meaning bringing life to you. When you feel a connection to yourself in meditation, you will experience this meaning. Develop a relationship between yourself and the blue sky, think positive, and say yes to life. It is evil to say no to life.

Why are some people so afraid to meditate?

Meditation is pure and simple, but some of you are so complicated. The obvious is not easily seen because you are focused on doing and doing rather than just be and let it be as the Beatles sang. You have to come to a certain level of new awareness, innocently and childlike, as if you had never meditated before. When you trust, and do not question, you will enter the Kingdom of Heaven. If there is a tendency, on your part, to proceed with your life without growing spiritually, develop a trust in meditation, and acquire the quality of understanding.

Your concept of the world includes your ego, and when it is dissolved, your whole worldview will change. So do not be alarmed or scared when this happens because as Jesus said, "The Kingdom of God is Within You." Let go and do not resist it; focus on yourself, and not on what you are experiencing because God will be with you when your ego disappears. Do not resist anything, because whatever you resist, will surely persist.

What is unique about your system of meditation?

Happiness is to want what you have in the moment, and meditation is to be in the moment. Return to happiness and appreciate what you already have. You are not required to do anything for happiness, or meditation, and there is no need for control of thought, concentration, or contemplation. All you need to do is to witness your thoughts. You have no control over *wisdom* and *ignorance*; the body is a good servant but a bad master. When you meditate you have no control over your thoughts, and you accept them, good or bad, whatever they happen to be. I suggest to you then, that happiness is the same, and I ask you to accept it for what it is.

Can you give us some tips for deeper meditation?

You drop your overemphasis on repeating some sounds and mantras mechanically. Then you reach a point of understanding in meditation. Support the process by doing nothing, watch your breathing, and refer to your personal mantra if you have one. If you feel lost because you are not doing something, then you have a problem. During meditation, your body might become numb, and when this occurs, you may feel that you are not the mind or the body, and the body and mind sensation disappears. If this happens, the world, as you know it, may dissolve; do not block it.

Why do you never give any instructions on meditation initially?

As a form of discipline, I want my students to learn to start with the body and not the mind. Watch how the body performs when you do things; if you upset the body's way of doing things, you could become ill. Acknowledge and understand how chronic disease is; the effect of over excitation of the body-mind system. Meditation is an understanding, and if you begin with the body, you will develop an opening or clearance for this understanding. Meditation is the beginning of feeling and understanding. You reach the peak of this awareness when you are walking with God, and you live in the reality of *existence, consciousness*, and *bliss*.

[1]   Sri Ganapati Sachchidanada Swamiji, Kriya Yoga, 2009

Chakra Six: Communication from God to the Souls from Mercury

· · · · · · · · · · · · · · · ·

The sixth chakra or third eye chakra (Ajna) is the foundation of our "psychic powers," and is related to how we can see and get an insight into the future. You could be lost in the visions and powers arising from your enhanced perception of a whole new world. Therefore, one can become enchanted and too attached to these "powers" and addicted to what they can bring to one's life, such as money and fame. You will feel as though you are rising in the sky of consciousness. However, the potential for falling is also high at this stage because the higher you rise, the steeper you fall.

You need to be watchful of the ego at this stage more than ever, since it has not dissolved yet. This can only happen when you move into cosmic consciousness, which is experienced at the crown chakra level. When this chakra blooms completely, you need to just watch it, be a witness to it (without judging), and do nothing. Miracles can happen. When they do manifest, don't get stuck to them, just let them happen, and keep meditating.

Note: Scripture quotations are from *The New King James Version* of the bible. Copyright© 1979, 1980, 1982. Thomson Nelson Inc., Publishers.

Section 1 - The Ten Commandments

Can you elaborate on the psychological importance of the Ten Commandments?

God said to Moses: "I am that I am." This could be understood as the first communication from God, as revealed through the third eye, through the Ten Commandments. This proves God's presence in the universe.

The Ten Commandments are like building blocks. When you pull one out of place, the building would collapse. The reason why they are structured this way is because all of the commandments are from a unique source. If you practice and understand them, you will be led to the highest point of dignity, and also gain a positive awareness with high self-esteem. In the same token, if you waver on practicing them, you will lose your high self-esteem, and if you break one of them, you will lose your self-image altogether.

The reader may wonder why negative language such as "Thou Shall Not..." is used in God's loving communication. *Righteousness* is very difficult to define just like love, but unrighteousness can be easily defined, and that is what the Ten Commandments indicate.

We will now go deeper into the profound nature of each commandment in order to understand it as a Soul from Mercury, and not from a religious standpoint. The opening of the sixth chakra is the prerequisite for the unfoldment of the seventh, and that is why we need to understand them from a universal standpoint, irrespective of your own religion. You will thus realize that these commandments are just as applicable in today's world as they were at the time of Moses, and will be applicable forever, in order to help one reach enlightenment.

#1. Thou shalt have no other Gods before me."

Who is the God in reference and who are the other Gods?

This commandment refers to God as always being in the present. "I Am That I Am" is transcendental. "I Am" never changes, but even if you alter it, the essence of what God is always there constantly. It is true that when your body disappears, the pure essence of you will move to another form or body or will dissolve in God. The experience of God is tantamount to truth.

If you are unable to see God, see what else you have made as higher priority than God. Is it money, is it power of the body, or is it power and prestige? Is there any other "god" that you put before "God" in capitals? Change your outlook, and do what you can to open your eyes and see the source of where you come from. Your goal is God. "Who is asking this question?" Who am I? When you know the source, you will become aware of the goal. If the goal plus the source is equal to God, then there will be "No other gods before God."

How did the other scriptures make reference to this important commandment?

In the Islamic tradition it says the same thing, "La illa illa Allah," which means, "There is no God but God." This will reaffirm in another faith and language, the One God. How about Hinduism? Do they not have many gods? It is only in outward symbols and rituals they use the many forms. Every Hindu who has read the greatest Hindu scripture called the Upanishads knows that there is only one God called the Brahman. Hindus actually know that there is only one God but manifesting in many forms. In fact they go beyond this and declare, "There is only God and nothing else." Everyone and everything they say is God in essence. So they worship the river Ganges as Ganga Devi and the Himalaya Mountain as the father of Parvathi Devi. These are symbolisms. The truth that there is only God and nothing else is not a philosophical statement but one that is realized in a state of Samadhi or unitary state of consciousness in self-actualization.

#2. Thou shall not make unto thee any graven images."

What was the meaning behind the word graven images or icons used in the Bible?

The graven image refers to all images that one can create in their mental horizon. It could be money, fame, or anything from which we worship as human beings that goes beyond a physical statue.

Let me give you a deep understanding why these words have created confusion and fundamentalism. The language itself is the "Word," and the language limits everything because of the opposites that exist in the illusory world. Let us go beyond the words when referring to "I Am That I Am," as used by Moses, and then there will be no distinctions. However, to survive and function in this world, you have to make distinctions. But when you refer to "I Am That I Am," be child-like. Go into silence and hear God. In prayer, you talk and God listens; in meditation you are silent and God speaks to you. Do not look for meaning; let it manifest within you in silence. There are no words that can support your understanding of God. He cannot be taught; he can be caught by your silent love, devotion, and surrender.

Do the graven images or icons spoken in the commandment have any relevance in the Kingdom of God?

Not really. Because all separation disappears in the Kingdom of God, which is the Samadhi meditation state spoken by all yogis from time immemorial.

This is where all distinctions such as inner or outer, above or below, man or woman, and the "other" will be present. In deep meditation and Samadhi, the outer and an inner "Self" become one, and in that "oneness" you enter the Kingdom of God. To be born again means to give birth to you, the real *you*, there is no other way. According to Jesus, you must be born out of innocence. There is no assumed picture of God and no created image of Him. You want to see God, and even though your mind will process an image, you will have to let go of languages and forms, conditioning and distinction to see God with no form in the state of union and unity, called in Ancient Indian Sanskrit language as Samadhi, the unitary state of consciousness.

Why do the Hindus make images and worship them?

Those Hindus who use the images of God for their worship know that it is a *temporary* form used for concentration only. For example, on the day of worship of the image called Ganesh, during the festivities in August throughout India, the people demonstrate this practice. They first take an image of Ganesh made of clay ormud, and perform the worship either at home or in the streets. Once this worship is completed, everyone takes that image to the lake or river nearby and let it go to dissolve itself. This can be applied to images used in the meditation process by using it as a means for the mind to settle down and dissolv their mental image eventually into nothingness. Only then the meditation process is considered complete.

It is only people with little knowledge of Hinduism that laugh at Hindus and think that Hindus are breaking this commandment. After all, a little knowledge is a dangerous thing, is it not?

#3. "Thou shall tot take the name of the Lord thy God in vain."

Can you elaborate on the psychological importance of the name of the Lord?

This commandment is a magical formula for developing and maintaining one's self-esteem. This commandment has indirect reference to the power of whatever we say. Such people who understand this do not use terms like "god damn it or I am so stupid" even once! Using unacceptable words such as these shows one's own lack of awareness in life and that is taking the name of the Lord in vain. It takes away your own power as these negative words drain our own energy.

It also refers to the commitment to what we say to others. We have to honor our commitments as best as we can, at least the ones we make in public. This commandment also refers indirectly to the words we use with others, which form the foundation of human relationships. Our words can help others or hurt others who are also children of God. Every word we utter should be uttered with full awareness, and there will always be truthfulness in our being and that makes the power in our words grow.

When I meditate on this commandment, I see so many dimensions of this and so many applications in daily life. The first point to make is that there is power within you to bring into reality what you want to manifest. You can also link yourself with God and perform miracles for yourself by visualization and affirmations and chanting of mantras as in Hinduism. This is actually taking the name of the Lord successfully and not in vain. The chanting reveals the power of the mantras. Be your authentic self, and ask for the highest in order to be with God. Be careful what you say and do not waste a single word. When God is first in your life then true joy, security and energy, time and money will come with Him. When one honors the name of God with positive words one also brings honor to oneself. Affirmations such as I am a unique soul, I am a masterpiece, I am a winner, etc, are actually using the name of the Lord correctly.

#4. "Remember the Sabbath day to keep holy."

Can the Sabbath day be any day of the week?

It really can be any day of the week even though the accepted day in the tradition is Sunday for Christian and Jewish gatherings. It can be any day that you choose to develop your mind and spirit. The Sabbath day is a "wholly" day (a holy day) for your development. Develop your body and become whole by eating a balanced diet, fasting, doing exercise, walking, and getting proper rest during the day. Keep your mind clean in silence, and nourish your spirit by reading the Scriptures from any tradition. Keep yourself clean and tidy, develop spiritual culture and always be aware of your connection to God on your Sabbath day. Let it be the day when you can see into your soul clearly and honestly. This is the way to make it different from the other days of the week.

What else can we do to deepen the practice and discipline of the Sabbath day?

I will take this commandment to the next step and recommend that we observe the Sabbath hour every day and to devote it to God. One should do meditation and reflection during this hour. Meditation times are ideally morning and noon when you are hungry and tired, and if you can meditate at that time then, do it. The meeting point of inertia and dynamics at noon is a point in time where nature supports you to meditate and reach peace. When night and day meet, it is time for silence, walking or running. The pinnacle of the meeting point of day and night is silence and music, and so use that Sabbath hour to rekindle your dreams as well.

#5. "Honor thy father and thy mother."

Why does this commandment refer only to the parents?

It really means that we should honor everyone. But psychologists know that our honoring everyone in life has some foundation, or the lack of it we hold with reference to our parents. If necessary, correct any alienation that may now exist relative to your parents. It is said that the famous mathematician Pythagoras was also a spiritual teacher. The maxim "Do not come in unless you are reconciled with your parents," was written in the front door of his retreat center. See why anger exists, and remove the seed of this anger, whatever it is. Not only do you honor your mother, who will always love you no matter what you do, but love also your father and your teacher; they are the first representatives of God in your life. The inner part of this commandment is based on the principle of the law of expansion and order of the universe.

Can you explain how this is referred in other traditions?

We can apply the Yin and Yang principles as the Chinese age-old system indicates. The Hindus call this the Shiva and Shakti. When the harmony and balance in your life is disturbed, you will get sick, and if there is too much activity involved, then sleep and rest is the Yin principle that you need to apply. You need a proper balance in action and inaction. "Honor Thy Father (Yang) and Thy Mother (Yin)," at the physical and nutritional levels. We need to balance the foods that are "Yin" with those that are "Yang." This system is known as macrobiotics in Japan popularized by Mr. George Ohsawa.

How does it refer to the two sides of our personality?

At the mental level, there is also a need to keep a balance between the left and right hemispheres of the brain. The father is the left hemisphere, which is the logical or analytical side of the brain, and the mother is the right hemisphere, the intuitive or giving side of the brain. Keep a balance in your thinking process because too much intuitiveness leads to madness, and with too much logic in your approach to living, you will not be able to relate joyfully to the world. Also keep a balance between the emotional, or the mother side, and the intellectual, or the father side in you. However, the dynamic or energetic side of you, which is the father side, is to be developed to bring love in action.

You have to practice regularly to develop the mind, the body, and the spirit. Listen to music and make it a habit to sing silently wherever you can let go, like in the shower, every morning, to grow in spirit. The sound of music touches the soul and will make you softer and happier. Listen to a nice song in the car and see how that tune follows you all day and keeps you in good spirits and in a positive frame of mind.

At the spiritual level, the mother represents the individual soul and the father stands for the whole cosmic self. There is a point of balance where you are no longer divided in spirit, and this point is between the cosmic spirit and your own individual soul. Honor the individual spirit (I AM) and the cosmic spirit (God/I AM THAT I AM).

You need to seek relationships whether they are physical with body contact, or mental stimulation among friends. You also need soul-to-soul relationships such as spiritual development, until the soul emerges with God. Until this happens, the human body is not complete in its evolution. The father is the vision you want for the union of your spirit with God. Do not forget God (Honor Thy Father), and do not forget yourself (Honor Thy Mother). Then you develop a balance between the world, yourself, and God.

#6. "Thou shall not kill."

Killing is the ultimate form of violence. However, all forms of violence is included in this commandment.

Is it possible to have no violence in us so that we fulfill this commandment always?

Yes. Let me address the very root cause why it seems impossible. You will have to get rid of your ego in order to have the ability to focus and be self-directed. The ego is an imaginary center, not the self. You personally cannot do much about the violence in the world, but you can move in the direction of self-knowledge and get to know yourself spiritually. When you reach the highest point of spirituality, you will automatically let go of any violence within yourself. When you are in the state of existence where the "other" is not, and you see only your true inner self, then you know who you are and you know what love means. There will be no offshoot of violence within you when you consider the "other" as your own self. However, when you consider the "other" as if he belongs to you and as your own, then you could not hate, be angry and be jealous. At that point violence just cannot be within you.

Will there not be some violence in connection with the body?

There will always be a little violence when there is connection with a body. There is no harm in eating, but chewing some fresh food life like bean sprouts looks like violence. Similarly, there is no harm in hugging a person, but when you go beyond that, it can be considered as violence. In fact hugging in public can be considered violence in some cultures. However, when you go beyond the body and the mind, ideologies will not clash and there is no violence. When you know "Who I Am," and you are neither the body nor the mind, then there will be no violence or fear. "Thou shall not kill" is lived when there is no violence in your heart. What exists at that point for you is love and love alone, and you live by all the Beatitudes told by Jesus. The Beatitude shows you who you are in relationship to others and in relation to God. It takes a lot of practice to search for "Who I Am."

Tell us some deeper levels where killing and violence goes on in a human being?

Tune into your teacher by practicing meditation, and be aware of what he did not say, which is more precious than what he did say. Recognize that, on your level, the counterparts of heaven are time, energy, and money. You have limited time because your life could end at anytime. Use this time to understand and increase your awareness to grow in truth, righteousness, and peace. "Thou shall not kill time," means you shall not kill the present moment burdened by the past and the future. You have been given unlimited energy but do not waste it. Use energy for inner growth. "Thou shall not kill energy" is an implied commandment here according to me. Use all the resources you have, including money and energy, for a spiritual purpose, such as helping others. Be an instrument of God and be a good manager of your own resources.

#7. "Thou shall not commit adultery."

How do you interpret the commandment thou shall not commit adultery in the Bible?

The bible says, "Thou shall not commit adultery." This has to be applied at a physical, mental, and spiritual level not just at a social level. When this statement is presented in a social context, it is understood only in a limited way. However, what is meant by *adultery* in the spiritual context is the *misuse* of your sexuality and the misunderstanding of sexuality itself. The social context only refers to the infidelity of a married person having sexual relations with someone else other than their spouse. According to the sixth commandment, you should not even have violence in your heart. So when you are concentrating on lust, your *thinking* is also adulterous. If you force a spouse or a partner into sex, it approximates to adultery. So if you or your partner are experiencing adultery or spousal abuse (sexual, verbal or emotional), seek help immediately from your closest relative or spiritual advisor. Harming or hurting your partner this way takes away the sacredness of sex and the profoundness of the experience. Also the love for that person will go away, and you may lose the person you love, and wonder why.

#8. "Thou shall not steal."

This is self explanatory. The only point to be made is that you will not only be stealing property of another, but you will also be stealing their energy and trust in humanity.

#9. "Thou shall not bear false witness."

Bearing false witness is harming another by telling false accusations about them. It is like another form of killing or character assassination as they call it in the media world. It is just another form of killing. You kill their reputation and character. This commandment needs no elaboration.

When the outside events and resulting feelings influence the manner in which you relate to others, then go to your inner core, where the "other" is seen, because you are not different from others. It is through yoga and meditation that you unify and stop dividing because you and the other are one even when you feel separate. In silence, this illusion will disappear.

What does it mean to be a right witness then?

Jesus was making reference to a great truth about right witnessing in his talk to Mary as reported by the little known Gospel according to Thomas. Jesus said to Mary after several days of silence and fasting in the high mountaintop, "If thine eyes be single, thy body shall be full of light." He refers to the pure witnessing or the right way of witnessing within our meditating space. Then our inner eyes are not two but one. Witnessing is not a thought even though you can think about witnessing. In true and right meditation, one simply reflects whatever is passing by like a mirror. Jesus refers to this problem that is encountered by every meditator. Many of us are habituated to witnessing in the wrong way. We evaluate and judge and verbalize and we think we are witnessing. Jesus says, "Let your eye be single, either it is thought or it is witnessing." When the inner mirror reflects totally without distortion the simple flower we see outside will be luminous and radiating light. William Wordsworth says, "For oft when on my couch I lie, in vacant or in pensive mood, the daffodil flowers dance upon my inward eye, which is the bliss of solitude." This is the right witnessing as it is deeper than the simple observation of what is going on.

#10. "Thou shall not covet."

There are different forms of coveting or desiring. Not to covet or desire at all seems humanly impossible. So we will take up a few practical questions and answer them. If to covet means to want to possess or have that which some other person already has, then is it not another form of violence? To covet then is the desire to possess things and people just for the sake of doing so. Does the word covet also mean to have a sense of possessiveness, or is it an attitude that you develop when you deal with ownership in general? Psychologically, it is the desire to possess things and people. You should use things and love people. Some unconscious souls just do the opposite; they love things and use people.

This commandment is quite clear; you shall not possess another person. You will be lead on a wild goose chase if you desire to possess. Why does man want to possess things or people? Is it because man is not the master of himself? You are always possessed by what you own because the rope is invisible. Why does this desire to possess and have power over someone or something lead you into darkness? You cannot have love for someone and possess that person at the same time.

Firstly, you will not have the time to enjoy life if you covet and desire things endlessly. Secondly, the richer you become the emptier you are inside, and the poorer you will be. What is true emperor-hood? It is the feeling of completeness and total adequacy with yourself, and you feel like a king or a queen. There is no need to possess anyone or anything when you feel like an emperor. Understand and live in this state and be able to say, "I am enough in myself." How can that be love when you demand something? If you are not bound by anything, you will be unlimited and enlightened with cosmic awareness. You will not know when, how, where, or in what form this enlightenment will take place, but when your ego disappears, violence, lust and the desire to possess will vanish, and you will be free from ignorance, prejudice, etc. When you let go of your ego and temporary "self" by spiritual practice, you are the master. You will just live in love and see the futility of wealth and possessions.

Will following all the commandments enlighten someone?

Following the eleven commandments for enlightenment is necessary but not sufficient. There exists two dimensions of your inner being, one that involves greed, lust, and possessiveness, and the other that includes compassion, love, sharing, and self-giving. Enlightenment is to live in the second sphere at all times because compassion and love feed on each other. Automatically, you will follow the Ten Commandments when you search for spirituality and dignity at all times.

This state is explained very well in Samuel Taylor Coleridge's famous poem, *The Rime of the Ancient Mariner.*

> "He prayeth well, who loveth well
> Both man and bird and beast.
> He prayeth best, who loveth best
> All things both great and small;
> For the dear God who loveth us,
> He made and loveth all."

#11. "Thou shall love one another even as I have loved you."

The eleventh commandment came from the very words of Jesus Christ. You can easily say that it sums up all commandments. He said, "A new commandment I give to you is that you love one another even as I have loved you."

He also said, "Love the Lord your God with all your heart, mind and soul, and your neighbor as yourself." If we practice this along with the teachings given to Moses, "I am that I am," then all of the Ten Commandments will fall in harmony like beautiful notes within an orchestra. This will become the way you discover beauty within yourself and beauty in others.

Note: For further reading on this, I refer to the book *Believe in the God Who Believes in You* by Robert H. Schuller. Thomas Nelson Inc., Nashville, TN. Copyright 1989 by Robert. H. Schuller.

Chakra Seven - Part 1:

·················

Prayer: Souls from Mercury Talking to God

The crown chakra (**Sahasrara**), also called "thousand petals lotus," is not even a chakra really, since nothing is whirling like wheel. You will feel for the first time that all the dualistic and materialistic desires are gone, and total peace dawns upon the Inner Being. The blooming process is now complete as if a thousand petal lotus has bloomed, hence the name "Sahasrara." True religion is also born at this level. In fact, all religions were born in the hearts of spiritual masters at this level. This is known in the Sanskrit language as "Soham," This is similar to the declaration of God coming to Moses saying, "I Am That I Am."

"I am one with the universal consciousness" is a typical feeling in the seventh chakra. By meditating on this phrase, chakra seven will start to bloom. This is in sharp contrast to the feeling in the first chakra where we get stuck with the feeling that "I am the center of this world and the whole world lives to serve me."

How are the chakras related to the Lord's Prayer in the Bible?

When you understand the Lord's Prayer as directed by Jesus in the Bible, then you will be aware of the relationship between God and man. The Lord's Prayer is not just a prayer suggested by Jesus, there is a lot more inner meaning and connection with the chakras. It contains within it all the angles of yoga, tantra and modern science. And here is a way one can look at the Lord's Prayer:

"Our Father..." Defines the nature of God and the nature of man; it refers also to the kinship of the other living creatures. By being the son, man has to be the same as the Father. Whatever man does, when he asks for God's guidance, it will be right there for him. Jesus established the brotherhood and sisterhood of all men and woman by using the words "Our Father;" all are equal in His eyes.

"Who Art in Heaven..." The word heaven, actually refers to chakra seven or the abode of greatest happiness; it is the place or a state of completeness.

"Hallowed Be Thy Name..." If God is whole, then man is wholeness (whole, holy, and healthy which comes from the same etymological origin), i.e. hallowed and sacred. His name is "AUM," or "Amen" or "Amin" and it is the primordial sound of creation. When you are in deep stillness you will hear the sound "AUM." Tune into the sound and his name, which indicates his nature, which means hallowed and wholeness.

"Thy Kingdom Come..." The Kingdom of God is the kingdom of unity and union, which is "oneness." When you have oneness with God, you will reach the Kingdom of God. Grow in spirit to reach the "oneness" with God, and let it manifest in all names and forms through you. Express yourself as God would do and allow yourself to be an instrument of God. You can say "thy kingdom come," truly when you surrender.

"Thy Will Be Done On Earth..." The word *earth* here symbolizes all chakras from one to six, and heaven represents chakra seven. It is important for you to have a clear understanding of the manifestations that express the Father's

will in your life. You will have total acceptance of people and events when this becomes your reality.

"As It Is In Heaven..." Let this expression on Earth be the same as the expression "in heaven." You will need to surrender yourself to God to allow this expression to also manifest on Earth. God's kingdom is already established in heaven and in the seventh crown chakra. It has not been felt in the lower chakras, which are symbolized by the term "earth." That is why this request is made in the Lord's Prayer.

"Give Us This Day Our Daily Bread..." means that you have more than just bread. You have a daily supply of fresh energy, in yoga terms, known as prana, that comes into you every morning. That is our daily bread. There will always be mental nourishment in the form of guidance from God, and if you are positive, you will hold on to this energy much longer.

The presence of God is always inside you, as energy, which is nourishment for the soul. Let go of yourself in meditation and you will touch God. To feel His presence is nourishment, but you must "eat your own bread," and generate your own prana throughout your life's experience. Just like exercising daily and eating healthy raw foods will generate more prana.

"Forgive Us Our Trespasses As We Forgive Those Who Trespass Against Us..." The reference to the word "As" is important here. The second part of the statement has to happen first spiritually, then mentally and physically, before the Father forgives our trespasses. Any form of anger or hatred will hurt you, and you are a prisoner until you let go of this. You will forgive others if you have the desire, the time and the willingness to let go. Unity is the Kingdom of God, and the opposite is your "trespass," which is to have no time for God. The ego in man forgets God. I remember someone saying that the three letters in ego means Edging God Out! To forget God is trespassing, and at that point there is no "oneness" with Him. Once that happens, the "daily bread of freshness, prana, and the life force" disappears quickly, and man feels starved and thirsty inside.

"Lead Us Not Into Temptation..." As you evolve, you will be tempted to have a goal and a path in life that does not include God; the focus will be your own interests. Living and working in the world should be an expression of what God wants for you. The mind is tempted to look at the past or the future, but your external life is happening now. It is very tempting to see and live in the

world as something separate and isolated from everything and everyone, but that is where the actual sin begins. Sin is not only in the action, but starts in our reaction to feeling separate from others.

Whereas, living in the "now," and seeing yourself as a part of the world and part of God, leads to "eternal" life. When the human mind is caught up in the past and the future, this is truly what is referred to by Jesus as temptation.

"But, Deliver Us From Evil..." Evil is another term for the ego. Therefore, delivering us from evil means letting go of our ego by growing in higher consciousness by praying and meditating each day.

"For Thine Is The Kingdom, The Power And The Glory..." The kingdom here refers to the settled state of mind, which reveals automatically the glory of all creations and the magnificence in all beings. The power refers to the power of transformation that God offers to us, if only we ask.

"Forever And Ever. Amen..." Forever and ever refers to eternal life as in the poem *The Brook* by Alfred Lord Tennyson. It states, "Men may come and men may go, but I go on forever." In other words, civilizations come and go, but God's energy goes on reverberating through humanity and its growth in consciousness. God is "Amen, Om, Amin. He is everything that is said and not said. He is alpha and the Omega. He is the known, unknown, and unknowable all together.

The reason why understanding this prayer is very important is because it makes you grow in your inner being. The words are old, however, the reader is asked to delve deep within themselves while saying these words so they can tune into chakra seven. Here is a recommended practice for the reader: chant and repeat this prayer ten times in a row while seated in a quiet place. You will already feel your inner energy, vibrations, and mood changing. All your fears, anxieties, and tensions will disappear and all your chakras will balance themselves naturally.

Chakra Seven - Part 2:

. . . .

Meditation: Souls from Mercury Listening to God

Is total silence needed to experience deep meditation?

We all want peace and we all want calm. However, there is noise and stimulation everywhere. During an experiment once done by John Cage and his team, a scientist at NASA, they made all efforts to eliminate inside and outside noises in a room to study the effects of *deep silence* on astronauts. This experiment was done to simulate the actual living conditions in outer space. All of a sudden, John realized that in spite of blocking out all these noises, he was still hearing something and he was wondering where it was coming from. Lo and behold, he suddenly realized the sound was from his own circulatory system, pulse rate, heart beat, etc. Therefore, the astronauts were taught to meditate so that they can easily get acclimatized to the silence in space.

From this example, we need to accept the fact that there is no total silent place where we can experience peace. Peace is not to be found from the absence of sound. In fact, when you practice meditation, you will experience your innermost core has silence and peace in it. We get peace by *acceptance* of what is. Do not let outside sounds, people, or things bother you. Accept things as they are. Accept everyone as they are. This is the master key to all the inner riches because then you have the platform to bring about the lasting changes that are needed in your life.

How do you attain authentic silence?

Authentic silence comes by being in touch with our own inner silence, which is experienced in meditation and in Samadhi. It is the feeling of being *at home* in our aloneness, in solitude. The blossoming happens *only* in solitude. Loneliness is not being alone; one may be around thousands of people and yet still be alone. Be stationary; be stable in your own silence, that's where the connection happens. Shankara Acharya says in his work *Naishkarmya Siddhi*, that real meditation is non-doing. If you are doing anything in meditation, that is, all preparation to meditation, but not meditation. Great Yogi Patanjali confirms this as well when he describes Samdhi in Chapter 1, *Yoga Sutras*.

Just like Buddha and Jesus took the time to be alone and go up the mountain for forty-one days, and came back into the city ready to talk to people. Please note that they carried back their authentic silence, and spoke from that silence. Jesus and Buddha taught the ultimate yoga, which is called *The Kingdom of God* or *Vipassana*. They brought new spiritual light into humanity by sharing these precious teachings.

How can we meditate better or become a Soul from Mercury?

You will have to change and be *willing to let go of certain beliefs* that are holding you to your present reality. Look deep within yourself, in *silence*, and see in what way these beliefs relate to your current thinking. You may have to end an attitude, dismiss a belief, or omit a thing and/or a person in your life, to take this major step. *Going within* can be compared to skiing where you descend down a slope. At that point, you need to lose control to succeed in skiing. In meditation, you have to go within and let go of the body and the mind to gain that pranic energy. Anger, jealousy, and lust in your daily life will take away this energy and power because they will keep you outside. It is said by most meditation teachers that, "You lose a lot of energy out of your eyes, so close your eyes to preserve this force." The Bagavad Gita talks about the four paths for spiritual growth, which are: Knowledge (*Jnana)*, Devotion (*Bhakthi*), Action (*Karma*), and Meditation (*Raja yoga*). Raja yoga is known as the King of all paths, the "pathless" path that leads you to the goal of Samadhi meditation. All of these, however, require a master, teacher, or coach. In today's world, you can use Google to locate a teacher or institution researching similar topics. Or you can find information at the end of this book on how to reach out to the author. As the famous saying goes, "When the student is ready, the teacher will appear."

Why is a Master or a teacher so important?

Even for learning to swim or riding a bike, you need a teacher. So what is wrong in taking a teacher to learn mediation? It's an opportunity for you to practice trust. When you know how to trust a teacher, you will learn how to trust God. A worthwhile quality in a student is the ability to trust his/her Master. The science of the spirit is a transmission beyond words, and it happens only in trust. There is one word from my Master's teachings and that is "playfulness." When meditating, you learn to "play" by taking it easy.

How does meditation provide healing or prevention from diseases?

Let us look at the word "disease." It simply means lack of ease. So, health manifests by the way we handle "dis-ease." The body heals in calm periods. The latest finding shows that cholesterol is no longer the optimum indicator of impending heart disease, but the C reactive protein (CRP), which is linked to anger. Creative energy starts when the reactive mode stops. We need to be close to God and our Buddha nature to tune into the creative source. We must tune inwards to hear our own silence. When you go into silence and asks what needs to be done, the right answer will come.

When you begin to meditate after you have found a sacred room, center, retreat or ashram, you will need twenty-one days of continuous practice of fifteen to thirty minutes to be able to see the effect of meditation on your physiology. This type of daily commitment and practice is known to prevent diseases, which has been proven by Dr. Norman Cousins, Dr. Dean Ornish, and Dr. Andrew Weil. For more details, please read their work.

I also presume that the healing related to particular parts of the body is directly connected with the corresponding chakra. For example, stomach disorders could be related to an imbalanced second or third chakra, while headaches could be related to chakra six. For further reading on this, please read the book *You Can Heal Your Life* by Louise L. Hay. It is very important to note, however, that healing modalities greatly differ according to each person and type of different diseases. What I can suggest to everyone for healing an emotional or physical ailment is to practice breathwork which consists of daily meditation, deep breathing, pranayama or a special *re-birthing* process developed by Leonard Orr in 1974.

Some people have claimed that eating raw food predominantly brought them out of the danger zone of the critical stage of the illness. Therefore, I highly recommend that you eat a good percentage of your food raw. Research has been done by nutritionists proving that the Mediterranean diet is more preferable for people seeking help in the area of chronic diseases. Other methods worth trying are replacing one meal with a healthy smoothie (e.g., kale) or raw fruit and vegetable juices. Recent works by cardiologist Gundry MD is worth a mention here. The power of prayer has also been demonstrated in my personal life as well as the lives of many whose stories have been published in Time Magazine.

In summary, I strongly recommend that a combination of all the above mentioned approaches could bring more drastic results in a shorter time. So if you want to heal yourself, wake up in the morning, do your asanas, practice deep breathing, do your prayers, then have a meal consisting of raw food. Next, laugh with yourself in the mirror, develop faith and hope, and take life lightly.

What is the source of tension in human beings?

The source of tension is the fact the we often live in *rejection mode*. For example, we often say, "The room is too cold, too hot, or too dark, etc;" always in the Yin Yang mode. But Buddha says, "Stay in the golden mean, neither this nor that." He also found that the source of all suffering is desire or yearning. This is the cause of vacillation from one extreme to the other—the constant craving for the new, which creates agitation in the mind. Tension is really held in the spine that results in the imbalance of chakras. The deep-rooted tensions will be released with Meditation, Samadhi or Vipassana.

How do you as a teacher manage to remain without tension and joyous all the time?

I know that *bliss* is beyond the Yin and the Yang, *pleasure* and *pain*, *happiness* and *sorrow*, *heaven*, and *hell*. In bliss, fear and hatred disappear. I ignore the differences in others, build on the similarities and accept myself exactly the way I am. If you are a slave of the mind, then you are also a slave to the external world because the perceptions that feed the mind *are* from the external world. I don't ever get involved in a power struggle because I know it is not necessary to convince people that I am right, or that they are wrong. I simply turn away and smile and be happy, no matter what. Would you rather be right with the resulting tension or just be happy? I always *avoid going to extremes* because I know it will eventually create anger within me. If we look at anger, it continues in us because of inattention to it, because we don't look into it. Once you see anger for what it is, and the damage done to the nervous system, then it will disappear. And I also know that anger is a cry for *love* and so I create more opportunities to give others more love, rather than react to their anger and constantly improve myself in my response to people and challenges.

Bernard Shaw once said jovially that he learned the greatest teachings from his tailor. The tailor would take a measurement every single time a person came, and suggested that something else needed to be stitched in order to improve the dress or suit. Always look at life with fresh eyes. Change and improvement needs to be a continuous process. Peace develops through the proper methodology of meditation. Create bundles of joy inside and covet the company of *balanced individuals* then you will derive the fruits of *devotion*. Realize that the universe is a friendly place, and as such, it will help you to reach your highest goal. I have the capability of doing everything because I have learned the *science* of doing nothing.

In any spiritual practice, what is the highest level?

In the spiritual practice of Samadhi, *silence* is the highest level. Hear everything and say nothing, keep quiet. The control of one's speech is both armament and ornament. It is in the depth of silence that you can hear the voice of God. It is said in the Bhagavad Gita, "In silence, between the thoughts, you can have a glimpse of the Divine, and there is always need for silence."

Just as when Pontius Pilate, who ordered Jesus to be put on the cross asked Him, "What is truth"? Jesus smiled at him with a chuckle, and remained silent. The chuckle perhaps meant, "How would you know about the enormity of the experience of any of the higher chakras, when not even the heart chakra is open in you?" Furthermore, you cannot give a better description for truth than through silence. So Jesus kept silent.

Is it not necessary to be a monk and renunciate to practice meditation?

Renunciation is not the track needed by every one. My Master says that renunciation in the way that is practiced by some monks is not the highest level of spiritual practice recommended for everyone. What is there to give up? Nothing. Because nothing is yours to begin with. If you become a monk to be extraordinary, you are on the wrong track. In fact there are no extraordinary people. My Master used to say, "We are all special or we are all ordinary." In a world where everyone is trying to be extraordinary, the ordinary person who revels in and enjoys his ordinariness is truly extraordinary!

Liberation is not a thing to be attained. The saints always said that when you drop all craving to attain something and the desire behind it, what remains is *salvation*. Zen says, "If you drop what you are seeking, you are enlightened."

We are born with the Buddha nature. We come from it everyday and go back to it every night. We muddy it along the way; we are not used to it. The state of enlightenment is an ordinary thing. It is finding the extraordinary in the ordinary.

What is in short the Samadhi meditation that you teach?

In Samadhi meditation, the body is separated. The mind is returned back to its source, which is consciousness, leading to the realization that all souls are one and separate. Lives do not exist anymore. And as long as the intellect is tossed between "this is right" and "this is wrong," "this is good or bad," "I like this," or "I don't like this," thoughts will continue ad infinitum. When intellect stops, the mind also stops like a pendulum. All creativity, all positive vibrations are born out of this state of no action, which is known as Naishkarmya Siddhi.

What is enlightenment in its essence?

The knowledge of this interdependence brings enlightenment, which manifests as a life free of problems and stress. The ignorance of this interdependence causes tension and stress. Enlightenment takes you to the point where you will experience all the events in your life as the manifestations of the *absolute love*, and back this truth up with your way of living as suggested by my friend Ron Smothermon. This is the spiritual path.

From your teachings, sometimes I feel that you are against knowledge?

I am against false knowledge that leads to illusion, delusion, and error. I am also against ignorance hiding as knowledge. Some of you hide your ignorance because you think you know, but you do not know. Understanding comes from within, and knowledge comes from the outside. The fact that you don't know what you don't know has the greatest impact on your life, and it belongs to the unknowable realm of experience. The levels of knowledge are the unknowable, the known and the unknown. The unknowable can happen inside you, but it does not include that which you cannot experience. The spiritual path is for the unlearning and the unloading, and the unlearning is very important in this pilgrimage as a first step.

Are you against the mind and mental powers?

I am myself a scientist and how can I be against the mind? I am only pointing to the limitations of the mind in handling areas of life where heart is the medium to understand. Some of you are so focused on the mind that you can never settle down. Meditation is nothing but a settled state of mind. You cannot clear water by stirring it. You must allow the contents of a container to settle first, and then the water will clear. Your mind is like the water during the unlearning and unloading stages, and meditation is just the beginning.

The mind is anti-meditative by nature and the heart is naturally meditative, then the heart is the space for Samadhi. If the mind is a beggar, as it is constantly demanding, then the heart is an emperor, because he is a leader, and the one who has everything. If the mind is the source of all insanity, then the heart is the source of sanity, balance, and harmony. If the mind is tension, then the heart is relaxation. If the mind compares, then the heart sees. If the mind is prose and text, then the heart is poetry and song. If the mind is a dreamer, then the heart is visionary because it builds on a base, and has the capacity to understand.

What is the master key to deepen our meditation practice?

The master key is to understand the difference between thoughts in meditation and those outside of meditation. The thoughts outside of meditation are the result of ignorance or the lack of *wisdom*. Your attention and attachment to these thoughts will maintain their existence. The proper way to deal with thoughts in meditation is be a witness to them, with no judgment or condemnation of these thoughts, but allowing space. If you don't pay attention to the thoughts, this lack of attention will turn into *awareness*. A gap will exist between two thoughts in meditation and this space will broaden as you continue to meditate. Witness who you are in this gap, which is *bliss* and *consciousness*, but make sure you do not try too hard because you may miss the *gap*. You must learn to relax in meditation.

What is the difference between thought and consciousness?

There is a great difference between thought and consciousness. Consciousness is like a sea and thought is like a wave arising in it. To be aware of something is a thought, and when this awareness is rolled back into itself, then you have consciousness. A thought is part of consciousness, and initially you created that thought within your subconscious. Then when you focus on the ocean of consciousness, the thought will subside. A thought, in its evolution, is transcendental, and exists only as a feeling in the beginning. There is a rising of a thought, the intermediary stage, and then the thought will expose itself, and once this evolution begins, it is impossible to stop it because you cannot hold back what you did not start. When you attempt to halt this process, you will only increase the energy that produces the thoughts. Besides the waking, dreaming, and sleeping states, there is also a fourth state of consciousness, which is between waking and sleeping. In Sanskrit this is called "The Sandhya" and it is this subtle meeting point where your level of awareness increases, and you are not there when it occurs.

What is the main reason that we are not able to get to the state of true meditation?

When you identify yourself with your thoughts, you have a major problem. I call identification as the only sin because the word sin just meant originally "to miss the mark." You think that you are the thought and you are finished. Someone gets a "voice over" in his or her mind, and even goes as far as to say that this is from God! Your power is high when you are witnessing the thoughts, but there is no power in the thoughts themselves. There is also a source of conflict in being identified with your thoughts because of the difference in the polarities of the observer and observed as pointed out by the great philosopher Jiddu Krishnamurthy. Then this is coupled with the basic polarities inherent in life and nature. Examples are dark versus light, life versus death, man versus woman, and action versus reaction. When the witnessing itself disappears, you realize that the polarities are just complimentary and that leads to enlightenment, and that is the transcendental point with God.

Awareness and meditation are important in the second or subjective stage of love. This is the stage when you watch to see how many ways you let go of love or even God, and observe how you act when you do. The first phase of love is the objective or possessive stage, and the third stage is the cosmic love relationship with the giver of life.

Please explain your polarity meditation?

There is a powerful technique called polarity of life meditation, which you can do either just before you open your eyes in the morning, or before you close your eyes to go to sleep at night. It is based on the principle of the polarity of light and darkness, which is a form of visualization. It does not replace your commitment to daily meditation. Use this process when you lie down to meditate or before going to sleep. As you begin to watch the breathing process, visualize a picture forming light-golden disk pouring down into the top of your head. When you breathe out, visualize a darkness coming out of the bottom of your feet. It is a form of dynamic breathing exercise that leads to a kind of progressive relaxation. You can imagine any form of polarity of life situation that is easier for you to visualize, such as warmth in and coolness out, or creativity in and rest out. At the end of the exercise, drop the visualization activity and say "one" when you breathe in and when you breathe out, it will help you to relax. This exercise is more beneficial when it is done for at least twenty minutes. Another activity is to look at your hands first when you wake up. As you visualize both polarities, say to yourself as taught by Robert Fritz, "I choose to be the predominant creative force in my life, I choose to be true to myself, I choose to be free, I choose to be healthy, I choose to be happy and helpful."

Is there a connection between meditation and the sound "OM?"

The sound AUM, in its natural state, is broken down into the conditions of waking for A, of dreaming for U, and of deep sleep for M. There is also a fourth sound, which is evident in meditation, and it is the tail end of this sound that has an impact on you. The waking and dreaming states are also transcendental to the meditation. The usefulness of chanting "om" is to teach you how to come to terms with your own aloneness, and how to let go. The first application of chanting OM is to come to terms with your nobody-ness, which eventually leads to oneness inside. Then you realize the non-separateness from anything. Meditation will teach you how to love yourself, but first, you have to appreciate who you are. The state you are in when you come from deep meditation is what can be called happiness. And this state leads you to balanced chakras automatically.

How do you bring the meditative awareness into daily life?

Meditation and prayer are useless unless you include them in your daily activities. Transform your daily work into a form of meditation. Yoga is a skill in action as Bhagavad Gita teaches, and if it is a philosophy with which you are familiar, then live accordingly. I will give you a quick summary of Bhagavad Gita as taught by Lord Krishna. You will always have the right to act, but not to the results. It is important to acquire the ability to direct your thoughts to God through daily prayer. You are happiness, and nothing outside of you makes you happy. No matter what you do to be happy, the action will always take place within you, and the change, from having to act to wanting to act, will happen. Therefore, yoga is the science of happiness, and meditation is the way to arrive at the point of contentment that leads to happiness no matter where you are or what you are doing.

Man has a natural tendency to create energy, overcome inertia, and keep his balance. The Bhagavad Gita calls it as Sattva, Rajas, and Tamas. It is up to you to become a witness to the events in your life, and to see yourself transcendental, and the person beyond the limitations of these three natural phenomena of the human mind. The state of being divine is within you, and to be human also is a plus point. Stop whatever you are doing from time to time, and go into silence and deep meditation to connect to truth. Recognize that the sum total of all that you perceive, know, feel, and think is not limited to a form of ecstasy. Give up your way of life and give it to God. You are not able to do it alone; you must have God. If you think that you are the doer, you are wrong; you are only the instrument. Think of everything as a happening, and not a doing. Be perfectly still and know that you are God. When you think that you are meditating, you are not. You are the soul, and when you are silent, you communicate with yourself. Let go of the thoughts that cause pain and reach the state of awareness. There is no way other than through silence. When you meditate watch your breathing, it will help slow down the thoughts. God is a *dynamic energy* phenomenon, so when you meditate there is one huge dance of consciousness happening. Nothing will remain at rest or correspond to the word "rest," and when you are totally in the dance you are at "rest." This appears to be a paradox. When you accept the premise that everything in the universe is God, then you are part and parcel of God!

Can the thoughts be a creative force as well?

The thoughts as a creative force within you are a gift of freedom given to you by God. Your present thoughts could change the pattern of your future through the visioning process. A goal is usually a consequence of the past, and vision is related to the future that is independent of the past. Therefore, a goal based on the past and thought is the negative part of you, and vision based on meditation is the positive part. Meditation is learning to let go, and to disappear. Meditation is to be in the presence of God, and to witness the silent prayer that the core of you is offering to God. Even though your thoughts have an impact on your life, these same thoughts have no validity in meditation. When you go inside yourself, you are the problem, the solver of the problem, and the solution to the problem.

Once thoughts are seen as a creative force coming from meditation, you will recognize that the source of all conflict in life is fear, and the cause of all fear is isolation. However, the opposite of isolation is inclusion, which is love, and if you are part of one family, you cannot blame others. You will now learn to live in love. It is said by a great teacher Sai Baba, "There is no reason for love, no season for love."

Does prayer have a place in meditation?

Prolong the presence of God after meditation by repeating a short prayer or a word. Prayer comes from your inner stillness. When you are calm and settled it is the best time to pray. The positive side of prayer is the quietness within, while you wait for the answer. Find a sentence from a prayer that touches a cord inside you, and say it right after meditation. When you concentrate on these words as a form of prayer, you will remain in the presence of God.

Does meditation help you to become a leader, a man from Mercury?

Now you can be a real leader for the first time. You have learned to lead yourself first and others next. You will not be a follower-meditator anymore. You will be a leader-meditator or a man from Mercury as I always say! The ability to lead is to exist as a healer, and to be a leader is to be human. The leader will provide the support, the space, and the opening to many to help them through their problems. You cannot be a leader and a warrior at the same time. The warrior may act with power and velocity but that is not enough, and the leader will perform with awareness, commitment and decision. You must be a man or a woman of Tao to go beyond polarities, to be transcendent, and to move toward the mystery, in a creative manner, in meditation. You will never win a victory over a mountain because mountains cannot be defeated. However, the real struggle for leadership occurs in your mind, and you can conquer your own hopes and fears. It is difficult for anyone to lead others further than they have gone themselves. "He who overcomes shall inherit everything, and I will be his God and he shall be my son." (The Bible Revelation 21-7)

Can you explain the inner self and the outer self, the terms you often use?

The inner "Self" and the outer "Self" are actually one, but they are always in conflict with each other. The outer "Self" has meaning only when the material world and the five senses are not satisfied. The inner "Self" has meaning when you are at peace and you have alignment and harmony. You need a higher point and a purpose to attain the total harmony between the inner "Self and the outer "Self." When the higher purpose and higher point is missing you will fall, but when you arrive at the point again, where is the higher purpose? There is no more an inner self and an outer self but one single whole—an authentic, connected and holistic Self.

Most of the time we live in the desire of wanting something more, better, different. Samadhi actually stops these three desires, and takes you to a point where you will live in love and not be in love.

In what sense do you use the word "God?"

In my teens, I bought a couple of books that had the word God in them, but could not relate to them or feel motivation to read further. But decades later, after my own realizations and unfoldment, I went back to these books that had the word God in them. One fine morning, it occurred to me, "Why don't I substitute the word God with the word love?" and then began my reading, which then made sense to me. I believe that using the word "God" *constantly* limits God, who is actually boundless and limitless. It is better to stand at the threshold of *unknowing*, rather than the threshold and cloud of *knowing*. Menachem M. Schneerson used in his book called *Bringing Heaven down to Earth*, the new word "G-d," instead of the word "God," because the word "God" is not God, it is just a word.

You can then *see* God for who He really is, which is vastness, unboundedness, and transcendental in nature, which means He is "outside of man's domain." Because man is not living in concordance with nature, he is unable to relate to God. So in order to be in concordance with nature, "sit under the green wood tree," and meditate in open-mindedness, and He will reveal himself to you.

What do you see as the future for mankind?

The future of my spiritual work is intimately connected with the future of mankind. We see so much chaos and confusion in the world today, and I see the root cause of this being a spiritual crisis in the inner being of man. I am willing to act as counselor to world leaders. As a person who can usher in a new perspective, which is the unity of world religions. I can see that it is already happening, and science is the bridge with all people belonging to all religions. In fact, I see that scientists will unite humankind when they wake up to the essence of world religions. For example, you can see evidence of this in the lives of the greatest scientists like Albert Einstein, Arthur Eddington, Max Plank, et al. I invite readers to read the autobiographies of these eminent scientists. A classic example would be the book *The World As I See It* by Albert Einstein.

Right now, we see there is so much difference between outer science and inner science. With quantum mechanics, this difference is already disappearing. When scientists start unraveling the mysteries of inner world, the science of the brain etc., they will see the value of prayer and meditation and other religious practices. You can see evidence of this in a number of articles in Time Magazine, where mainstream is beginning to see and appreciate the efficacy of prayer and meditation in people's lives. I myself predict, that meditation will be seen as a pure energy medicine. People will then have only two options, *meditate* or *medicate*.

Conclusion

Charles Darwin, author of the book *Origin and Evolution of Species*, published in 1859, spoke about the *history* of mankind. But what did he really say about the *future evolution* of man? In our survival of the fittest and our moods of aggression and competition, will we end up annihilating ourselves as a species? That could be a bleak future, but that is not what I see. I concur with Darwin who said we are social animals, and we will grow as human beings by showing *empathy*, *kindness*, and *compassion* for others. We have grown and will continue to grow in that multifold, which is god-likeness. Therefore, the more we meditate and go in samadhi, which is being in the state of silent witness, the more we will develop and display the qualities aforementioned.

So if this book can create in the readers a thirst to become a Soul from Mercury, I would have achieved the purpose of writing and publishing this book.

Raju's Spiritual Journey

· · · · · · · · · · · · · · · ·

This chapter recounts my life journey and gives glimpses of the miraculous way in which all the various events and experiences unfolded in my life. This section consists of informal conversations and interviews conducted by my close friend Mona in a journalistic style.

Monica: (Called M hereafter)
Raju: (Called R hereafter)

M: Master, tell me about yourself.

R: What do you want to know?

M: Where you were born and tell me about your childhood.

R: I was born in a small village called Krishnapuram, not far from Chennai in TamilnaduIndia. I already had one elder sister and three more were born later on. According to my family Guru, there is mystery behind my birth. My parents prayed a lot for my coming. They arranged for a special pooja[1]done by this Family Guru so that a great soul like Adi Shankara will be born to them. I was born in October 1946 on the last day of the nine-day religious festival called "Navarathri. At a very young age, I started reading all the Scriptures. I was also exploring the religious teachings of Christianity, Islam, and Buddhism and I go freely to their religious gatherings.

M: There is a mystery about your birth as told by your father, what is it?

R: My father R.A. Subramanian and my mother Lakshmi are a very religious couple. My father actually worked as a Commanding Officer for The British Army in Ceylon. In the last week of his stay there, he went deeper into the forest taking his official vehicle (Jeep). In the middle of the journey, he saw three elephants which suddenly chased him. He got down from the Jeep and ran for his life. He saw the entrance gate to a big organization, opened it and closed it behind him to prevent the elephants from getting in. He went inside and found that it was the famous temple of the famous six-faced God Subramanian who is the son of Lord Shiva. He went inside and prayed for an hour and then returned. He started going there every day, and one evening, the temple priest came to him and asked him if his name is Subramanian and if he is from the land of Sage Agasthya, Shakti peetha, the Seat of Cosmic energy, which is in the south. My father answered in the affirmative. Then the priest revealed the dream that he had the previous night. He said he was told by the Lord himself that the Vel, the shakti weapon which he has in his hand should be given to that person with his name and who comes from Shakti Peetha. So my father got it and came back to India. He was guided to seek a particular teacher who would instruct him on the way to perform worship of this spiritual weapon. He continued to perform the worship as given by his spiritual Guru. About one year after, I was born on Vijaya Dashami day, the tenth day of worship for mother Divine in honor of how divine and positive forces were victorious over the demonic and negative forces. The term Vijaya means victory, Dashami means the tenth.

M: How long did you stay in Krishnapuram?

R: I stayed there with my auntie and my grandparents up to the age of fourteen. Then my parents took me to Hyderabad to study in Nizam College. I stayed with my parents until I completed my engineering degree.

M: Is there anything specific that you want to relate about the child Raju?

R: As a little boy, the moon always fascinated me. I wanted people to get it for me. So my grandmother would fill a plate with some water to show me the reflection. I always wanted to go to the moon.

M: So it's no accident that you ended up working with projects related to NASA (The National Aeronautics and Space Administration) in the USA and in India in the early days?

R: It is true in a sense that it was a mere realization of my childhood dreams.

M: Tell me about your awakening and intense journey along the spiritual path.

132

R: It was a full moon day called the "Sravana Poornima" and I was outside the village temple. There was Divine Mother worship and a celebration with the recitation of a thousand recitations of the Gayatri[2] mantra by the Brahmins. When the ceremony was over and everybody had left and I was alone near the Bilwa[3] tree, an incident happened! Suddenly I felt a strong energy coming to me from the nose ring of the statue of the Divine Mother and I fainted and I don't know how long. Fortunately one of the neighbors, a lady named Sitama, was around and she took care of me until I regained consciousness.

M: What is your understanding of that incident?

R: I understood that Divine Mother would guide and protect me every second of my life.

M: Tell me more about Sitama, who was she?

R: She was a widow who was living close to my home. She used to invite me to her home regularly so I can read the Scriptures to her, in particular the advanced ones dealing with Vedantha and Upanishads. I did that for some time, assuming that her eyes are weak and she could not read by herself. Years later, I visited her unexpectedly, and I found her reading a book by herself. I was amazed! She had a lot of explaining to do. I understood that Sitama was my Guru in some past life and she wanted me to learn the Scriptures, that is why she made me do all those readings for her.

M: Master, can you please tell me about a similar incident involving the Divine Mother which you told me in the past.

R: Oh Yes. It took place at Cape Kanyakumari where there was and still is another temple. Once I went there and the priest asked me to do the chanting on his behalf. I was slowly becoming unaware of the surroundings through chanting the prayers intensely for hours. At one point I felt that the Divinity gave me a kiss on my cheek and I was in a state called Samadhi.[4] I came back to normal state of consciousness after the priest called my name several times.

M: What is your understanding of that incident?

R: The light from the Divinity went right through me, and filled me the same way it happened before in Krishnapuram. But this time I was not unconscious of the outside world. From that incident I learned that I can live in this world but, not be of it, similar to the way Jesus said. It gave me a sense of completion that nothing in this world can take me away from it.

M: Once, you mentioned an incident about sage Agastya but I don't remember the details.

R: One day when I was sitting on my front porch, Sage Agastya came to me while I was chanting the Soundarya Lahari, a great work of Adi Shankara. He squeezed water from a rudraksha and asked me to drink it and I did. Then my grandmother came out of the house and asked what I was doing. I wanted to show her Agastya walking. But he disappeared right in the middle of the street. I was struck with wonder and did not realize who he was until years later. My father's teacher explained to me that he was a teacher of Mahavatar Babaji who was my teacher in the last birth. That is how the priest in Kathirkamam identified my dad as the one who is from the Shakthi Peetham of Courtallam. (Read *Autobiography of a Yogi* by Paramahansa Yogananda).

M: Did the Sage introduce himself as being Agastya? How do you know he was the great Sage?

R: Later my Guru, confirmed that it was Agastya because only sage Agastya and Babaji of the Himalayas have the 'kaya siddhi,' the power to materialize and dematerialize physically at will.

M: Tell me about Sage Agastya.

R: He is a great saint sent by Lord Shiva to live in South India moving from Kailash to Kanyakumari. He was considered to be the Guru of Baba Ji referred by Paramahansa Yogananda in the book *Autobiography of a Yogi*.

M: Why did the sage pay you a visit?

R: Agastya did that to energize me for the work I had to do then and continue to do today. The Agastya Nadi predicted that I would teach the way of enlightenment to the world. The Bhrigu astrology also tells about this material life and it is said that I will also work for corporations.

M: After completing your Master's Degree in Engineering, what did you do?

R: There was a Space Agency program which was starting in India at that time. I joined that program in Trivandrum. It's called "The Thumba Rocket Launching Station," India's center for rocket research.

M: What made you decide to come to the West?

R: It was through the same Space Agency program which had contacts in Toronto, Canada.

M: How did you come to work for NASA? What was your specific responsibility there?

R: When I was working for the Thumba Rocket Launching Station, I started developing joint programs with NASA Together with NASA; I was responsible for introducing a new system of Total Quality Control called NHB standards. I worked with the committee that wrote the NHB standards, which assured that only the highest quality and most reliable systems were used for rocket research. You can't afford failure in rocket launches. If even the smallest thing goes wrong, it can mean the loss of millions of dollars, not to mention human life upon which you cannot put a price. Later I worked with a company called Spar Aerospace in Montreal which worked on several programs with NASA such as Canadarm, which picks up satellites from the space station, also launching of satellites for Canada such as Anik D and so on and also Radarsat.

M: At all of the companies for which you have worked, you've carried out some spiritual teaching activities in parallel to your responsibilities. What are the fundamental principles of your teachings?

R: My teachings are to learn to keep a balance between spirituality and worldly activities. Some people think that they have to be only spiritual and neglect the human aspect of living; some others don't incorporate any spirituality in their life. My teachings reveal the ways to bring balance between the two dimensions. It also describes how awareness and love are like the two wings of a bird, and foster people's inner and outer development.

M: How did you end up getting married?

R: I wanted to lead a life of celibacy. When my parents tried to introduce me to or match me with girls, I always turned them down. But one day, I changed my mind. My close friend had a high position in the government and was reporting to a minister in the government, and he was looking for a girl to marry. He had seen around twenty girls with no success. Chandrika's father had put an advertisement in the newspaper looking for a husband, as it is common to do in India. My friend asked me to accompany him to see the girl. Whilst in their home, I saw Chandrika's great grandfather's picture on the wall and that brought back a past life memory to me; it was Subramaniam Bharati. Anyway, my friend was not interested in the girl and asked me to take the bad news to her grandfather. I went back and told her grandfather: "I have bad news, my friend says no. But I also have good news; I am going to marry her."

So I got married at the age of twenty-six. Chandrika became very disappointed with the life I offered her. She was stressed and very unhappy. Now she is okay with the situation. I told her that I will always keep my commitment towards her. My son matured from the situation and became very independent and has a take charge personality.

M: Some people do not understand why you sent him to India for seven years far away from his parents?

R: It was for his own good and Chandrika could not manage everything. Things were too difficult for her. I went through the same experience as my son; I lived fourteen years with my grandparents in Krishnapuram.

M: How was this period with your grandparents?

R: It was a tough time. My grandparents were strict disciplinarians and I was not allowed to be with other kids and play with them. I was forced to be by myself, playing marbles alone inside or sometimes with other children but only inside the home. My grandparents were very afraid that something bad would happen to me. So they did not take any chances and let me lead a normal child's life, like other kids of my age. They were thinking: "What would we tell our son if something happened?" When they were hard on me, when I was caught playing outside, my auntie Subbulakshmi was always my savior.

M: Tell us some incidents from your time as a boy in the school?

R: I showed signs of learning everything quickly and with ease. The villagers used to gather to listen to me as a young boy speaking on advanced topics in Vedanta philosophy. I was inspired by Subramania Bharathi who was a great poet; he was quite prolific and very famous. I read and memorized most of his poems when I was young by just reading three or four times! I wrote some poems myself until I started being involved publicly in spirituality. Looking at my keen interest in spirituality, my parents had concerns about what I was going to do with my life. I became a Biomedical/Aerospace Engineer and I continued to be involved in spirituality. I think I did not disappoint my parents and neither did I disappoint my Guru.

M: Master, who decides that a great soul has to come back to be a spiritual master, and when it will come back?

R: The desire to help brings it back. God will decide when it comes back.

M: When I embarked on the spiritual path, I wanted liberation, mainly to escape from pain and suffering. It's hard for me to understand why someone would want to come back into this world of misery.

R: Those who choose to come back for the sake of humanity know about it and they are capable of handling life's difficulties.

M: How is it that Swami Ganapati Satchidananda from Mysore is your Guru? What is the difference between him and you?

R: He perhaps has some connection with Mahavatar Babaji and he has mentioned about it in some private talks like the one that happened in Mt. Shastha USA meditation session. He is operating at a much higher level than me. So he gives me energy and supports me in my level of operation.

M: The other day I asked you why it is so easy to relate to nature and animals while it's much difficult for me to relate to people. You said that it's because I don't know myself. When I mentioned that it seems so easy for you, you said "It's because I already knew myself when I was born." So, why did you go to so many masters and call them your gurus if you already knew yourself when you were born?

R: I went to so many masters or gurus to give them my unconditional love and support. Only Datta is my Guru from time immemorial.

M: What about Bhagavan Sai?

R: I wanted to learn from him, in what way I could serve him. He told me: "You are a scientist, there is a big hole in the ozone layer, it is very dangerous for the planet, and you have to do something."

M: So, what did you do?

R: I was part of the team that made the ISO 9001 standards happen in the year 2000 through the Technical Advisory Group in the USA. I continued to work in this group until 2011. There are things in which I want to make a contribution. What I do should have a global impact; it's not something I am doing to make money. What I do should have a tremendous impact over the coming years. So the ISO standards became a part of the standards of quality of most major companies in the world. Almost a million of them! I get involved in this kind of work.

M: You don't consider J. Krishnamurti as your Guru?

R: No, he would not even accept anyone as a disciple. He is a great thinker. Anyway, my mission in this life is to support everybody because everybody is doing my work. Now I want to know how I can serve Swamiji.

M: Master, Swamiji called you "Datta Yogi Raja," and you mentioned some parampara lineage. Can you please go over it again?

R: There are sixteen manifestations of Dattatreya. One of them was Datta Yogi Raja. After giving me the title, Swamiji actually said, "I don't like giving titles to people because people misuse them. But when I first saw you, I knew you were a Datta child."

M: What did he mean by that?

R: Swamiji meant that I am truly a child of God. I live and experience life in that way.

M: Tell me about the circumstances under which you first met him?

R: I have heard about him in 1985 from my dear teacher Rishi Prabhakar. He gave me some of Sri Swamiji Bhajans tape and extensively used them at the retreats held in Canada, USA, and other countries. But it was in June 1993 that I actually met him in Canada at the inauguration ceremony of a Datta Yoga Center. He gave me a mantra initiation at that time which practice gave me lot of inner peace and tranquility. Ten years later, in the year 2002, he invited me to India for the Datta's birthday celebrations and gave me a new name and title of "Datta Yogi Raja."

M: Thank you. Master, can you tell me how can I get rid of my ego?

R: Just the fact of realizing that ego is there is already an important step. You cannot destroy it, but you can realize that in this universe, you are nothing. You are just a dot in the immensity of the universe. When you realize that, you become one with everything around you and you will reach the level of being a servant of the universe. It's a tremendous realization. Then you become responsible for everything and everyone in the universe. At that point you feel the minutest pain, suffering or disturbance around you as did Mother Teresa.

M: How do I reach this state?

R: By service. As long as you think "I am doing this, I am doing that, I am better than others, the ego is there."

M: You said you don't like people touching your feet. But I need to put my ego at your feet.

R: That's why I allow you to do that. It is a support for you to be able to drop it. Actually, I am very happy to support you this way. But I am always watching that my ego does not flare up.

M: How can I purify myself?

R: Meditation, humbleness. Always see yourself as the servant of the world. I go to Swamiji to surrender to him, to teach you to surrender yourself. It is the only way to teach you, by surrendering myself to somebody of a higher caliber.

M: You said "I have never thought of becoming a spiritual teacher." How come it became the main activity of your life for so many years?

R: It started a long time ago. At the age of thirteen, people from the village used to gather to listen to me. I knew all the Scriptures. Near home, there was a church, a mosque and a temple; I used to go to all of them. They used to wonder how I had known their Scriptures.

M: The first time I came into contact with you, I was fascinated by your spiritual knowledge. I was thinking "how does he know all these things?" So how do you know all that?

R: My knowledge comes to me from the cosmic energy every time I let go of my ego.

M: How do you explain that everybody does not access knowledge from the cosmos, like you do?

R: You have to drop your ego completely to be open to the cosmos.

M: You have said that the Gita and all other Scriptures are included in you. Why did you go to the whole Sadhana process?

R: I never do any serious Sadhana; I came only for the sake of the world, to bring the light to those who can receive it.

M: So all these poojas and prayers are to set an example, to be a model. Tell me about your previous incarnations?

R: In every critical time, I am always there.

M: Did you ever stop coming, or you just change clothes all the time and then come back?

R: I just change clothes and come back.

140

M: Changing the subject, you said you helped people manage stress in companies where you work, what did you do with them?

R: Since 1981, along with Rishi Prabhakar from India, I have introduced a unique program offered to corporation employees entitled "The Science of Doing Nothing;" it's really simple. What it involves is fifteen minutes of sitting down doing nothing, before your daily lunch break. Any corporation can introduce it. Of course people find it very difficult to do nothing, because even though the body is still, the mind continues at a frantic pace. I trained them to witness their thoughts. The whole training takes about three days and contributes positively to the productivity of the organization. Many people have reported to me that their afternoons are totally different when they do this. They don't feel tired or bored, and they have much more energy with which to work. I also introduced humor to all technical and administrative meetings in corporations. People who become too serious automatically become unhappy.

M: You said once that I am reacting negatively to people because I don't know myself yet?

R: Yes, it is just a way of being, it is not a title, and nobody can give you the title. What I believe is what I do. The way you are is the way that you live, in bliss, in love, and in peace. It is a sign that you are in touch with the Self, the soul, because your Self is all this. You are love, you are joy, and you are peace. So when you live that way, that means that you are in touch with your inner Self; there is no other proof. Even though you are a teacher, this does not automatically mean that you are in touch with your inner Self. You can be a teacher who knows people, but that does not mean that you know your Self. If you fail to live in love and peace with everyone, it means that you are not in touch with the Self, the soul, with your inner Self.

M: How come we are disconnected from the Self? Why is it so difficult to always remain in touch with the Self?

R: It is actually very easy, although it has been made difficult. It is so obvious but you don't find it obvious and easy because you make it difficult to begin with. You make it into a task, you make it into a chore, you make it into a hard thing, and you make it difficult. A child is naturally loving, joyful. It is not difficult for a child. When I was little, I told myself "I am not going to mess it up! I am not going to grow up." I have done nothing to attain this. I just decided it; I just told myself "I don't want to be a serious adult."

M: But you are an adult. Children don't get married, children don't have another child. Children don't have work responsibilities; this is quite confusing for the world (laughing).

R: It's only a play. It's just like child's play. A job is a play for me. Getting married is just a play for me. All those are sorts of plays.

M: You are looking at it from a different perspective; but what about the world's point of view? Because the person who is with you at work doesn't know that you are a child in a man's body, playing a game, etc.

R: They don't need to know. Why do they need to know? Some people come to my house and ask these questions. What do I do? I teach them to be innocent and childlike; take it easy and be enlightened. I tell them this week after week. Others may not know; I can't do anything about it, but if they ask, I will tell them. But they don't ask. I am not here on any mission. See, you call me Master, right? People call me Master. Did I ever tell anybody to call me Master? Think! It is up to everyone to decide that they should pay respect to me.

M: We are calling you Master because you are bringing the light into our lives.

R: I don't deny that!

M: You are guiding us systematically or invisibly. I don't know how to put it, but you are doing it.

R: I agree about the fact that I am bringing the light! What I am saying is that I cannot be forced into thinking about exclusively being a teacher; you see what I am trying to say?

M: No, make it clearer please!

R: I don't want to see myself in a box thinking "I am a Master" and behave in a specific way.

M: So you don't see yourself as a teacher?

R: I teach myself; I see myself as someone who loves you, all of you, including your spiritual teacher. I am not an exclusive student of any particular teacher. I am not the exclusive teacher of anybody also. I am beyond being the student and the teacher. I am just here to serve! I want to be the foot soldier of my spiritual master to bring peace and love around.

M: Okay!

R: I am beyond being a father and a child! I am beyond being a husband.

M: How can you say that you are beyond that?

R: Because all those are roles and I don't accept any defined role. I am indefinable.

M: Who are you?

R: I am Atmaram, the Self, that's all! I am the Self that resides in all beings, all transient beings, and all living beings; I came here to tell you that. There is the Self within you also and you need to look at it very carefully; and be in touch with it and enjoy the life that has been given to you as a gift. I am not falling into any trap.

M: But when life is painful and difficult, we don't see it as a gift.

R: The Big Self gives you life, right! The Self gives you this life. Did you make this life? The Self gives it to you as a gift. But the Big Self has come to tell you, "don't waste it," I am that. Self always guides you too, that is why I am that sometimes. I choose to be that. You will only know the Self when you know who you are.

R: You are asking me who I am; "Who are you?"

M: I don't know (laughing) I don't know who I am really Master. That is why I am watching you because I know that you are something that I would like to be.

R: Yes, I agree! That I don't deny. The only things I deny are all these roles that I have. To be a Master, I have to act like a Master; I have to function like a Master. I cannot say to myself that I have to chant only certain mantras. I have to do only certain spiritual practices. I deny all that as I respect every spiritual teaching and every religion and I am a very inclusive person.

M: This is how we perceive you. To me, you are my Master.

R: You have the right to see me as your Master, but I am telling myself that I don't have the right to be your Master. Even so, you still have the right to take me as your Master.

M: Okay, Okay!

R: No problem, no problem. I don't create any problems for anybody, thereby indulging your right to be. I think that everyone has his or her perception of what the Master is or should be.

M: I agree with that too.

R: I am not here to match anybody's perception about who I should be. There is no reality, it's just perceptions. I am who I am; I am not here to confirm what everybody says I should be.

M: Our filters of perceptions are so inappropriate. It would be pitiful if you had to go down there and match them.

R: Right! Right!

M: And there are so many filters! It's not possible to match all of them.

R: How many filters can I match? If I match this one filter, I will not match the other filter. If I match the Brahmin filter, I won't match the non-Brahmin filter. If I match the household filter, I won't match the

Sannyasin filter. I want to be boundless. And, I am boundless, and I choose to continue to be boundless, because the Self is boundless.

M: But anyway, you have chosen to play with limitations. Just being in the body is a limitation.

R: Oh yes! The body itself is a limitation. So when I am with other bodies, I am automatically limited, right? But this is only a play.

M: That has nothing to do with the real you.

R: The real me! You said it.

M: Because, some people look at you and say "He has this weakness, that weakness, he is so ordinary." But sometimes it is apparent that you are so far away from being ordinary.

R: In reality, I am beyond the category of ordinary and extraordinary. And I don't want to claim that I am ordinary or extraordinary, the Self just is!

M: Uhu, uhu!

R: I make no claim.

M: I know you make no claim, but the world has created so many categories and they try to fit you into one.

R: All that I say is "Listen to me; whether there is value or not. If there is no value, you can also challenge me."

M: Why?

R: I am saying if there is no value, some people can even challenge me too. You are free to do that. It doesn't mean that I will accept the challenge, or necessarily conform to the requirements.

M: (Laughs).

R: Today I have chosen to work, tomorrow morning I may choose not to work. Today I have chosen to be in Chicago. But at any time I may choose not to be in Chicago. I was in San José years ago, and people in San José thought that I was going to be in San José forever. I came back in exactly 365 days. I am not bound by any city. I don't want to be bound by any country. The whole world can claim me. And I don't think any one country should claim me either. I am not an Indian; I may talk like an Indian, with an Indian accent, but I am not Indian.

M: You eat like an Indian (laughs).

R: I am not an Indian; I am the child of the universe. I may speak from another world of the universe who wants to claim me as her child. Yes, I am open to that and I surrender to that. My only mission is to love and be loved. I have no other mission. Whatever mission I take up, if that mission is followed, there is no other mission necessary on the planet. When you are in love, you are automatically at peace. If you are in love, you are also automatically in joy.

M: Everything is included in love!

R: Yes, what other mission do we need? Do we need to fix any other problem? Do we need to fix the hunger problem? When you fix the love problem, the hunger problem is solved. The lack of love that is leading people to not sharing the available food with each other is the problem to be fixed. There is already enough food on the planet for everybody, so why should there be hunger in the world? Fixing hunger should not be a mission. Love is the mission, which should be taught to all.

To complete what I have already said, I do not belong to any one of the four different castes either. I am not a Brahmin because I do not follow any particular rituals. I am not a Kshatriya because I do not fight wars; I do not want to fight with anybody. I have no conflict with anybody. I am not a Vysya because I am not skilled in any business. I cannot even maintain the simplest thing. I am not a good Sudra; I cannot do any heavy work. I cannot even lift a small box. I don't belong to any category.

M: You are in the category of the child. (Laughs)

R: Yes, yes! I am in the category of the child.

M: So you are a Master, always teaching.

R :   (Laughing) All "being" is teaching." My love itself is a teaching. There is no other teaching. All other forms of teaching are only commentaries.

M: Some people don't understand why you don't create an organization around you. What is the reason behind this?

R: There are so many organizations. I love them all; I want to support all of them. When I was six years old, I supported the Shankaracharya Peetham. And when Shankara came to my village, I went to every house and I put up a welcome sign. I enjoyed doing that. I support so many teachers, as you now know. I went to so many teachers to see what I could do for them and how I could support them because they do such wonderful work. I want to help everybody. I am not choosing one person only, saying: "This is the only one I am going to support." I am here to support everybody. I am here to stand with everybody, every organization.

M: Yes I do.

R: They are all mine.

M: They are all doing the same work, maybe in different formats. I understand now. The question arose because people think you're going to those organizations for yourself, but you are going to these organizations for them; to serve and to support them.

R: Like everybody, I have nothing to give except the opportunity to serve.

M: Someone said: "He can do his own thing; why is he going to this master or that master?"

R: There is no "my own thing." "Doing my own thing" is a part of ego, I don't have this part of ego.

M: It is people's ego!

R: It is all people's ego. The people around me can say: "You have to find this; you only to work through that." It is their ego. I don't want to live according to their egos. I am here to teach them that this very ego is a barrier. See? The whole world is my ashram.

Some people said: "You have been doing this for so many years, and you don't even create your own ashram!" The whole world is my ashram and the people around the world are my ashramites, without being my followers. I don't want followers. It's not a matter of where they are, who they are or to whom they belong; they are all mine.

M: How do you define followers?

R: Followers are those who stick only to what I tell them to do.

M: (Laughs) Nobody does that!

R: If anybody does do that, I say "Please don't do that!"

M: So you have no followers.

R: I have only friends.

M: In my opinion, there are so many people who have been blessed with your love, your kindness, and everyone who has had the chance to know you or just to be with you has expressed that just knowing you have been a blessing in their life.

R: Because my love for everyone is unconditional; that's why. Love radiates.

M: It's radiating hugely. Master, there is something I have to practice. I have to learn to live in the uncertain, in the unplanned. We have so many things that we had planned to do tonight and now we are doing this interview.

R: I really don't know what I will do!

M: We planned to do the groceries, we planned to clean and organize your bedroom.

R: I don't follow any plan.

M: Yes I know, that is what I am saying.

R: I go only with the moment. I live in the present moment.

M: You said you don't consider yourself as a teacher; do you consider yourself as a spiritual leader?

R: Because a teacher needs a student to be a teacher, a leader doesn't need the followers. I think that my very being is a teaching. I don't need a particular program and all that. That's why I say that I am not a teacher. I don't have a particular teaching to offer, a specific dogma, a certain opinion or certain methods, saying it's my method. I don't have that to offer to the world. I am still a spiritual leader. I said yesterday that I am living as the self, the spirit, so I can certainly live according to the very being of who I am.

M: How does being a spiritual leader affect your life?

R: It gives me lots of fun working with people, both men and women. I experience fulfillment, learning from everybody. I have learned the process of how to work with people; how to live and be with different types of people.

M: How has that affected your relationship with God?

R: That does not affect me. They are two different things.

M: How come it doesn't affect you?

R: Being a spiritual leader is actually representing God. It means speaking for God. So in a way, being a spiritual leader does not affect me. I have to be with my statement.

M: Do you think that if you were not a spiritual leader that it would have affected your relationship with God?

R: Not necessarily. It remains the same; that does not change. For, being a leader or not, my love for God remains the same.

M: Yes, I know. I am asking for the sake of the world.

R: Because being an expression of God's love means being a spiritual leader. That means being a spiritual being as well as a spiritual leader. I am only doing the work that God wants me to do and ask me to do.

M: Are you God?

R: Everybody is God in his or her essence. I also have God in essence in me. I don't really think about being God. I only think about the creation, the godliness, and the divinity in all beings.

M: What is your favorite Holy text, passage or prayer?

R: The Lord's Prayer in the Bible is one of the best because it covers so many dimensions. The next one is the Gayatri mantra, which is also a very powerful prayer. It also touches many dimensions. It is very powerful when it is chanted.

M: Have your favorite prayers changed over time?

R: Definitely, because I read about so many different religions, I have learned different types and sorts of prayers. Islamic prayers left very indelible impressions in my mind; all of them left imprints on me. Some Buddha and Hindu prayers have also impacted me. I relate to all of them equally, without singling out any one of them.

M: What is the purpose of human existence?

R: You should ask God; I did not create this existence. Why are you asking me?

M: But you know it. I pretend that you are God and I am asking you.

R: The purpose of human existence is to know oneself. Existence exists to know itself, to be conscious of it. It is to be aware of itself, and to multiply and expand itself.

M: To multiply itself?

R: Existence is constantly spreading. It's not manifesting itself in some place sometime, and then stopping. It is not spreading in one place while leaving a vacuum in other places. Sometimes there is no life on some planets while there is life on other planets. So like that it is spreading. That is the purpose of life. It is all a play of consciousness; that's the purpose of existence—its expansion.

M: So by multiplying and expanding, is this how this purpose will be achieved?

R: Through the multiplication and expansion, there are so many varieties of creation, so many types of animals, beings and birds, so many colors, so many things everywhere.

M: What is the purpose of your own life?

R: I don't need a purpose to live; I just enjoy life.

M: So the purpose of your life is to enjoy life?

R: Yes! That's the only purpose, to enjoy life in all its essence. Not only the sensations, the thoughts, the feelings, but also life that is beyond this; the transcendental life. I am transcending all this.

M: You can enjoy life at this level, but is this kind of enjoyment accessible to anybody?

R: Not necessarily. I can only talk about the purpose of my life. And I said that the purpose of my life is enjoyment. I enjoy life both in the way it is manifest and non-manifest.

M: That is the part that we miss; the non-manifest part. What are the practical components of a holy life?

R: To be whole. First is the love component. That's why I was telling you that you are not whole. If you are fragmented; you are not whole. When you are integrated, you are holy.

M: What are the greatest obstacles to human happiness?

R: Living a fragmented life. Living life based only on thoughts; living life in a constant state of conflict.

M: How can it be overcome?

R: It is overcome by manifesting the purity within oneself, the unity with all, and the unity with everything; by at least raising the divine potential.

M: What is your central message of faith to believers and non-believers?

R: My central message is to live and let live. It is to live life intensely and passionately. Love life intensely and passionately. What else is there? That's my message.

M: To non-believers, what do you say?

R: This is what I tell everybody. Make and keep life simple, straightforward. Do not complicate your life. When you complicate your life, you don't appreciate life and you fail to enjoy life. To be religious means to appreciate everything, to be fascinated by everything. Being religious means to be in that intimacy with all beings, all things. That is to be enlightened. A life lived without enlightenment is not worth living.

M: Is there any function that you chose to fulfill and upon which others depend as a spiritual leader?

R: It is love and all that which is compatible with it.

M: How can one integrate that in oneself?

R: You can do that by connecting yourself to God. Because God is love, that love will flow within you automatically and you'll feel it.

M: How do you connect to God?

R: Meditation, prayer, contemplation, and absorption are all ways to connect to God.

M: In your class you make people talk a lot, why is it so important that they talk so much?

R: I make them talk to cleanse them of their problems and their concerns because they are full of garbage. It is to make them ready to receive what I want to give. They have to ventilate and empty their mind of garbage before being ready for silence. Silence is a second level. Nothing can be poured in a full cup.

M: What is certain in this world?

R: Death and taxes!

M: (Laughs) You are right!

R: There is light beyond that too.

M: There is light beyond that? How can you be certain of this?

R: Because there was light before. So, as far as I know there was light before my birth, to that extent I can see light after death.

M: How can you be certain that there is light before birth?

R: I am able to see it. I can feel it. I felt my own light before my birth. I remember descending down the waterfalls of Courtallam in light form before I was born. My maternal grandmother told me that I didn't even cry at the time of birth. They were not sure for a few minutes if I was alive. I did not cry because I had no major complaints about this life. I saw and see all that was positive in this life and the life to come. So this is how I know about the future, because it's a continuum. Life is a continuum; it's not isolated.

M: Can anybody feel this connection with this light?

R: They can feel it in silence; by working on it and spending enough time looking into oneself, into one's own dreams, one's own patterns.

People's Experiences with Master Raju

· · · · · · · · · · · · · · · ·

Here are some interviews from the many "Souls from Mercury" from around the world who have been touched by Raju's teachings. (Mona's contributions are greatly acknowledged).

Mercy, Teacher (Montreal)

I met Master Raju through a friend he had invited to the introduction of a spiritual program he was going to teach in June 1996. I attended the program out of curiosity because he had mentioned that it can lead to enlightenment if practiced. I wondered about what could be in that program to make it as powerful as he said. So I decided to test the program to see if anything would happen to me. From June to December 1996 I attended a few retreats with Master Raju. I think it was at the third one that my curiosity shifted to a deeper interest. I found him profound and I thought that he might probably be able to give me something valuable from a spiritual standpoint. I noticed that he had a vast knowledge and thought that he could teach me or guide me on the path in which I was already engaged. I continued to attend more retreats. And in those days, he did different levels of retreats which led to increasingly deeper spiritual cleansing. I was fascinated by what was happening at the retreats and was enjoying them, and would not miss any of them. I started trusting him as a teacher. It was not a personal relationship with him. I think the personal connection came three years later when he invited me to visit him in Chicago. Master Raju has his own way dealing with each student and I think it was his way to bring me closer to him. I perceived him as someone very spiritually knowledgeable and I felt great respect for him and my relationship with him was a student-teacher one. I have never seen him as a friend because to me friendship is between equals. Now, after ten years of being around him, I can say that he represents the Divine Mother Energy in my life, even though he is in a man's body.

What kind of impact has he had on my life? When I took the basic program, I was going through a difficult time and I was lacking energy. The first impact was a surge of energy after I put his program into practice regularly for a while. I associated the improvement to the breathing exercises and the meditation he taught us. I was amazed by the results. I wasn't merely experiencing so much a psychological transformation from the program, but rather experienced a physical feeling of being highly energized as well. I felt I could carry the world; no more fatigue. And as I was integrating the new concepts of the course, I also noticed that an irrational feeling of joy came over me. All of this made me think that perhaps he was right when he had said that the program was very powerful.

At the very first retreat, I learned a new concept when I asked him how to deal with difficult people. He said: "You can handle it through inclusion." I had no clue what he meant. He explained this way: "It is feeling enough compassion and understanding for the person in front of you, so you treat him or her as being you." By being around Master Raju, I learned how to be aware of the impact of my action on my surroundings. That includes the way I treat people, nature, and animals. On many occasions, he pointed my behaviors out to me when I was insensitive and unaware that I was being that way. Gradually, he is taking me to a higher level of awareness; awareness about there being no such thing as others and me, or the rest of the world and me. There is no separation; I am this world, I am others and I should feel as them and be sensitive to their misery, pain and, cries because those are also my cries. This universe is also me, and it is part of my responsibility to be a good model for this world. This has been a considerable insight that Master Raju brought to me. This unlimited responsibility to do whatever is required to create a loving and peaceful world. Before I knew him, I knew that I was responsible for myself and the people depending directly on me—my parents, my children, and my extended family. The rest of the world was none of my concern. I never felt that I was responsible for the world as a whole, whether close to me or far away. Not only should I not inflict pain, but I must create a better world wherever I am as well. It is not a distant project; it is something that I have to do right now, every day, by increasing my sensitivity towards the surroundings.

Once, during one of my visits, as he was leaving for work, Master Raju said "I want you to tie the plants." He has too many plants for his living space and they were growing wild and out of control. I did not have much time for the plants at the time because I was helping out with other tasks, so I did it hastily and it was poorly done. When he noticed it he said, "Mercy, why did you do that to the plants? They will curse you." Then he added, "I cannot bear to see

156

anybody suffering." The way you tied them makes them suffer, and when you are suffering, you curse because the pain is too much." That meditation was material for me; to help become aware of the impact of my actions on the surroundings. Once more, I learned that I should be careful of not hurting, not causing pain, or creating mess around me. I had chosen to ignore pains around me because I had been comparing my life experience to that of the rest of the world, thinking: "I went through so much pain and suffering and I survived, so everybody can work their way out of their experiences as I did." I have now learned that all these examples of compassion were to lift up my consciousness. It was about opening my heart and feeling the world with my heart and not with my head. It was about my approach of feeling insensitive and separated from the surroundings. It was a way to teach me how to love the world unconditionally just as it is: things, plants, animals, and people. At that point, I realized how immense his compassion is. I also became aware that I should not compare my life experience with the rest of the world. I just have to love unconditionally; that should be my main and only concern, not judging and comparing.

Incidentally, he taught me how to change my attitude towards people and see the good hidden behind negativities. When I witnessed him talking to two parents and their teenagers, he told the parents: "The best way to help children is to see them manifesting your highest vision for them. Do not get confused by their weakness or mistakes. See your highest vision in them; see them manifesting the qualities and the behaviors you want to see in them. Then miracles will happen."

An aspect of Master Raju that I found intriguing is his capacity to read your mind or some events that are happening thousands of kilometers away from him. I have noticed it on many occasions where it was materially impossible for any common individual to know what was going on. For example, I might be having some questions in my mind; Master Raju would turn towards me responding to them as though I had voiced the questions loudly. There was a situation where Master Raju had been a victim of disrespect which I could not accept and I was trying to protect him. After the incident, I thought why are you disturbed by this? Master is okay with it, the whole world is okay with it, why does it bother me? These were my "private" thoughts. A few months later, I was seated near him alone for just two minutes, and without any introduction, he suddenly said: "I have emotions. I only do not allow them to come at the surface." I heard him and understood perfectly what he meant and I also knew he was referring precisely to that incident.

Because of Master Raju's teachings, I developed a special connection with all forms of nature; be it the sun, the sea, the trees, the mountains, a stone, etc. Wherever I am, there is always this silent peaceful friend nearby. This connection created a sense of security in me. I feel that there is always something around who loves me and protects me. Gradually, this awareness has generated within me a different approach towards life.

Master Raju is living the same kind of life as most of us, but his approach towards life experiences is a model for us. Behind all life activities, his main concern is spirituality. With great subtlety, he will adopt the attitude or exhibit the behavior commanded of a spiritual being. Despite his high academic qualifications, he always acts as a very humble and very simple person. He is an open book, not paying attention to the judgmental world in which we live. He is very careful of not hurting anything or anyone, and he is always authentic but unconventional. Whenever he is attacked or insulted, he always has a unique ace card to put on the table and display compassion. Many times I have witnessed him saying: "I can only offer my compassion." This is something that I wish to be able to practice because in my life, I mostly deal with difficult situations by hitting the "delete" key whenever someone hurts me. He is so perfect in these kinds of situations that you wonder if he feels emotions like all of us. Patience, love, and compassion are his dominant personality traits. When someone fails to be adequate, he sees you as a spiritual child who needs his help and he will never punish you. His cheerful attitude is waiting to welcome you.

His thirst to spread spirituality has taken and continues to take him everywhere on the planet. Where there are people hungry for spiritual growth, he will go. Case in point, Heidi, one of his disciples, took him to Venezuela in 2003 for a three-day program. He spontaneously accepted her request. On business trips, he always reserves his weekend breaks for spiritual seekers. Although sometimes he is physically exhausted, he will never turn down an opportunity to spread spiritual wisdom. His childlike cheerfulness, spontaneity, and candidness are contagious and are first nature to him—as automatic as breathing. If you are depressed and you come into contact with him, your spirits will be lifted. However, don't be mistaken of his childlike nature. In my opinion, he is not an ordinary individual. He is a very powerful being capable of performing miracles in your life. This aspect of Master Raju is hidden, disguised as simplicity, and playfulness.

Most of Master Raju's teachings revolve around achieving inner peace through silence. Something about Master Raju that I want everyone to know is to do your best; to be 100% present when you are in his presence because he is always 100% present for you. Whatever he is doing or not doing, whatever he is saying or not saying, that is the lesson; he is teaching you how to be in life. And when he talks, weigh each word. He never says or does anything without reason notwithstanding that he is acting, playing a role in the cosmic show.

I will always be very grateful for his supportive and compassionate guidance. I wish for many more people to be blessed with the same opportunity from which I continue to benefit.

Lillian, Artist (Montreal)

In 1996, there was a personal development program given at my friends' house. My husband attended it, and I joined it three days later. However, I have to redo the next session because some health problems prevented me from completing the course. In December 1995, I had ended up in the hospital emergency room. I felt very weak, as if life was leaving my body. In April 1996, Master Raju came to give me healing light. At the end of the session, I felt a movement inside my body like an organ had been lifted up. From that point, I got a significant relief from the problems I had and followed the full course. I went to more retreats in June and October 1996. After that retreat, I noticed some improvement in my meditation. On the 5th of October, he blessed us by doing a pooja in my home. I participated in another retreat in 1997. In the meantime, I met some others Masters like swami Satchidananda at a concert in Toronto, and also Yogi Ramaiah and Arkaji.

In June 1998, Master Raju started giving a new program. As I attended these programs, I started noticing some transformations within me.

I visited him in Chicago in August 1998. It was the most significant trip of my entire life as I got to know Master Raju a little more. A personal experience that happened there made me realize that he was taking care of me spiritually. Chandrika, Master Raju's wife, spent some time with us in December 1998 before she joined him in Chicago. During the whole time she spent with us, we recited the Divine Mother's a thousand names every day. That was a good support for me.

By his example, Master Raju taught us how to have balance between spirituality and secular life. He gave me the hope that one can purify oneself and become a divine person. He helped me to improve my relationships with other people by making me being aware of their feelings. He is a very committed person. I had read the Adwaita of Adi Shankara, and Master Raju made me understand it much better by his way of living.

I have greatly benefited by his presence and I wish everybody could be blessed by that opportunity for their spiritual upliftment. He brought faith into my life by clearing up the doubts I had.

Master Raju is a person whose thoughts, words, and actions are all linked to each other. Sometime people think one thing, say something else, and do a totally different thing, but all relating to the same matter. He is not like that. Whatever he thinks, he keeps to and remains committed to. He has the special quality of a Master: always taking care of the disciples' spiritual needs. Master Raju has brought so much change to my life that I consider it is a great privilege for anyone to come into contact with him. He is a blessing from God. God shows us his affection through him. Lots more people will meet him and take his guidance; that's why he has come on this planet again.

Actually there are many great spiritual Masters roaming the Earth, and they are doing so well to humanity. Master Raju had brought so many opportunities to my life, allowing my soul to grow. I can see the changes within me: I am doing so many things I would have not done before. I am going to different places and meeting people. I feel so transformed and know it is because his energy is with me. He has put me in contact with different people, different books, and other different forms of support according to my needs. This has enriched my life; otherwise I would have not become wiser. So I feel the presence of Master Raju all the time and have gradually come to know his divinity. In the beginning, it was very difficult for me to talk to him or to invite him to our home. I think ego was in the way. Even though it is still there, he helps me reduce it. He is progressively removing all the bad and negatives things from me with his pure and great energy. He is supporting me in overcoming lots of things. This is a good thing, because when we do things without guidance, we do not know if it is right or wrong. When the divine energy is doing it, she is always working for the growth of the soul and she is always right. So I am very pleased and I feel very happy. I have never been this happy in my life. Before I met Master Raju, I was a lost cause! I used to be happy with all the materialistic things, but it seemed there was always something lacking. Now,

I can say that my happiness has been expanded. There is still more growth to come before I reach saturation point. There are still more practices to be done, and the Master just gives you the energy so you can follow these practices although they remain your own responsibility. Every time I meet my Master, he brings my energy level up by different processes, which has been a very great blessing. I have nothing to give back to him because I feel inadequate. I would not give him material things as he is totally above those things. The only thing I think I can do—which is like an offering to the Master or "guru dakshina"—is to prepare myself to support his work. I think this state of my life is also coming as I do not worry about anything now. I just follow the practices and the rest comes by itself because his grace is always there during the process. When my body is unhappy, he helps overcome that. I think it's a great thing to look forward to, reaching the same level of purity as the Master. This will be a very wonderful stage to attain. I think that anybody who reaches that stage will find happiness. But to reach such a stage, one must have total focus on the goal. When circumstances put you in a non-safe mode, it is at that moment that practices must be intensified. However, the Master's grace will always be there to support you. Master Raju has said that he will be really happy when a disciple no longer needs his guidance. He wants his disciples to arrive at his stage and be able to act in whatever situation they are put, as he would. I think there are lots of people ready for it, but they just have to do their practices. Master Raju has already reached out to so many people; his energy is slowly working miracles. If something you desire is not happening today, he will make it happen at a different time, through somebody else, when you will be looking in opposite direction. It might happen because you have already expressed your desire and he has heard it and he will make sure that you get what you wish. There is no doubt about it. So many things have happened to me. Once a Siddha Guru has touched your life, walking on the spiritual path is much easier if you surrender to him and allow him to take you to the final goal.

But there are also many people who have come at the last stage of their spiritual journey, and after this birth they will be realized and will merge with God. Master Raju has come to touch all these people or jivanmuktas. This means to realize divinity whilst still living in this world. You don't have to wait to die to go to heaven; it is already here in this world. Many people will come to Master Raju, and they will have a great life, because he has touched them.

Tulsi, Manager (Toronto)

I think I met Master Raju in 1983 or 1984. Someone from another workshop on the enlightenment also took the course. He gave me a telephone number and that number belongs to Master Raju. He and Chandrika, his wife, was helping facilitate the course. They were living in Scarborough at the time. This is the year Master Raju just got his job in Montreal at Spar Aerospace Center, and he was still commuting between Toronto and Montreal at the weekends. So when I took the basic initiation course he was still commuting to give the program in Toronto. I took the course in Scarborough.

What impact has he made in my life? I will begin with generalities, and then I will go into specifics. I think in general he has been a friend, a teacher or guide, you know pointing me in the right direction. Regarding his course for example, I think that I benefited more from him when I chatted with him. In 1994 or early 1995 he directed me to go see a great saint in India. I don't know what I got out of him tangibly or physically but I like to think that there is something I have benefited from, yet can't quantify it. I cannot name it. But I do hold the saint as the modern day avatar. Being in the man's presence, things may have shifted, I don't know. I can't personally say what has shifted and how it has changed. I feel that Sadhana has shifted tremendously since 1995 to now, but I cannot directly attribute it to him. However, I don't know to whom? But suffice it to say that Sadhana is unfolding the way it is, so who knows? Okay! This is not how some people would report—"Oh I met the saint, I saw this great light, I did this, he manifested that for me, this way I found the new job. You know none of that!—But the way I see it, something must happen when one is in the presence of individuals of his caliber. When I say these things, they may sound trivial, but I don't treat them trivially. So in 1995, with Master Raju's direction, when he said, "You should go to see Bhagavan, he is an old man, and who knows how much longer he is going to be in his body." So I went to his birthday. It was quite an experience in itself, and we could discuss more about that, but to get back to the original question of what kind of impact Master Raju had on me, that's one by directing me to go to see great saints. In 1996 or early 1997, he also directed me to a kind of a Sadhana, a pilgrimage, something I had to do. I did not get anything tangible out of it, but hey, I was there! I met Swami Ganapathi Sachidananda once again. He also told me to go to Sringeri and that is the genesis of Adi Shankara, it is the first spiritual centre established by him. So I went there. The first tour was strictly one ashram in South India. The second tour was of many other places plus the previous ashram. As a matter of fact, I even went to see Master Raju's father. It was a very specific instruction to go to Sringeri. At that time, he did not say why. Afterwards he told me why. He said, "To jog your memory" when I was there. He continued "I did not want you to go to Shankaracharya just for the heck of it. It was for the vibration and to jog your memory and see if you remembered anything." I remembered nothing!

Again, I think my propensity does not have a lot of what do you call that? You know how people remember past lives, past history, and so on? I am not into that kind of stuff. I don't remember past lives. I may have certain inclination that I would dismiss it as a joke. I will say, "Oh yeah, in my past life perhaps I was a monk or something like that." But I don't give it a lot of credence. I don't take it seriously, but I don't take it lightly either. So he asked me to go to Sringeri to jog my memory and I recalled nothing. When I went to visit this 800-year-old temple, there were a lot of poojas happening. I have a lot of reverence for that, so I went outside and sat around the temple for some time. I remember sitting at one specific spot very quietly; there were not a lot of tourists around. As I sat in that place, an incredible amount of devotional feeling, what I would call the tears of Bhakti or devotion, came over me and resulted in lot of tears which was not the first time that happened to me. But in Sringeri, this was a unique experience for me. I sat there. I was there and that was it! These were some of the impacts when he specifically asked me to go to certain places. I saw value in all of these experiences of visiting temples in 1995 and in subsequent trips. I met a lot of people along the way. I also experienced so many things when I went to Ramana Maharishi's place in Arunachala. So all these things were sanctioned and blessed by Raju. In a way, without his direction, the trips may have not occurred, but because of him it all happened.

T: I also read in Scriptures that those people in this life, who have done enough Sadhana, can come to the point where certain emotions will totally just vanish where, when the chakras are opened up and are so purified, there will be no possibility that the inner tranquility can be disturbed by the outside turmoil.

M: You reach the point where you are not like a sponge anymore. I mean the point where these emotions don't get into you. He explicitly said that to me in a context where I was thinking: "He should put his foot down and stand up, that would have helped the situation." He read my thoughts and out of the blue he said, "I have emotions, only I don't allow them to come to the surface." I was very surprised because all this was going on in my mind silently.

T: They do not affect you. So my recommendation to others would be to hang out with the man. He is a loving guy. Certainly it's a tremendous contact. If you sit quietly enough and you talk to him, there is something that happens with your contact with him; something that reminds you of who you are within yourself. It happens in a very subtle way. During the communication, he shows you which direction you should go.

M: It is very interesting what you are saying. Recently I was telling somebody that Master Raju is not an ordinary person. I told to that person, "Be around him, don't miss him, you will surely get something from him. Something will come from him to you. I cannot say what that thing is, but something will pass from him to you, and you won't ever be the same again."

Arnold, Manager (Toronto)

A: I came to know Master Raju in 1985. I was forty years old, and my children were just being born. My daughter Vanessa was three years old, and I had reached major burnout. I was looking for something different. I wanted to learn yoga but I could not find a teacher, so I got some books and tapes. Locked in my room, I tried to focus on the flame of a candle. I had been teaching myself for a few weeks when a friend of mine told me about some yoga classes, which were going on. He said, "Why don't you contact this fellow?" This is how I took two weekend courses from Master Raju. The things he had taught at that time are still in my mind.

M: Tell me about your relationship with him?

A: My relationship with him is very deep and very personal. Over the years, I have followed different masters. I followed Pandit Ravi Shankar and someone called Mohanji from India. I followed Mr. Karl Green who introduced me to Buddhism. I learned from each one of them. But Master Raju has been a constant in my life since the time I met him. He is a very personal Master. He is always accessible and my relationship with him is very mixed. In one sense, he is my Guru. I always look for guidance from him. I always ask questions and he is always there for me. I don't need a retreat to reach him. In other ways, he is like a good friend. I am very close to his family and I try to be with him as much as possible when he is around.

M: He is the Master, but also a good friend!

A: Yes! I think since I met, him my life has shifted 180-degrees. He introduced me to spirituality. He started the fire, and lots of people stoke it. But he keeps on stoking it. But you know how these things go, it's like when a child starts to walk, after that you don't have to hold his hand and you know he knows how to walk on his own. He has changed my life. I remember before I used to love ghazals. You know ghazals?

M: No, I don't.

A: They are different types of songs; songs of love and romance. Indians have this kind of song, which are metaphors of music. Every young person loves this kind of music of love and romance. When I started with Master Raju, I just forgot about all that stuff. I listened to and now sing his bhajans and nothing else. I left behind every other kind of music.

From his teachings, I notice one constant; that is love. It is something which is always challenging me. He has always spoken about love and I could not understand it. I still do not understand it fully. But his message is always the same and sometimes, at the beginning, you don't grasp it at all. Then you begin to grasp it little by little. He used to say, "When you face people you don't like, that precise moment is an opportunity for you to generate the highest amount of love in your life." It is a very difficult concept to understand and to live with, but maybe, after fifteen years, I think that I have understood some of it.

M: Even when we understand it, living by it is another thing!

A: That's what I mean. By understanding it, I mean you have internalized it and you put it in practice. His message of love is constant in his being. I have always been touched by his gentleness. I know his life is very difficult but he never says anything bad about anybody. I can say to people about him, "If you would meet God face to face, that's what God would look like, with a smile and gentle face reflecting love and compassion." It takes the best of you to teach these things, they must be deeply part of you.

I can see the difference between him and many other masters; it is that he is very accessible. He cares for your personal life and he is always there for you. The difference between him and some other masters, who have millions of followers, is his accessibility. One is very lucky to have somebody of his caliber to be interested in your personal well being. He is only at a phone call away. You could not get that kind of attention and access from other people of his caliber.

He is always very gentle and very responsive of people's needs. They would discuss personal and spiritual issues with him. But I have seen him also come and make a very forceful statement. And I have never seen anybody else make a statement as categorical as that. I remember one day, eight or nine years ago, he was with a small gathering, I think it must had been in his mind because he said in the first few minutes of his talk, "Without meditation, spiritual progress is not possible!" And later on in the same meeting, he said, "Unless you can see God in people, you cannot have spiritual progress. It will happen to the extent you see God in other people." That is very strong and very categorical. It's not half and half. He does that from time to time. And yesterday, remember when he said, "When you feel love, it's God acting through you." And I think you can extend it to whenever you do great things. You have not done anything; it is God who has done it through you. You are only the medium.

M: Exactly!

A: I think it's very categorical and not everybody catches it.

M: Who has to catch it, catches it (laughs).

A: Of course, you know, I don't always do what he asks me to do (laughs), but I pay a little bit of attention. It's like catching fish. If you put your own net there, then the probability is very high that you may catch fish. (Laughs) You don't have to be sitting there all day. (Laughs) That always impresses me because a few people make such a statement that get to you. You don't need to remember everything that everybody says. You only need to latch on to a few things. You can internalize a few things to propel you into outer space. That's how I see my good friend Master Raju.

Vanessa, Student (Toronto)

M: Vanessa, tell me, how did get to know and become close to Master Raju?

V: I have known Master Raju for most of my life. I knew him in a different context when I was younger. I grew up with him and his son Arvind. When my dad started getting involved in the personal development program, he was encouraging us; my family, my mother, and my brother to get involved too. As my father would say, "Call him Master, touch his feet, do this, do that." I never did because at that point in my life, that was not who he was to me. He was uncle Raju, and I kept it that way. It's only recently I started to call him Master. I matured and I actually went to see him myself to see what he has to say, and to discover for myself why people think of him in the way they do.

My relationship with him was still in transition a little while ago, from the whole uncle figure to the Master figure. I think I am still a kid to him, and I think in many ways, he talks to me the same way a father would talk to his daughter. In a sense, he guides me, as he does with many people. But my case is a little bit different. I don't know as much as other people are, but I ask him questions on various things, and we have a good relationship.

He has taught me so many things about the way a person should be in life. Although I knew about "being good," I was not sure how to go about making a contribution to the community. So many people think it's impossible actually to be that good and for anyone to be that kind of person. But he is such a good example, and he has shown me that is possible to live life in such a way that you are truly helping people; how we can be kind and true to each other. He has really shown how to be the kind of person I want to be. He himself is so nice to everybody.

He taught me by the way he teaches. He does not preach but presents himself as a knowledgeable person. This is so different from the way it has been with my parents and the way I was brought up. When I go to temple with my parents, I don't understand what is happening there; I don't understand the language. With him, his teachings are so practical to daily life. He talks about relationships, about love, and even about science. I remember when he was talking about science and about how that can be applied to daily living. One can live one's life through what you learned from his teachings as they become part of your daily living. For example, the questions that we discussed at the class today, I think you can see what those questions can do for you. When I asked myself those questions, I can see what I actually realized about myself. I think that mainly his teachings are a part of it.

When I talk to my friends about him, I tell them who he is to me, who he is to lots of people, and that he is an inspiration. He is such a great example to the world; of what a person can be. He shows you how one person can make a difference. This one man has made so much difference in so many people's lives!

If I can tell this to people, if I can share the things I have learned from him, that would be great. I think he has the ability to make a great impact in people's lives, not by preaching but by the way he presents himself as the person he is. He does not tell you "This is right, that is wrong, this is how you should live your life, this is what you should or should not do, etc." He just makes you question yourself. He makes you question what is right, what is wrong.

I am so amazed by his humbleness. We all think that he knows so much but he is still open to everything. The way he reads many books, the way he is interested in so many things. He also can be so many things to so many people. The way he is a father and at the same time he is an employee, a Master, and an uncle. He is this, he is that, and he does it all so well. The way in which he handles all his roles, he is an example. I think he shows how to keep a balance in life. He shows he leads a good life and he lives it in the middle path. He teaches by being an example, and shows how we could all be the same.

M: Do you want to add something on how you feel about him?

V: I just want to say that I am so grateful. I am so thankful that he came into my life at the point that he did, because he came at the point when I was really searching for who I am and when I was trying to figure out what I wanted from my life and what to contribute. The fact that I have him as a guide is the best thing that could have happened to me. He has taught me to see things in such a different way, in such an amazing way that I would not have done normally. I wish that everyone could be as lucky as I am.

Rosa, Teacher (Toronto)

R: We came to know Master Raju at Sheila's place in 1993 or 1994. She had talked about the personal development program and him constantly. One and a half years later, she had arranged for course at her home and she convinced me to take it, claiming that it would change my life for the better. I had been through some tough times in my life and she was aware of it. She thought that the program would help me and my whole family.

When Master Raju presented the course at Sheila's place, it was a commitment for three consecutive weekends. It was an important commitment for me. With God's grace, we took the course; me, my husband, my mother-in-law, and my little daughter Gloria. It was my first meeting with him, and it was amazing. The best thing that happened to me was that I knew he had the power to change my life. For a while, I realized that I was ready for this change, but it took me some time before I could make a commitment to it.

I have to thank Sheila for being the vehicle who made it happen for me and my family. If it wasn't for her persistence, I would not have been able to do it. Master Raju was great with Gloria, she came to every class and Master Raju played with her during breaks and made special bond with her. She was the only child in the course, and Master Raju spent quality time with her. He gave true meaning to the quote "Without the guidance of a Master, one cannot receive true knowledge in life." It was through the Master that I could understand and start my journey toward self–realization. I am very grateful to him for that.

What it means to me is energy, it is God, it is light, and it can be anything. But to me it was the ultimate self-realization; basically he bridged the gap for me. He brought it to me through light. He made us aware of it. I am still working on what he taught us. The last day of the program he said, "Your real homework will be when you leave this room." You will think what you have learned here is over, but you will have to apply it in your lives. He made it simple to understand for me. Even though we went through lot of material, it went like a smooth sail for me. It kept making sense and kept "clicking." I had always known that a door existed, and I also knew I had to go through it. With awareness, I realized it was something that existed beyond my comprehension, beyond all which is visible to my mind's eye. But I did not know what "ultimate" was until then. But I knew once I met him. Once the door opened, I also became aware that I could not have found it without his guidance and love. I love reading, learning more through books as there is a wonderful collection of knowledge. But it all made perfect sense once he opened that final door. Books alone cannot teach all he has taught. The simplest way I can describe is that I had this lock and did not have a key to open it. He brought the key and opened it for me. I had gone from book to book, and people to people, but found out he had the key to my lock of ignorance, and his love was the key that opened it for me.

We have been blessed with his presence through the courses and lectures and also through private time at home. He has been very kind to us. He has been a grace for my family. He had given us the opportunity to take care of him sometimes, to cook for him, to have his presence in our home and do pooja for our home. As we spent more time with him, the need to ask questions diminished. His presence is enough; he always gives without asking for anything. He has taught me to be aware of all my actions, good or bad, whatever they may be. The most important thing is to be aware of it. He also taught me that God is not outside or a separate entity, he is inside us, we are it. At first, this came as a surprise to me, and then once the thought sunk in, it made all sense. Today, now I know I am it. It is deep inside us. It is not separate from you. I did not know that until I met him.

During my third weekend, I had asked him to write something in my class notebook. He blessed my book and my journey with this note, "Always see God in each other." Doesn't that say it all? It was enough for me to understand what he was trying to say. It became my motto for life. Whenever I face a challenging person, I try to see the same God in them as in me. All of a sudden, the negative changes to positive, and compassion replaces the anger. It has given me an insight to what all the Vedas are about. If I can do this simple action all the time, I will love everyone with the same compassion, even people I have challenging relationships with, and whom I cannot forgive easily. This has made it all possible for me. It is the sole purpose of my existence in this world, to completely adapt to this logic. It helps me in any crisis situation.

Now, when I have to face people I do not want to deal with, or wish some of them did not even exist, I look at them as lessons that I have to learn and to overcome, to go to the next level. The person in front of me is the challenge. The challenge is my ability to overcome the situation or problem. It is God's way of teaching me. Today, I have started walking towards this path because of him coming to me at that particular time in my life. I was ready, and he appeared. It is as simple as that. I have made myself available to go where my Master wants to take me. I have not reached it yet, but mind you Mercy, I am totally aware of this wonderful feeling of where I am going. I have my map now, my Master. I am not at a crossroad where I am questioning which way to go. Instead, the doubts are gone. It is my complete faith in him that drives each and every activity of mine. The confusion is gone; the fog has been lifted. That is what he has done for me.

Even though we do not see him often, I do not miss him. He taught us well. In the beginning, I was concerned about what we would do without him. But since I have put myself in his humble hands, I am carefree, safe, and at peace. He has made us love him as he has given my whole family unconditional love. I love him without any attachment. I always carry him with me wherever I go. I talk to him all the time, asks him advice, and he always answers me. I would not have understood any of this if I had not walked the road on my own. He gave me the confidence to try out on my own.

M: He has given you confidence.

R: Oh yes! It is not only that. It's clear now what is happening, and I am able to see it as a project not only for me but for all the people that I met or will meet: in the streets, in the grocery store, at the office or anywhere I go. It is like a contract given to me to help, and to be there for everyone. I now have that chance, that opportunity to do something to help each moment. And spend it with total awareness. I am not sure if it was there before or not, but now I am aware of it. He has turned the switch and put on the light, so to speak.

M: It is so wonderfully said.

R: It is as simple as this: I feel like a mother to the whole universe. I am able to feel the pain of each creation of the Lord who can feel pain. I think of all the children of the world who do not get one square meal a day. In my small ways, I try to make a difference as Master has taught me. "Help the world," he said. "The best way to help God is to serve his people." Each day I try to show my children the awareness that Master has graced me with. Every single day I teach them to love and respect nature. By helping it to flourish, we in turn will flourish. As I try to extend and share the awareness with my family and friends, it will slowly extend to my street, my town, my country, and to people everywhere. I believe that was the lesson he gave us and wants us to spread to the rest of the world.

M: You are practicing the sense of responsibility as he taught us?

R: Yes, definitely. He taught us that responsibility does not only finish at our own home. He taught us how to extend ourselves to all around us. Every chance I am given to show this, I avail to the fullest. Isn't that what it is all about?

M: Hmm hmm.

R: I am very thankful that he came into our lives as he did and made such a difference.

M: Hmm hmm.

R: Through this book, I think he will find out how much of an impact he has made and how his efforts are bearing fruits. It is my connection to him.

M: Is there anything else you think that could be inspiring to other people? Something you received from him and you wish that everybody could benefit from?

R: Yes! That would be awareness. Just the way that we should love ourselves, we should love what we have, what is inside, what is around, and thus awaken love in other people. For what I feel is that there is so much pain in other people. It is not that they cannot love other people; it is just that they do not love themselves enough to love beyond themselves. He taught me that you cannot love anyone completely if you do not love yourself first. You must first see good qualities in yourself to be able to see them in others. If people could love themselves and forgive

172

themselves more, then everyone would benefit from it. That would be a tremendous contribution to the world. This is what Master is doing.

M: Exactly!

R: He is trying to make us aware, to love ourselves. And once we do that, we will be able to truly spread love all around us. It starts within your own homes, then spreads to your garden, to your street, city, and so on. The pictures get larger and larger to include the whole universe.

M: Can you tell me about how you see Master Raju, the man, the engineer, the ordinary person who has an ordinary life like everyone else?

R: You know what he told us when we first met him? People were so curious about him and started asking personal questions. He just laughed and said, "Forget about figuring out your Master. You are here for bigger things." It is about a good year and a half since this happened, and I still did not know anything personal about him. The only thing I knew was that this person had come in my life with the key to a lock I had, and had taken me on a journey that I was supposed to go on, which is everyone's goal. But I did not know that then. This man was full of love for all the people around, for nature, the country, and the universe. He had no ego in him. I had, until then, never met a man of his caliber. He had so much to give to people if they were ready to receive it. He was this pure being whom one could trust and believe in, listen to and learn about the truth of life. He has this wonderful habit when he first walks into the room. He stands with his right hand on his heart, and looks around and makes eye contact with each individual in the room. It is the look that fills you up with love. It is the look that gives you a silent blessing. It is the look which says "I love you just the way you are." And this is how the message keeps coming from him. This is something that lives inside him as much as each one of us. That is the person you get to know. The rest does not matter.

M: You know, sometimes when he is there, I feel like telling people "Look at him, don't miss his look." There is so much love and compassion flowing from him. I personally told someone I took to a class "Be careful, look at him, and don't miss his look, all is there."

R: I felt that, the minute he walks into the room, my eyes are glued to him.

M: When Master Raju is there, I don't want to miss a second of his presence. Sometimes I don't hear properly what he is saying because I am deaf in my right ear. But it does not matter. For me, just being there is enough to receive what he knows I need. I am glad you mentioned it too and that I am not the only one who feels this way.

R: Everybody that I had taken to him always feel like that. They feel they are so special and loved. And I am sure that many people in the room feel the same way. They feel he is there for them alone. You can only feel that way once you have recognized your true person inside; I mean one who has realized himself. And that is a sign, because he radiates that to me, it cannot be put into words but only experienced.

M: I know.

R: The only thing I know is he takes me where it is safe. I feel loved, I feel that I can do anything, and everything is possible. Also, I am part of him; we are not separate from each other. It is this feeling that has guided me to love others around me with the same love and ease. I am so full. I can now give love to people I never imagined I could get along with. He has taught me to love for the sake of love. Things that hurt me before do not hurt me any longer. He has made the picture wider for me. The little details do not matter anymore; we now leave them behind. It is happening for us. The more we let go, the more we are able to love freely. I get invited to hear different spiritual leaders, and I am sure they are all great, but the need to find more answers has gone. I do not think anyone else could tell us anything more than he had told us. I can now make it my life's work to bring his teachings to life. He is with us all the time, guiding us, and I try to follow all he has given each day of my life. I have reached that mode with him, you know.

M: You got it?

R: I don't know if I got it but I don't care anymore.

M: You got all you need I mean?

R: I have everything. I feel now I am ready for the "silence." I have grown to appreciate not talking, I used to be the biggest talker you know, and

I would not wait for other person to shut up, I was just going on with it, sort of, you know what I mean.

M: Uhu.

R: He brought silence and its values to me. He made me think of what is truly important and made me sit down with myself, and look deep within myself to see what I am and who I am. I kept what I liked and let go of what I did not like. It is wonderful to be at this stage. I am working on and on as I consider everything, and the more I explore in this journey, the less I feel I know. In other words, I will be a perpetual student. I do not want to stop learning! And I hope God will be graceful. We do not get disturbed by little things in life's up and downs anymore. I live in a family and I have three children. One is Christian and the two are Hindus. I have been divorced, and had a lot of struggles in my life. Then this person came into my life as a friend and later became my husband. It is the best thing that happened to me. I did not know one could be loved just for what they are as Kevin has loved me. He was my friend, and we still remain the best of friends. During my pain, I offered a special prayer in 1983—to be loved for what I am, just the way I am. It was granted to me a few years later. Even though life was a roller coaster, I never asked "Oh God, why me?" I always believe God does not make us suffer, but gives us challenges so we can learn what we came here for, and he did that wonderfully. God was listening to my prayer. He sent Kevin, then he sent Master Raju to guide us to better and bigger things and we have never looked back. Kevin asked for a gift, which was to make a home where there was also place for his mother, as she was living with her daughter then. In our culture, if one has a son, one should not spend old age at a daughter's home.

M: Because the son has to take care of his parents.

R: Exactly. He had too much trouble in his previous marriage and could not do this for her. But it was his dream to give her a happy home. It was a turning point in my life living with her, getting to know her. Even though she is tough, as she has seen lots of struggles in life herself, she does not love anyone easily. Master Raju helped me to love her just the same and see God in her just as in anyone else. We all took the course together and Master Raju could read our minds and give us pointers when and where needed, which helped us all tremendously. We had our own share of challenges with three children, a mother, and a new home. With Master Raju's silent help and guidance, we have managed to create a peaceful home and a place where all are welcome and loved. We could not have done it as well as we have without Master Raju's blessed hand and guidance. He always said just the right thing to make it easier for all of us. And that was amazing. There are a million stories and I could go on and on; all are fascinating and magical. Master Raju came and the magic came into our lives. As they say, "When a Master comes in your life, things start to happen," and they sure did when he came into ours.

M: Happen and happening are words I learned with Master Raju. Now I really cherish it because things just happen and life is so easy this way. We do not have to do anything, just be with it, and be with what is there in the moment. No more fighting against the current of life.

R: It was always easy. However, if one expects difficulties, then there will be. Today, it is so obvious, but we made it so difficult for ourselves. We had to go through the learning process to appreciate how easy it could be today. He made it easy for us because he made us aware. He made us accept things as they are. That is the way to make it easy as we are not fighting anymore. We are just "going with the flow" so to speak. Before, we used to say "Why this? Why that?" now none of that, just "Why not?" You know, in every situation, one can choose to cry or complain, or you can accept it. Complaints are less beneficial. Awareness is more beneficial. Now we do not hit our heads against the wall asking for something other than what is given.

M: Something different than what is there.

R: Yes. That's the difference in attitude that has come to all of us. I do not speak just for myself, I mean my whole family. We are calmer; we are more able to deal with different things which would have made us crazy before. It's a big improvement I think because life will always be stressful. It is still full of challenges but our attitudes are different now.

M: I am hearing that since you have known Master Raju, he has brought a lot of greatness in your life, a lot of peace. It is just too bad we cannot bring him to everybody, to the whole world! (We both laugh).

R: We will bring him to more people. I thank you for bringing forth the idea of doing this book. This will bring him to people, by the people who love him and whose lives he has touched in such positive ways and which made all the difference. It is not for him to know but for the rest of the world to know. It does not make a difference to him if this gets done or not, but it is wonderful for the people to get to know him.

M: I believe Master Raju knows everything. It is now becoming sometimes a little difficult for me.

R: He can read everything?

M: No, no, not that. He is not a common individual from my experience.

R: I knew that too.

M: Now that I know what he is, I have difficulty treating him as an ordinary person. He knows all about my life. He knows all my thoughts, all my weaknesses, and all my strengths, all of me. So what to tell you? He already knows everything and he pretends being a simple individual. But I understand that he has to play it when you have to relate to pre-scholars like us, you have to go down on the ground.

R: That's amazing Mercy! Once when we were travelling, we were curious but I did not have the courage to ask as I respected his privacy. My friend used to talk about his personal life sometimes, but not much though. Then once when I picked him up at the airport to take him to Sheila's place, as we were talking about things in general and listening to bhajans tapes, he would sometimes sing along with it. One day, suddenly out of context, he started talking about himself and his family. Until then I did not even know his wife's name. He talked about his son and what his name was, which university he attends, and what he does, etc. I must admit he had read my mind as I was curious. But it's like you said, he is aware of your thoughts. (Laughs) I was wondering for few minutes, but I did not ask the questions. I took it as him showing me respect; he was gracing me with information about himself. So I got to know him as a father, as a husband to someone out there. I felt very privileged to hear all he told me. And he went on sharing about his life.

He shared that he wanted to write about the good uses of a vegetarian program and diet. It was so different to see this side of him. Our initial encounters with him were only as our spiritual father or the Master. By knowing the individual side of him, it gives us a holistic picture of the man behind the Master, so to speak. He once mentioned to me of being a Brahma Kumara. I am not sure if I am saying the exact term.

M: It's the exact term.

R: One day he said, "I was made to be a "Brahma Kumara." I said "You are kidding? He said, "No, no, that's the role I was supposed to take in this life. I was one of those, believe me I did it." He added, "I also used to wear flat, belly-bottom pants, flat pants, etc.," he laughed when he was telling us these things. He continued, "I was not meant to get married you know." I said "So, how did you get married?" He shared he had just gone with a friend to see Chandrika as a matrimonial match for his friend. When his friend ended up saying no, and in our culture it is not considered good for a girl to be rejected like this, Raju volunteered. (Laughs). I said "You did what?" He repeated "I volunteered."(Laughs). I said "That means, you were meant to get into the marriage circle and go beyond that to get where you are today." It was a wonderful feeling seeing him sharing so innocently like a child. This whole conversation was over the dinner table, and we had such fun.

M: I remember when I was doing the interview with him, I asked all the questions I had prepared in order to get specific information I needed to know. I did not ask that question as I put it to the end of my list. I already knew that he was married to Chandrika. They were in the group with me when we went to India in 1992. But I asked, "How did you get married?" He reacted as if he was waiting for that question. He said, "Finally you come to this question. It is a difficult one." I replied "I don't find it particularly difficult." Maybe, as usual, he was reading my mind, and had seen that I was not too happy to invade his private life. I had to ask the question for the sake of the book, for posterity. The curiosity I had about him was regarding his divinity. I felt he was not a common individual; I wanted to know with whom I was dealing. I was not really bothered about his private life.

R: He said that he considers his wife Chandrika as his Guru.

M: He considers her as his Guru?

R: Yes! She considered him as her Guru too, because as a spouse, we teach each other things. We have books which are my gurus: Paramhansa Yogananda is my Guru. Vivekananda is my Guru. Everything which gives you insight becomes your Guru. My son is my Guru, my husband is my Guru. He taught me patience so he helped me grow.

M: So I asked the question because I wanted to hear the answer from him. Hearing things from a third person, it can become their perception of the truth and can be a little distorted from the reality. So he told me what you said.

R: He did?

M: Yes, he told me.

R: Then Chandrika's mother met him and they were married.

M: When I met the couple in 1992 I did not know who he was, or better what he was at the time. Since the women were separated from the group of men, I got to know Chandrika a little more than him. I had the opportunity of seeing her interacting with people. But I did not know much about either of them.

R: His universality is the most beautiful thing about him. He helps everyone out there irrespective of their background. He touches everyone no matter where they come from and what they believe. He manages to touch every soul. He says he was programmed since his childhood to be where he is today and to do what he is doing. It was his destiny, so to speak. His Guru also told him he would go out of the village and even out of the country to spread the teachings of the sages to the whole world. This is exactly what he is doing.

M: He won't stop. He will go around the world.

R: Yes. Because there are so many people who are waiting for him to come into their lives.

M: Master Raju is the one who wants people's experiences to be in the book. When I told him that I wanted to write about my experiences and relationship with him, he said, "You have to include other people's experiences too, those who have been close to me." I thought at that moment, "How am I going to do that? I will have to bother people; I will have to invade their privacy." And then I thought, "Maybe it is a test for me. It is the ego that I have to drop. It's not a personal business. It's about him being an inspiration to the world."

R: Yes, and you get it! He is the man with no ego. And the book would have not been complete without other people's experiences; the most important thing is that he does not belong to anybody. So these experiences belong to everybody. And that is what is wonderful about this book.

M: Yes, it's very clear to me now.

R: I am so glad you are sharing so much love and devotion for Master. I cannot find appropriate words to tell you how I feel about this sharing. I thank you from the bottom of my heart.

M: It's a mutual thanks because I am realizing that by meeting people and questioning them about their experiences; it is becoming a wonderful and very enriching experience for me personally. It is another way for me to remember and learn how to integrate his message.

R: My husband did not know Master Raju until then. Master Raju managed to make such an impact on him. Many times, when we get stuck with things, we would stay in line with Master Raju's teachings. We keep all we have learned from him in the backs of our minds and it is like an instant guide being with us each day of our lives. He is in everything we do or say to anyone. It's like gardening; we are growing new things and seeing them flourish in front of our eyes. He once told me, as I had asked him, "How can I find ultimate peace?" He said, "By service to others." So I ask God each day, "Please, it's a new day; use me for your work." So Mercy, use me for this book as much as you need. I am there to help you with anything you need. Please use me.

M: Thank you very much. I will, don't worry.

Kevin, Manager (Toronto)

M: Tell me Kevin about you and Master Raju.

K: There was a session at Sheila's place, Rose, my wife, and mother decided to go, and I gave them a ride. I was just going to spend some time and then come back. While I was there, I thought, "I should listen to what Master Raju has to talk about." It was quite impressive. He was talking about lots of things, which I have believed all my life. I found him interesting. The next day, surprisingly when they were going again, I said, "I am coming." My wife was kind of shocked and she said, "Are you sure?" I said, "Yes! Yesterday I went there for you, today I am going for myself." I enjoyed the sessions and many things that were taught relate to the way I have perceived life and have seen God. More than anything else, I was interested in Master Raju himself because he is not a saint who sits in a cave somewhere or has cut himself out of society. He continuously pays his dues. He went to school to educate himself, and after that he decided to pay back society. Coincidentally, he is in a similar line of work as me. Most coincidental is that, most of the places where I have worked, he has also worked. It became a sort of bond between us. While giving him a ride back to the airport, we talked about technical things. He knew people in the places I worked for, in India and Canada. So, for me, it was amazing and it seems like a coincidence, but we know this is no coincidence. It's all planned; it's all God's grace. Since then, we have thoroughly enjoyed being with him and have never looked back. His philosophy and the sessions we had with him changed our lives and our goals. We believe in him and we follow him. We follow the principles and the teachings given at the sessions.

M: Tell me about your relationship with him? Who is he in your life?

K: I think he is a very good teacher. I have met a lot of teachers in my life and tried to listen to them, but most of them, in spite of how good they were, were not able to make things as simple as Master Raju did. He teaches people at their level. In other words, no deep words or complicated theories, no high philosophies, but simple things that he can give you examples of in daily lives to which one can relate. Being a technical man, he can give explanations scientifically which I thoroughly enjoy because I believe in those things. Then he became a good friend.

More than anything else, I have enjoyed his company because I think I found a man without ego.

M: What kind of impact has he made in your life?

K: In life, you meet people as you go, and I now believe strongly that it's God's plan to bring these individuals into your life. Those who are going to teach you new things or affirm what you already know from the beliefs you already have. Master Raju is one of those men who have great impact, not only in my life but also in my family. I, my wife, and my mother have had several sessions with him. We have taken our children there and his simplicity with them touches me. He is open to questions or doubts I have, and he has been able to clarify them for me. Everybody always has questions and it's difficult to find the right person to answer them because you have to be comfortable with that person. I usually don't even need to ask them, they are answered automatically. It seems like he can read your question and give you answers. Also, there are lot of things he has taught which have been with us all our lives, it's just he has reconfirmed our beliefs.

M: What especially did you get from his teachings, his being that you are applying in your daily life?

K: It was the first time in my life that I was introduced to the breathing exercises. Now we think back, it makes perfect sense to work with the Supreme power that is everywhere and in touch within us through the life force or prana. That is basically the only connection between us and the Supreme. By doing these exercises, I got a lot of energy to deal with my daily activities and in a much more confident way. It has given us a lot of calmness in our lives. He has also taught us how to listen. I personally feel that in society, nobody takes time to listen to anybody. Everybody wants to talk. I have worked on myself all my life to listen. Master Raju's teachings helped us to listen, not only to hear, but to listen and see differences. So that has helped in my day to day life. I make more friends. I am calmer, and any time a situation comes up even if Master Raju is not there, I can talk with him just like I can talk to God. Anytime I think of Master Raju, he helps me make the right decisions.

M: From your experience with him, what can you tell people to inspire them?

K: I can talk for a long time about that. He has inspired us; we have talked to lot of our friends about him. They have seen changes in our life, noticeable change and talk about it. Everybody who comes to our home finds peace there. People feel relaxed when they visit, and it has a lot to do with what Master Raju had taught us. It is felt in our day to day life with our family, friends, and children. There is a lot more harmony in our home. An incident happened recently which I would like to mention. I have not talked much to my next-door neighbor who just moved here. While outside one day cutting the grass, she came over to say hello to me. I had been talking to the husband but not to the lady of the home. She came to introduce herself and said, "We have been living here for so long and have not talked except to just say hello and goodbye; your family seems very peaceful!" I said, "Is that so, how do you know?" She said, "We always hear laughter coming out from the house. We also see a lot of your friends coming in and everybody seems to be happy, you must be doing yoga or something alike." I said, "Yes we do!" She said," I am coming to your home whether you like it or not!" What I am trying to say, getting back to the point, is that people see changes in us, they feel it. Even though I did not go and talk to her in the beginning, we became good friends. We bought books from her; she is very heavily into yoga and has traveled extensively in India. When people are into it, they notice each other. Our friends are noticing us. I introduced a lot of my friends because they wanted to know why we are always in a happy mood. Everybody wants to be in that mood, and I have introduced a lot more friends to Master Raju's teachings and they are finding peace. As I said, this is his charismatic personality, he is so simple. Such an educated man and he does not show it. He seems such an ordinary person and it is great! Most of the time, anybody who is a little bit knowledgeable starts showing it off. Master Raju is a man totally without ego.

M: What did you get from him that you think everyone else can benefit from?

K: I don't go out and advertise Master Raju, but anytime I see anyone in need or I feel people can use his blessings or knowledge to help them, I go out and suggest they take time and come see him. We have brought many friends in his company. And once they are there, they see when they listen to him. What I am saying is there is no fixed agenda. Everybody is welcome to ask questions. Somehow he can satisfy every individual, and people go there with their children. Master Raju is especially great with children. He makes a quick bond with people. In the sessions, everybody feels when they come away from the sessions that they were the one who got special attention from him. So Master Raju has this charisma of being in a session of thirty people but still giving each individual that special treatment. That is a very great quality he has in himself. People can learn from him; they can learn what can help to improve the quality of life.

Dr. Paul Vyas

Mercy: Paul, tell me when you met Master Raju for the first time?

P: It was more than ten years ago. We had already taken a first retreat with another teacher, but this was an important one. It took place approximately sixty to seventy miles from here. I believe it was from Thursday night to Sunday night. Anyway, that day, one of our very good friends had a heart problem. We went all the way to the retreat, put our stuff there and then drove thirty to forty miles to see my friend, then came back to the retreat. That was the first time I saw Master Raju. When I met him, he appeared to be plain and ordinary, and we did not think much about him at that particular time. During the retreat, he started explaining to us the meaning of the new philosophy. Master Raju was the one conducting the retreat. When one starts listening to him, one realizes the depth of his knowledge, his understanding of the Vedas, and his understanding of life. Not only was he very knowledgeable, he also explained that we could use his teachings in our daily lives. He taught us how to look inwards, and how to use this knowledge in our professional lives; how to deal with colleagues and how to be with family members and more. He always appeared to be very energetic and full of life. He took us to a different level of life, from what we learned at that particular retreat. This retreat was extraordinary. That's the way I came to know him and respect him.

M: Tell me about your relationship with him? How you became close to him? What role he plays in your life?

P: When we met him at that retreat, it was our first meeting. At that period of time, he was living in Canada, so lots of people from Canada came to the retreat. After that, a third retreat had been scheduled in Chicago at Grace Lake. At that retreat, we got to know him better, and then he decided to move to Chicago. I cannot tell exactly when. Do you know when it was?

M: Yes, it was in December 1996.

P: He moved here and started working. When he settled here, he initiated a Bhagavad-Gita class. He used to come every Sunday to talk about the Gita. He also started teaching in a small place in the Lake Forest area. It was amazing to know he did not prepare anything in advance. He just started with a shloka or verse from the Gita and he would elaborate. He teaches with examples of what it means and how it applies to your daily life. He was not using any notes or prompts. He was speaking from his heart, and he explained everything very well. People were coming every month to attend the class; looking forward to hear what he would talk about next. There was a period of time he came and stayed with us for a while. You know the exact timing?

M: I think it was in September 1999.

P: The time he lived with us is filled with lots of good memories. Because he was with us, we would do pooja every day. We would talk about different religious things and different philosophies of life. He is brilliant mentally. He would also talk to my children who were growing up. You know, everybody goes through different emotions. But he was very instrumental in explaining things to everyone. He was very good with people. I might have a very hard time talking with my daughters but he has no problem. He could talk to anyone, and relate to them in a way they would understand, and accept. It was wonderful. He had been here for a while and then it was time for him to go. He decided to move to California. We were very sad.

M: I know you were in tears at the airport.

P: Yes. When we took him to the airport, we were all in tears. He said, "Hey! Don't worry. I'll be back in a year." And that's exactly what happened, he came back. So that's how I knew him, he had been my spiritual Master. He had taught me and had given me insight. According to my family, I am a very difficult person to live with and understand. He has given me insight on how to deal in day to day life; how to deal with stress; how to deal with people and family members. He has had a very calming effect in my life. He showed me also what is really important in life, and what should be one's priority in life. And he was still working with me at that level. In my life, there are lots of stress—work, relating with my children or other people—whatever it might be, he is very soothing. He will show you a better way so you can focus and do things the right way. That's the big impact he had in my life.

M: If you have to tell people about him, what would you say to inspire them, or to make people know him or benefit from him?

P: All the people that I know are in the same boat as I am. They have the same stresses in life, whether it is job related, family related or about bringing spirituality into their life. Then I would tell them, "If you need a catalyst, go to him, be with him." As soon they spend some time with him, they immediately feel the difference and think how lucky they are. They realize exactly what they need to do. He improves their potential tremendously just by being with them when they spend a little time in his presence.

M: What do you know about him, as an ordinary individual, his personal or professional life?

P: He works for a Fortune 500 company in Chicago, and he can learn things very fast. He can adapt to new things quickly. You know, when he moved to California, there were different challenges there; different departments, different people. When he went to work, he took the people of the whole department to a different level. He inspired them and made them work as a team. He is very good in putting team spirit in people. He is wonderful with people.

I have met his wife, Chandrika, she is a wonderful lady. I think they have a great influence on each other. I also met their son; he does his own thing and has a good relationship with his parents.

I know Master Raju came from a very religious family. I met his nephew Anand in Milwaukee when his son was born. We went to visit him and spent some time with them. I also spoke to Master Raju's dad and mom on the phone. I noticed that every time they called, they were just finishing pooja and they would bless us. His father's voice is so deeply affectionate and full of love. I have not met them yet. They are very religious people and they have a temple in their home where Master Raju grew up. He had learned all the Vedas and Scriptures at home at a very young age. His inclination for religious activity started very early in his life. We have talked to Master Raju about many things. He spent time with many spiritual Masters. Just name one; he was with them some time or the other.

M: Do you know anything about his implication in some kind of program at the level of work, social, or international that would have made a difference on the planet?

P: He started basically this personal development program that teaches how to live your life. He is the one who has spread this program in North America. He promotes well-being and teaches people how they can transform their lives. He is not only teaching, but he is always there for you, whether in social life or work. He does not hold on to any one philosophy. You will see him with many different organizations also like Chinmaya Mission and others. He has broad knowledge of all different religions and the role they play in promoting the well-being of the human race. This is what he does.

      There is something else about him I noticed. Anytime he comes in my home, he always brings something. He never fails. It might be some flowers, some juice, or some candies for children. It is not a question of price or anything, it is the thought. He always remembers to bring something for people, wherever he goes, and he always has a message to give you.

M: Some people see him as a prophet, what do you think?

P: It would be a way to look at him, definitely. Because he has a message to give, and that is the role of a prophet. If they think of him as a prophet, it's perfectly right.

M: According to you, could he be an avatar?

P: I think he is an avatar because of the way he conducts himself and the way he is. Now, I see him going with Swamiji. Even this time, when Swamiji came, I realized Swamiji has full trust in him and he had given him responsibility in his organization. I believe Swamiji sees lots of potential in him. I would never have met Swamiji if it were not for him.

M: Are you talking about Swamiji Ganapathi Sachidananda from Mysore?

P: Yes! Master Raju is working with him, but my guru is Master Raju. When I saw Swamiji giving him responsibilities, I realized that Swamiji knows who he is. Swamiji knows from his previous life who he was, and what kind of progress he made. And these progressions have continued into this life. Swamiji also wants to free him from his worldly obligations. I believe this and I think this is what is coming to him. He will spend more and more time working with Swamiji. When I was there with him, Swamiji gave him a special respect. He recently gave him a title also.

M: What title did Swamiji give to him?

P: Swamiji called him" Datta Yogi Raja" in front of thousands of people on December 19, 2002. When Swamiji was here in Chicago, he wanted him to be in the West Indies when the Hanuman temple is to be opened. Swamiji definitely wants him to be with him now, and I feel he might be taken away from us. He might go with Swamiji. But I am somehow reassured because Swamiji needs Master Raju in North America to spread his messages. Swamiji knows also that Raju has a lot to give on his own; you know. Swamiji's messages and Master Raju's messages are the same.

M: Definitely!

P: Swamiji also realized that Master Raju is very articulate. Swamiji wants someone who will spread his message. That's what Swamiji wants and that's what is going to happen. I believe Master Raju had been a very great soul in his previous life. Do you know that he and I have the same birthday, but he is one year younger than me? But he is far ahead of me in the game though.

M: (We both laugh). We cannot rank with him.

P: Even if he never mentioned anything about his previous lives, I assume he must have been a very advanced soul because he is very knowledgeable. You cannot learn everything in one lifetime. He must have learned lots of things. The most important thing is that he wants to spread his knowledge; he wants to help other fellow human beings. He never considers himself superior to anybody. He never thinks that he is higher than you or anyone. He always considers you equal, with or without your knowledge. He never brags about his knowledge. He only wants to help you, to hold your hand; he wants to pull you up. He is always there. He is like a dear friend for you, and he would do anything to help you. He understands when you are down or when you are up; he knows you very well. He knows everyone around him very well. He is there for you anytime when you need him. You can always count on him.

When my father in law passed away in India, I was in Colorado at the time. I was in a meeting. Immediately when he heard about it, he came here to my home. I was not here and I could not get back before the next day. When I arrived home he was here consoling Padmaja and the children. He talked with me on the phone telling me, "Don't worry, I am here," and he was indeed there supporting the family.

It's amazing to see. When he has so many different people around him, yet he never complains about anything, whether it be the kind of room he has or the kind of bed he is lying on. He never complains like me. I am complaining all the time! He never complains about the food he eats, whether he eats in restaurant or whether he gets any food at all. He always has a smile and no complaints.

M: It's like he is in a state of permanent bliss!

P: You know he takes everything as it is. I have to drive half an hour from home to go to work in the morning. He drives two hours, and he gets up smiling. I have only a half hour to drive and I am complaining. This is a quality in him, the understanding of life, and that's the only way one can be so satisfied. People can barely do this. Is he an avatar? Yes! I think he is and he is going to do lots of good work. I am glad that I am with him and a part of his mission. Hopefully I will be able to rise above this and reach him to some extent. You know, this is what I want.

M: I heard that you are supporting him in building a temple here in Chicago. How did this idea come up? How did it start?

189

P: Here in Lake County, in a place called Mandeland, we have had a land to build a temple for some time now. We have been working to build that temple but nothing worked out. We have had to sell that land and get a new place. We finally have this in progress now. But two years ago, Swamiji came all the way here and did his" bumi pooja" on the land and he said, "There will be some obstacles in building here but the building will go up anyway." He blessed the land and told Raju, "Now you get involved in this project." He also told other people, Raman and Lakshman to get involved. Swamiji knew that it would not happen unless an extra amount of energy was extended to the project. Now we think Master Raju is totally behind this project. He is very good in getting other people involved. Something is happening and I believe within a year and a half we should have a temple built.

M: My questions are over unless you want to add something.

P: Thank you, it was wonderful!

Mrs. Padmaja V, Chemist (Chicago)

M: When did you get to know Master Raju?

P: I do not remember exactly when, but it was through the personal development program.

M: Tell me about your relationship with him.

P: Over a period of time, it became a very close relationship. Master Raju started having classes in Lake Forest every Sunday morning for two hours on the Bhagavad-Gita. That was for the I.C.A.

M: What does I.C.A stand for?

P: It's for Indian Cultural Association. It was about eight years ago, and he used to come here regularly once a week. That's how he became more or less part of our family.

M: What kind of impact did he make in your life?

P: He introduced me to different spiritual things like Divine Mother worship, the repetition of Divine Mother names. He taught us not only the rituals but also their meaning. Through him, I met Swami Ganapati Satchidananda of Mysore in India. Through him I also get to know Amma from the Jeevana Dharma Yoga organization in Bangalore. So he had been instrumental in bringing those spiritual Masters to me.

M: What did you get from his teachings or his being that you are applying in your daily activities?

P: I learned meditation and working on chakras. He is the person who listens to your problems. At the right moment, he would give you the right advice. He also brings positive energy and right attitudes to my life.

M: What would you tell to people to inspire them?

P: I would say that he brings such a positive vibration, such a positive energy with his teachings, and with his presence. Just by being around him will change your way of thinking in many aspects. He sometimes talks about food; even that brings changes in your habits. It's not only religious levels, but he covers much more in different aspects of your life.

M: Some kind of holistic approach!

P: Yes, something like that.

M: What else did you get from him you think other people could benefit from?

P: I have really appreciated his way of being in the present moment and his loving attitude towards everybody; this is what creates the positive vibrations.

M: Do you know his implications in some kind of programs at work or at the social or international level?

P: Yesterday he was talking about introducing all these quality programs in the company at work. He thinks it would make a big difference in the kind of product the company is bringing to the market. He also introduced the personal development program courses in Canada,

Chicago, and California. He is travelling to other countries too and he is spreading his teachings on how to live life in a better way.

M: Do you want to add something that can express our gratitude towards him and make the world know more about him?

P: I would say that he has made a big difference in my life. Whenever I was in need, he was there to advise or to give positive energy, to help my children and my husband turn towards spirituality to some extent. I see him as a father figure in my life. He guides without you even asking. He just shows up at a time of crisis; he is always there at the right moment.

M: Thank you very much.

Nitya Vyas, Student (Chicago)

M: Nitya tell me, when did you come to know Master Raju?

N: I can't remember the exact date, but I think it was far back in 1998 or 1999, and it was through my parents. He was giving a workshop. That day, I heard a lot about him from everybody in the group. I was not there, but I met him when I went to the retreat in1999.

M: Tell me about your relationship with him.

N: I think our relationship evolved as all relationships do, and it changes from one way to another. In the beginning, when I met him through my parents, it was no more than knowing the presence of anyone else. At that time I was in my early twenties, about twenty-two or twenty-three years old and was struggling with my own self.

M: How old are you now?

N: I am twenty-eight. After that retreat, I slowly opened up. What was neat though, I was able to take what I wanted to take out of that relationship. Even though I was not buying into his whole philosophy and religious concepts he expected that of me, and it surprised me. He was able to see where I was in my own path, and in my conversation with him, he gave me the guidance I needed. Do you understand what I mean? Does it make sense?

M: Yes, yes, it does make sense.

N: I did not want the religious part.

M: What kind of impact has he made in your life?

N: He made a tremendous impact on me. If you remember earlier we were talking about Masters who come in our lives and if we are not receptive at that time, we miss the boat. Everyone is a teacher in some shape or form, right? He is an obvious teacher.

M: Mm, hmm.

N: At that time, when I was not even receptive and not looking for anything, I had been able to get an insight and I realized the benefits. I accepted him. I remember in 1999 I was going through a hard time. We sat upstairs in that room where your were seated for dad's interview, and I have notes from that time where we talked about "God created world, man created world," and I wrote down these insights which I came across the other day. I became aware of the way it seeped slowly into my own consciousness, and helped me blossom into my own path. That's why I think I have got most of the basis of the foundation of what he teaches—not necessarily all the rituals. It did not have to be a structured method of learning, but it is there for me to use at the right time. I learned something, you know . . . a story here, a story there, from the Vedas also, but that comes to me sporadically.

M: Can you tell me what did you get specifically from his being or his teaching that you are applying to your daily life, something that makes you line life from a different perspective?

N: I think he opened me up to a different way of thinking, towards more peace, to a grounded peacefulness. I have come slowly to trust and love him. When I first met him, I had no trust in life or in my inner voice, and now, not only has he provided the seeds, but he allowed them to flourish without his control. In any other environment, it would not have flourished. I don't like the structure of most things and of most people. Anyhow, this happened four years ago. If you had asked me that question prior to that time, I would not have been able to say because my outlook was different. But now I can say he gave me faith and grounded me.

M: What would you tell people about him to inspire them?

N: I think that my piece of advice to anybody who might come across him or anybody else, who has something to offer, is to be receptive. By being receptive, one will appreciate the benefits reaped.

M: What else do you think everyone else could benefit from?

N: As long as you go to him with an open mind, you will benefit from him. He has love, patience, and understanding for all, and upon one's acceptance, the path of life becomes more enriching as one evolves. We have the ability to benefit from his inspiration, and we should use this as the key to success in life.

M: Do you remember any anecdote about him?

N: Last night, I woke up at 3:00a.m., and I felt I was not in a good place. It was raining. I went outside at 3:30 a.m. I saw the light in his bedroom turned on. I was hoping I had not disturbed him. Seeing the light turned on at the same time that I was going through something made me feel attuned, and that there was light in my life just when I need it. I did not need to talk to him. I did not need anything, simply that light. That has occurred on more than one occasion in my life. In this case, all I needed was to see the light. It was raining, it was dark. I was in the driveway; I was not in a good place. The light turned on. And I knew he was there, and that was enough. Just that light reminded me who he represents. The metaphor is perfect. Another thing that happened in my life is whenever I needed someone, consciously or subconsciously, even in my silent moments, he is there, and he makes an impact right away. Yesterday I knew immediately, I have come a long way to notice the difference. I can now go back four years and see what I wrote down at that time, and I can say I needed to hear what he said then, although at that time it did not mean much to me.

M: Some people see him as a prophet, what do you think?

N: I don't know. Do I think he sees and feels and knows more than most of us? Yes! Could he possibly tell what is going to happen in five to twenty years? Yes, probably. Do I think he will tell? No, there is no need for him to tell us. He may be a prophet. He may know. But he would rather let it evolve and let it happen and be there to guide everyone. Even if you won't call him a "prophet," it doesn't matter. He won't play the role like most prophets.

M: Could he be an avatar?

N: What is an avatar?

M: It is what we call God taking a human form and being with us just to teach us or guide us or bring a specific message. Some come more grandiosely, some come in a simple form or anonymously. This is my definition.

N: Could it be? Yes! Could we all be? Yes. That's why I am saying we all have the potential.

M: At a very early age, they came with these tools like Bhagavan Sai, Sri Swamiji.

N: Yes, he went through difficulties in life. I would not expect perfection in an avatar, look at Jesus Christ. Each soul has its purpose and will fulfill it. I never even had the notion of an avatar. We all have to clear the clutter. The potential is there for all. It may come easily to some and not so easy for others.

M: Feel free and comfortable to add anything else you want to say about him.

N: From my experience, I would say that the greatest thing he has brought and the message given in the philosophy of life is acceptance. I have learned that from him even though it is difficult. He judges no one, neither does he preach. He just accepts each and everyone on their path, wherever they may be, and guides them through.

Donna, Computer Specialist (Montreal)

When I came to Canada on October 1996, everybody in my family knew Master Raju, from my aunts, uncles, cousins to my grandfather. I knew that he was already part of our family. I had seen him while he was giving a course at my cousin's home. She invited me to her place to help me with my résumé. I saw Master Raju there. At that time it was funny, because everybody was bowing down to Master Raju and was talking to him. I bowed down to him. You know this entire guru thing was quite interesting. I wanted some kind of communication with him. I told him that I wanted to do his course. It was the last course of this format he taught in Montreal. He just smiles, he speaks in telegraphic style, with the least possible detail, one sentence here one sentence there and that was it.

Later on, I went to a job fair at the Queen Elizabeth Hotel in downtown Montreal, and I saw him there. He looked so formal in his suit! "Oh my God! He looked so handsome there. I thought "Hey! This man! He is here!" He looked at me and we just exchanged smiles. I thought that he was there as an executive looking for employees for his company. Later on, he told me that he had blessed me to find a job. The job fair happened.

Soon after that, Master Raju moved to Chicago. I attended the September workshop. I had lots of questions in the class, and I think maybe it was not a good idea that I attended that level of class. I had so many questions to ask and I was pulling the group behind. Those who had done many sessions with Master Raju wanted to go on to meditation or to a higher stage, and I was asking all these questions. That was the real communication I had with Master Raju. There came this question about commitment. He said, "What are you ready to commit in your life?" Make that statement. "I am committed to be a good person; I am committed to getting up at 6:00 o'clock in the morning." This question was so hard for me to understand. I was thinking, "How can somebody make such a commitment?" To me it's like if you make a commitment, you cannot fail. So I could not understand how I could make such a commitment knowing that I would fail. And it's simple; you fail. You stand up again and start all over. Master Raju gave me one nice scolding in front of the forty people saying, "Your flight will never take off." I was so mad. I was so upset. I spoke to my friend, to my cousin, and my grandfather about it. They gave me good advice explaining what he meant and how he was. They saw my perspective, they motivated me and I attended the next day. It was amazing to see how people adore him and really want to be with him.

Master Raju made such an impact in my life that I can't imagine my life without him anymore. The same way one can't imagine life without the sun. We can imagine living without our parents. If one doesn't know God, we can imagine life without God. For me, today I cannot imagine living without a connection with Master Raju, who is God to me.

Master Raju gave meaning to my life. He taught me how to appreciate life. When Master Raju came into my life, I was in a deep depression, but I did not know I was depressed. I could not get up to go to work; I could not get out of my bed. Maybe it's because I was working sixteen hours a day. I don't know. I am trying to explain how I felt at that time. That Donna died sometime in 1998 or 1999, and a new one has been reborn. The person who seems to be Donna is the one Master Raju had brought out. I did not go to a physical death, but I got a new body with a different energy. I got a new perspective, a new meaning in life.

If Master Raju had never come to my life, I would have died a premature death. I would really have physically died. He saved my life. He is like a mother to me. He had done so many things for me, and he does with so much love and compassion. It is like you are doing him a favor by giving him the opportunity to help you. He is taking care of you, it's like he is benefiting from it. In the meantime, retreats continued here in Montreal and slowly my connection with him became deeper.

In February 1999, Master Raju taught us the ten fingers meditation. When I came home, I tried this new form of meditation. I felt a lot energy flowing through me. I felt like writing a poem and singing it, but it was a transient state. For one hour I would feel good, and for the rest of the day I would feel very tired and unhappy. And the worst part of it was that everybody around me told me that I had low energy and that I looked morose. I felt that people did not want to be around me because my energy was too low and I looked too sad. I was not complaining, but they could feel it.

Then in 1999 I got access to Master Raju while he was living in Chicago. I remember the first time I called him and the first question I asked him was: Does God exist? Who is God? How do we connect to God? Is all this philosophy? He was having dinner at that moment. He took his plate with him and went to the living room; from there he talked to me. He did not bother about the people who were there around him and were having the meal with him. I was a person whom he didn't really know, and at that time we had not bonded. For him, it was just this little girl who had all these questions, and how can I help her? He spent more than one hour explaining those things to me. He came from a PhD level to a kindergarten level and explained it in a way that I could understand. While he was giving all these explanations, he was doing more than that. He was also transferring energy to me; he was charging my energy from inside. He was doing two things at the same time. I felt good after speaking to him. I found him very nice. The talk continued once in about every five days. I really don't remember. This was the period between February and July 1999. He had a great impact on me already.

In June, I took my vacation because I was still not feeling too well. I called him and said, "I want to do this, I want to do that." He said, "Good, do it." So I said lots of prayers and shared some experiences with him, not much. In July, he was going to Sheila and Simon's house in Toronto for a weekend course. As usual, I went with Mercy to the retreat, and I think this was the most important experience I had with him. I was sitting there asking Master Raju about Brahmacharya, which can be defined as many things. One is being celibate, or taking the vow of celibacy to God. Master Raju said, "I am not concerned with what you do but with what you are, whether you marry or not, that's immaterial. How you are and who you are, is more important." But at the same time, he said that I have the potential of being unmarried and he blessed me for that. The next day he was doing a Sri Chakra pooja. I was humming some bhajan and when he saw how innocent I was he said, "Hey, you come to my room." I went there, and to me he looked like a saint from India. I felt that I was in front of the saint. I told him that and he smiled with no comment. He gave me his picture. I then showed him the pictures of my family and I asked him to bless them. At the end of the day, when it was time to leave, I had the ultimate experience. We went to say goodbye to Master Raju and I was feeling like a five-year-old. I raised my hand to wave goodbye to him; he was talking with somebody at that moment. Master Raju also saw me as a kid and said, "Hey come here, give me a hug before you leave." I went to give him a hug and felt this strong ball of energy bulging into my heart and my heart caught it. I felt like a ball implanting itself in my heart, and I could feel the weight of it like when you catch a ball thrown to you. I was very puzzled and did not know what was happening. I went home and I was very happy. But I was thinking, what is this? The very next morning, Master Raju called me from Mexico. I was flattered and thought, "This man has left Toronto and I am connecting so much with him; someone that I call my Guru, calls me all the way from Mexico!" I told him what I felt; the ball experience, the ball of energy. He said, "Yes! That's why I wanted to call you, to make sure you are okay, it's Shaktipat." It works in a mystical way.

From that day on, I had a permanent bound with him. He is my mentor, my guide, my guru, my parent, my child, he is everything. Sometimes he acts like a child. You have to take care of him, you know. He is so innocent, so happy. When I look back now, that was the most important day. The day not only changed my relationship with him but also changed my life at the energy level; transformations in communication and much more. And he did not stop, my behaviors, the kind of person I was, all changed. My life was not the same after that.

Behavior change is very hard to notice. Some people have a lot of willpower and can change something in one day. But knowing myself, it takes me a long path to operate changes. Every little change takes lot of time, and it's very easy to fall back into my old patterns. Even today, after so many years, some people may see no difference in me; others may see lot of differences. But I know where I am coming from. I know who I was, who I am and who I will be. Each person learns differently. For some, a little bit of teaching is enough. For me, it does not work. I need to see and to observe. Most of the learning I have learned from Master Raju is by observing, by relating to him. And he has taught so much. I don't know how much purification I have achieved up to now as it's so long to cleanse oneself. When I was angry with somebody, I used to have so many problems. I would think that I will be angry for the rest of my life. He is working with me on that. Now, Mercy, slowly, slowly I am learning. I can see also bigger transformations around me. Like I told you, people at work treat me much better than before. If there is a misalignment around me, if somebody is rude, or if something they did made me feel bad, Master Raju taught me the importance of positive thought. But I learn from action each time. Let's say, from July 1999 I had spent a lot of time with him. I think I am the only person who had more time with him in terms of quality and quantity. I haven't seen him angry, even once. I haven't heard him raise his voice even once. He always comes from, "How can I help you, how I can serve you? How can I improve this situation? Can I make your life more beautiful, more cheerful? I have love, have my love."

You know there are energies, light, and darkness. You also have hatred and love, they are both energies. Energy is not good or bad. Darkness is a slow and dense energy and light is fast and weightless. There is higher and lower energy. For example: if you don't want me in your life, then I don't want you in my life. Master Raju had been teaching me so much. He lives by the principle of bringing love and he believes that love is the only solution for any problem in life.

All this is very good in theory. What makes Master Raju different to me is that he is constantly practicing love. Although I am a difficult person, he has given me so much time and energy. You know Mercy, there was a time I used to call him so much. He had to communicate with me every day. I was like a child having tantrums, having all these demands. Master Raju is not my blood, he is not related to me, he is not obligated to me by any social relationship, and he had pressure on himself for giving me that much attention. People would say, "Why are you spending so much time on the phone with her? Why are you giving so much time to Donna?" All he knew was, "Here is somebody who has her needs to be met; I am going to help her." So many times I laughed with him. We have a joke and I told him, "I am your toughest challenge. If you can improve me," which I think he has done, "then any other student will be very easy to handle." It is like a joke, but it's true and I had been bad, bad in a sense of being selfish. I had been inconsiderate in that he needs time to eat, he needs time to sleep, and he needs time to be with others.

I can tell you something, there is nothing like such a relationship. You cannot be in a relationship with a person who is constantly in demand, right? The beautiful thing about him is he could see that I had the sincere desire to improve myself and the genuine desire to understand spirituality. He came to my home once and I wanted to do a guru pooja to him. I even did not know that such a thing as a guru pooja existed. I suddenly asked him, "Why in our tradition do we offer kumkuma (the red powder) only to God? I feel a need to offer it to you, can I do it?" He laughed and said, "Of course you can do it. You see the problem in this world is they don't know about worshiping a living thing. When you are dead you become great, when you are alive you are nothing. It is a big ego problem for human beings to have to bow to another human being. I am not a human being. I am the principle of the Lord. I am just energy. If you think that you are bowing down to Raju Ramanathan that is wrong. And if I think you are bowing to Raju Ramanathan, I am also wrong. It is the main principle in devotion, it is surrender. Surrender what? Surrender the ego. You have the desire to do it, do it! I had nothing at home for the proper offering to the Master. I had only Kumkuma.

I did what I could, and offered it to him. I am doing guru pooja but he is the one reciting the mantras. He is the one saying the right prayers because

I don't know them. He is the one telling me what to do. He accompanied me with his heart. The idea for him was. "Whatever this girl wants, let her do it." And whatever people may think and say, I was like a three-year-old kid with him. For me, I was applying kumkuma and was massaging his feet. Doing that made me feel mentally and physically like a three-year-old. It was only then I could get myself to that level that I could relate to him. Maybe I did not know how to relate with him in any other way. I was the first person who did the Master's offering to him. In October 1999, I went to visit him in Chicago for the first time. It was his birthday. I was always asking him to come to see me. He would always say, "No, you have to come to see me first." Here also a funny thing happened. I wanted to go to visit him in September and for some reason, things did not work out and in my typical behavior, I just sent an email saying, "Hey, I didn't make it." I did not call him. I didn't say anything and they were worried. They called me the next day to find out. I said, "I thought you would have read my email, I could not make it." Then he sends me a strong email saying, that for important things, I should also phone because they were concerned about me. I have to tell you I was totally inconsiderate of the other person. That's how I was or how I am. But little by little, with love, understanding, and full acceptance—because it's the only way I can learn—with so much patience, and giving me as much "food" that I can swallow, he taught me. His commitment is not for months or years. No, it's a lifetime of commitment, even when my training will be over.

When I was in Chicago in 1999, I noticed how Master Raju was appreciated by everybody. Before I went there, he said, "Come, but you have to let me study for my examination for The American Society of Quality." I went there but never allowed him to study because I was always questioning or disturbing him by just being around him. If I was at his place I would think, "Why is this person is taking all my time, can't she understand and give me some break?" But he was 100% with me, Mercy. And he never admonished me by saying "You did not let me have any time for myself." I have never heard one negative sentence from him. It has always been this way with me. By seeing him so patient and compassionate with me, I thought, I have to emulate him; I want to be like him.

By being in my life, Master Raju has made me a whole or complete person. I mean, he made me know myself, accept myself, to feel okay about myself. Because in society, what do you have? You have people complaining about you, criticizing and putting you down, especially if you are a weak person. I was alone here in Canada. I did have some amount of confidence, but still, there were too many things for me to cope with. Master Raju took care of me so lovingly and his support made me more aware. I was not like that. Now, every time I am aware of what I am saying, what I am doing, what I am thinking. I am becoming more considerate of others. In every little way he taught me to be human, forget being divine. What are human beings like? He taught me everything by setting the example himself. People can break. I cannot imagine that he is a human being and be fooled. He was not perfect; he was a whole human being. His teachings were perfect, even if he had some deficiencies in being human. But his being is whole. The outer personality may not be whole. How come he spent so much time with me on the phone? How come he can't find his papers and remember where he puts them. How come his nose is like that? Oh! The body is not perfect, that's a human's limitations. But the being inside him is complete. So he taught me all that at my level of understanding.

To inspire people who would get in contact with Master Raju I would say, "If you want changes in your life, if you want to know divinity, he will take you there. You might be fooled because he is very humble, very plain, he will do anything to hide his divinity. But he is like a magnet. If you hang around him and be with him, you will discover by yourself. He will let you grow at your pace, and without you noticing it, he will make you grow. Where are you going to find such a Guru? I don't' know any guru who can manage a forty-hour schedule , travel all over the world, be everywhere, and give so much of his presence and love to everybody. There is no other guru doing what he is doing, living totally like us yet doing much more than us. So if you want to practice spirituality in your day to day life, Master Raju is the perfect example.

As an ordinary individual, he is very sensitive and alert, noticing every little action you do. He may not say anything, but he has noticed it. I went to visit his parents in India. They are very proud of him and feel very well-treated by him. For his mother, he is perfect. Even in India, he has travelled a lot and had been involved in many organizations: the Brahma Kumaris, Gurumayi of the Siddha Yoga, Self- Realization of Paramahansa Yogananda, Nirmala Devi,et al. His father is a much evolved soul also. I noticed that every time he communicates with him, it is always such a happy communication. It is not what the matter is or is not, it's about the fact that they enjoy what they are talking about. Even his father has much respect for Master Raju and his role in this world. His parents have seen how so many other Masters also like him namely: Sri Ravi Shankar, Arkaji, Swamiji Ganapati Satchidananda of Mysore, and Amma of Jeevan Yoga from Bangalore.

At the physical level, Master Raju has a very tiny stomach. He eats very little but still likes a variety of food. His favorite food is" idli," but he also enjoys North Indian cuisine and he deeply appreciates any little expression of love that someone would manifest towards him. At work, he is very much appreciated by his colleagues and people feel more confident when he is around.

Right now in China, the Communism political system and religion is not much practiced and there is a real thirst in the people for spirituality. He wanted to give them something without affecting the political structure. So, when he went to China recently, he spoke with a well known Zen Master. When he found the finger bone relics of the Buddha in some corner of the museum in Xi'an, China, he told the authorities—in their language—how it would affect tourism positively in their country. He made them build a fantastic Buddha temple to develop tourism. It is still a museum, but now people have a place to go. Buddha's finger bones have become a place of worship. It is no longer lying there in some corner. In fact, he even taught yoga and meditation classes there. I think in a country where there is no temple, and to have them built one in such a short period of time—because he was there for only three weeks—he has the capacity to put enough energy into something, so that it will happen. That shows how efficient he can be.

He has helped many organizations: Yogi Amrit Desai of Kripalu Yoga Organization, Sri Ravi Shankar of the Art of Living Organization during his initial stages, and Rishi Prabhakar of Siddha Samadhi Yoga. He is now supporting Swami Ganapati of Mysore and Amma from Bangalore. He is genuinely interested in the world. I was surprised to see, when the Columbia accident happened in February 2003, how it affected him so badly. Events of the world affect him in a different way. When the discussions on the war started, he went in silence and meditation and sends healing energy to the victims. He is very deeply involved much more that it appears to us. Master Raju is always ready to help any spiritual activity. Right now, at work, his boss is involved in educating people about vegetarianism. Master Raju is implicated to encourage whatever he can contribute to create a better world.

Sheila, Marketing Specialist (Toronto)

I met Master Raju by God's blessings at the Sivananda Ashram in Val-Morin near Montreal. I went there for a weekend and met a friend who introduced me to Master Raju. That was the first time I met him, and I had a very brief conversation with him. The next time was when I took the personal development program course. My profound experience with him was when I went for a silent retreat. I remember Master Raju was in silence, and we were all in silence. I was going through a very difficult time. It was my birthday in December 2 and I was going through tough times in life and I had to make serious decisions.

It was 1992. One night Master Raju spoke, after which everybody left. Since it was a silent retreat, we left in silence and Master Raju kept sitting in his chair in Samadhi kind of state. I quickly got up and sat again. I felt his energy, his light flowing from him to me. Then tears started to flow from my eyes like (she is crying) it is doing now. And I did not see him. Suddenly he said, "I will be with you." He added, "I am with you." I felt a lot of love, a lot of light, and peace at that moment. Then he silently got up and walked away. I also got up and left. I do not know how, but I felt my soul was connected to him and I got his blessings. Since then, I never have difficulty to get into meditation. I never ask Master Raju questions; if I have a question in my mind, Master Raju always answers it before I ask. I always feel his presence, his guidance, and love whenever I need it. That was my experience with Master Raju.

He is all in one for me. He is a Master, a friend like Lord Krishna was. Sometimes, he is a child who needs to be protected. But he is my Master and I truly have had many experiences with him, and they are wonderful. One of them happened when I was in meditation, and I started writing a prayer but the words were not my words. It was not from me, it was him, through the pen. It cannot be said in words. That's the kind of experience I have with him very often.

His impact in my life is very huge. The result is who I am today. My spiritual being is the result of all that grace. His teachings, his words, his Pooja, have made a lot of difference for me.

I got a lot from Master Raju. Finding who I am and what I want is the biggest impact for me. His class on "vision without boundaries" had the greatest impact on me. In his presence, I was able to go within myself and to forgive myself. I learned to meditate with Master Raju, and how to prolong the experience of meditation in my day to day life. He gave a silent retreat in nature and said, "Be with them, be with the trees, be with the river, and be with the flowers, be the poet!" It was all about enjoying nature. All came in his presence. I have learned to experience nature every day. When I am going to work, I am with the nature all around. Oh! There are so many things in day to day life.

Sometimes I feel I am an extension of him. Well, my life has been totally transformed by him. Everyday his teachings are practiced in my life. Every day you go through that experience of life where you take responsibility for everything that you do. Master Raju has been there through my sickness.

Recently, I was talking to a friend of mine and that came out. She follows her Guru. She said, "I always feel very safe in my Guru's presence, and I rely on him to find answers, he will tell me." After listening to her, I thought "Master Raju is very different." He taught us to rely on ourselves. He taught us to make direct connection to God and get direct answers. Every time we want to reach God after Master Raju had left, his blessings are still there. He has taught us to connect directly to God. And that is the difference. That's why I tell people that Master Raju never makes you dependent on him. He gives us enough, so that we can handle our lives ourselves. That's how I find Master Raju changes your life and it benefits you so that you are self-reliant on your direct connection to God.

I would like to add that he said, "First, just find your own self and your own soul to find out who you are. Make your direct connection with God through Pooja and meditation. God within and love within yourself." And he gave us one of the most powerful tools in "vision without boundaries," which makes you realize that you can achieve anything that you want in this world. There is no limit.

I do not worry about who he is. He is my Master, and his presence is wonderful. I never have the need to know more. To me, he is totally a Master and there is no need to know more.

There are hundreds of people like me whose lives have been touched and changed by what he had given. He has done so many great things for me and my family. My children's lives have also been so touched by him.

I want to add, from my experience with him when he said to me, "I am with you!" He is there. I remember I was studying downstairs and I needed some answers. Suddenly I said to my husband, "Look Simon! Master is saying this!" There are so many times when I have a question to ask and it comes through very loud and clearly to me. See! I surrender to Master and he definitely guides. It is not that you don't see him for six months and you are not guided. His guidance is always there with me. As he said he is always with us.

Vicky, Pilot (Toronto)

Mercy: Tell me how did you get to know Raju?

V: I met Raju in 1986 when I was working for Paramax, a Division of Sperry Aerospace. They were building Ships Control System for the Canadian Navy. Raju was working under the director of the Quality Control Service. I was the secretary of the director. I worked with Raju and we became friends. He and I had many discussions, especially about spirituality and the Godhead. He is very structured, and he also helped me to meditate very deeply.

One day I wanted to test him. I wanted to know how psychic Raju was. I did something very naughty to test him. I went in the ladies room. What women do in the ladies room? (Laughs) Then I mentally called Raju while I was doing it. I just concentrated on him. I was not sure about the reaction I would receive from him. When I came out fifteen minutes later, he gave me a dirty look. So he is very psychic. I knew from that moment forward you don't mess up with Raju! You don't play around; you do not abuse his sensitivity. I thought before, if he did not know, there would be no reaction. If he knew he would give me a dirty look. I had a nothing to lose and a lot to prove either way. (Laughs). But I had no way to know before that time, now I have a proven test.

M: Now you know how far you can go in your tricks!

V: You can't just send someone a message with no way to check or control, what you want to look for; it has to be a very vivid physical picture. And he caught it like that! Okay! Now I know Raju knows, Raju really knows. From that point forward, I realized I could reach Raju anytime I wanted to.

M: Anytime! Anywhere, as far it can be.

V: Yes. For instance, after I left Paramax in 1988, I went to Victoria, in British Columbia for a few years. There I pursued my flight instructor training. First I achieved my commercial pilot's license, followed by my instructor's rating license on July 6, 1992. At that time Raju, was in Europe on business and was flying from one place to another. While there, he sent me a postcard of an airplane. That card arrived the very day I had achieved my rating and had my license signed. He was congratulating me upon my success and he had written and mailed it several days previously. In other words he knew way ahead of time what the outcome of my examination would be. Only the very, very best of friends can have this closeness. Raju is obviously a very astute sensitive man and we have a connection of souls that is very harmonious and deeply aligned. Once Raju enters your life, he is able to bring about changes quietly and effectively without one ever being aware of anything happening.

M: Can you tell me more about the kind of person he is? The man, the engineer, the colleague?

V: He is fragile; he is what you call an ascetic. He does not eat a lot, he does not have strong muscles, and he is tall but slim. He is almost like a dancer, with a very large head and very big eyes, and full lips. Thus, his communication to the world appears large. Both features are large but the rest of his body is very slim, like a yogi. You know, in his life he discharges his body. He understands the world from another level. He doesn't use his body to transport his message. This is how unimportant his body is to him. He always keeps it very healthy; he feeds it enough to be able to transport him from point A to point B. I could not live eating only what Raju eats. His energy is entirely spiritual, so his body is almost an artifact. This is obvious, and a one mark of a great spiritual person. His energy is very balanced.

As an engineer, I understood that Raju was a prophetic child. He told me about his childhood. He was raised by his grandparents. He was the best student and was always loved by his teachers and was a very favorite student of his class. And you can see why! He is one of those people you cannot possibly hate.

M: You can't not love him.

V: Most people have something in them, which can be irritating to some people. But Raju is not like that at all. Working as an engineer, he was extremely effective. Some people, I have known and my husband too is like that, they are very brilliant. It seems they do not have to work as hard to achieve the same amount of productivity that others have to do. Raju achieved a great performance because he could assimilate information very quickly, and he could use that information to produce or make a tangible product. In the office—you have to understand it's a huge office full of engineers—you have also to understand how different engineers are sometimes; my husband is an engineer. They often have a bizarre personality. They are very self-contained, quiet, and within themselves. They are also pretty dominant and protective of their work or their creations or intellectual property. There were several fractions who just disagreed all the time. They just could not get along. There were crisis coming to my boss Francis all the time because they could not get along. They have different elements that pertain to electrical or some computer base, and so they just could not meet. Sometimes differences resulted in arguments. And when two people are arguing you can hear them. But when Raju was in the office, and was not on a business trip, there was always total peace and people did not misbehave. Raju's energy calms everybody and makes people more willing to discuss their differences rationally. When Raju left it was like "daddy" had gone and everybody misbehaved. That was another extent of his power, his personal aura. He believes that meditation overcomes anger. There are certain cities where there are fewer crimes because people meditate, like in Shambala group, the Buddhists and the Taoists. They meditate in large groups of over hundred in blocks of cities. If you can imagine that many people rising above quarrels, it is quite an achievement, and Raju could keep peace within our office. He could calm people. He could make them more productive and help them to focus on what was more important, what had to be achieved. That was the engineer Raju.

M: Okay, that was very interesting to see how he can influence people to bring out their best in different contexts. What else do you know about his life?

V: I knew that he was married to Robin. Robin was the exact opposite of Raju.

M: Robin?

V: Yes, his wife in India, Arvind's mother. His son is Arvin right?

M: Robin? It's not Chandrika? Her name?

V: Raju always referred to her as Robin. She called herself Robin too when she was in Canada. I met her twice.

M: Okay, I understand. Some people prefer to carry a more common name, rather an exotic one.

V: I think it was an arranged marriage. He is a Libra and she is Aries. They are diametrically opposite. Robin was always sick. I think she suffered from chronic fatigue syndrome.

M: Oh! That's sad.

V: Robin and Raju were the vehicle for Arvind to come into the world. But Arvind does not relate to them. He is not going to be a spiritual master as his father. And I will not be surprised if he becomes a millionaire. He has that in him. I know about Arvind's past life when he was in California. He is an industrialist; he is from an industrial age. Raju is from a long time ago. Raju was always very gentle towards his wife. But I think the marriage was stormy because of Robin who could not be pleased. She was very unhappy in Canada. Raju was very good and he sent her to India. I think she is happy there and lives a good life in India.

M: So she has lived in India for a while.

V: I don't think there is any romance in Raju's life. He cannot be a yogi. He cannot be! What do you call Raju these days? What is his title now?

M: You mean Spiritual Master?

V: Yes.

M: He is a Guru.

V: No, there is another word. Anyway it's what they call him. He is not a yogi, a guru.

M: Yes, he is a "Guruji." Ji is a suffix we add for respect. He is a Guru, a Spiritual Master.

V: He cannot be a Guru, a Spiritual Master, and be married; you are looking at a spiritual society. You see too much emphasis placed on the physical Raju.

In his marriage he was a good husband, kind and, he was honest with Robin, and he still is. He is a good father. Although he knew he could not raise his son. He always found people who would love Arvind and could give him strong leadership, good direction, and good influence. And look how he turned out! It was how he got Arvind to start exercising and help to grow as he is growing. He has got a kind and loving father. Raju is good at that, he lets Arvind be Arvind and does not expect him to become a little Raju.

M: I think he is like that with everybody. He does not enforce things on you. He only brings things to you, to help you expand, but he is not enforcing.

V: If you can see into anybody's soul, then you can see where the path leads to the path of least resistance. You will seem like a miracle worker if you can nudge them. But none of us can see inside the soul of another person. But Raju sees inside the souls of people. He just nudges them along the path and that makes him seem like a miracle worker. It is a miracle when you think of all the obstacles that we set up for ourselves and then we try to overcome these barriers. If somebody leads us to the gate and opens the gate to our potential, doesn't he seem like God on Earth? He does, and this is what Raju is, he is patient and he has vision.

M: I think so too. You have touched the next question a little bit. Tell me more about your relationship with Raju?

V: The relationship I have with Raju is not like anyone else. I have watched Raju grow in his influence with people from a man that I respected and admired to a man who people now kneel before. I mean they literally get down on their knees and perform obedience. It's amazing; they bring him gifts, flowers and stuff. This is not the Raju I know. What I have with Raju is interesting. I have been in one or two of his spiritual meetings. There was one in Montreal, at a lovely home. I sat way across from him and did not enter the group. Because Raju tends to attract many people who are sick and with great needs. A room full of people like that is hard for me to join in. Raju's work is not my work. I cannot open myself to these people the way he does. What lives within me assimilates with the illnesses of others. But Raju can adjust and give unconditionally to people, without discrimination. Anyway, from what I saw in the session and the Raju that I know, there is a huge difference.

There is nothing that I need from Raju. What he gives me I accept gladly, but what he needs from me he will always have in great measure.

M: Did Raju's teachings have some impact in your life?

V: Oh! Yes! I paid close attention to Raju from the very beginning. I was receptive to what he was teaching. I had been trying to learn all that stuff on my own. And I was beginning to teach myself how to meditate to cope with my life. But everything that Raju was teaching, I was very sensitive to. I wanted whatever way Raju could change my life. I accept it and in whatever way it is offered. He encourages me. He was just starting to get into this and felt that he was at the end of the cycle of being an engineer. It was the beginning of the cycle of becoming a Spiritual Master and it was a difficult transition for him. It can be a painful transition too, and I was always there to encourage Raju to enter this path at his own pace. I could see well ahead that it was something he needed to do and that the engineering part would allow him to travel and meet people and spread his light. It is interesting that Raju knows how to use his presence to fill the truth of his words and that they can only have an impact on your life. I felt if he has this effect on me, he must have this effect on everybody. So I felt this is something great that can only grow. So I encouraged him. He helped me to become more sensitive. But I think Raju helped me in ways that I cannot really know or understand.

M: So you feel that when you need help from him, his help comes through from within?

V: Like a gardener who plants seeds. The seed in the soil has potential and with the right environmental factors, it will grow strong. So he is able to do that. He helps me in many ways like you say; he brings you to your own gate. If you open the gate, you are on the path. I think his way of doing things is extremely subtle. And you cannot know about your own karma, and how the decisions you make now will affect you in the years to come. You cannot know that. But with Raju I believe he has protected me. I fly. I am an aerobatic pilot, and so far nothing bad has ever happened to me. Not because I pray to God for his protection every single time, but also because disasters never occurred to me in my life. I have noticed that for example, certain illnesses that are in my family never happen to me. I also made decisions to be healthy, but ever if you exercise you could still have a heart attack. I think Raju has protected me from disasters and congenital disorders. And he made it possible for me to arrive at this point. I don't think it is something he did consciously. I think he just gave me his love, God's love, and however that worked in me, it healed me. It kept me strong. It is like a great gift to me, and my husband is also a gift of love that Raju wished upon me. Raju said that I will never have this kind of love in my life. I will never have anybody else, and love anybody as much as I love my husband. You will never know. I mean this is the type of gift God will give you because it is perfect.

M: Okay! The other day, when I called you, you started talking about Raju and you said, "Raju is a prophet." What brought you to that conclusion?

V: I guess he is similar to Deepak Chopra. Raju still has the ways of a prophet. He can see ahead, he can see down your path where you cannot, and more than half of the world cannot. He can guide us to avoid certain disasters that we cannot see.

M: Is there anything you could say that would be an inspiration for other people, like what good they can obtain from him?

V: Okay! In order to obtain, not only from Raju, but from any other person like him, the best possible enriching experience, you have to be completely silent. You have to stop thinking all together. Stop wanting, stop wishing, stop hoping, stop praying, and be still. Let him do his work. The more noise you have in your soul, the more noise you have in your mind. The more you are diminishing the effect. You are diluting the effect of his power. So as Canadians love to say "Shut the puck up!"

V & M: (Laughs)

V: Because you might get some effect, but like pouring water on raspberries; the more water you pour, the more you dilute and less taste you get. What was the question again?

M: The question was, "What you could say to people to make them benefit from Raju. And you started saying that they should be silent. You were saying they should stop the noise.

V: With Raju, and I think people make that mistake over and over again and that's why they don't get it. They get a little bit; but they don't get a lot because they don't shut up. They don't stop chatting, they don't stop doing anything. When they are meditating, when everybody are meditating, I know, I can feel it when they are not completely quiet. The room is noisy, they are noisy. They are like snow, okay! And Raju is trying to instill calmness into them, but they are still noisy. It is what he wants to do with them.

In the Lao Tzu Tao Te Ching, there is one great full thought, and that is to open you to the Tao. To trust your natural responses and things will fall into place. Okay! This is very profound. To open yourself to the Tao, you have to be receptive to the force that is out there and which cannot enter you unless you are still. If in your life you go from crisis to crisis; it is because you are interfering with the work of the Tao, by not being quiet. Raju is a lens magnifying the force of the Tao. Through him, much will change through your life and the life of the group. The work of Tao can be accelerated, but you have to stop trying, period! You have to stop thinking that you know what to do. You don't know what to do, okay! Give up, just give up. Go quiet, go within and let his power, the power that he is trying to channel to you, enter in you. Trust that this hour or two you are spending with him will bring enormous change in your life. Be like an empty glass, and he will fill you. And stop trying to giggle and make things happen. You can't, you have no power in your life. Or you would not be with him, okay!

M: (Laughs)

V: But through the power of Tao, allow that to work through us. Let it be. A tree only bends in the wind because it lets the wind go through it, and it remains the tree. A tree when the time comes and it's cold loses all its leaves and survives winter. And the next spring it will be green again. It allows the circle of nature to occur through it and it has its charm constantly. So, in the same way, allow Raju to flow his power through you. Trust that two hours spent in absolute emptiness is not wasted. And then wait for the sign in your life tomorrow. And then changes will happen.

M: It is so well said, what more I can say!

V: Raju said one thing about himself. "That life is the bow and he is the arrow, and it propels him. When life propels him that's where he is."

M: It's beautiful. I get it. Last week, when I was in Trinidad, I saw something beautifully written on a wooden plate. It was very inspiring. It was from Kahlil Gibran. I wanted to get it for him, but we were in such a rush to do something else I thought I will come back tomorrow and take time to choose properly. When I went back, it was gone. I thought, "Anyway it's okay, he does not need it, anything I can find on the outside he already has it within himself."

V: When people go to visit Raju at one of his seminars or gatherings, they bring him things, but they never give him anything he can use. Do you understand that?

M: Yes, They feel some devotion, some gratitude towards him and they want to show it, and they are clumsy in the way they do it.

V: The thing you should give Raju is something of yourself. Give up the things. Give a little of your own energy, like a bouquet of flowers releasing its fragrance, don't bring him material things. Give him what empowers him in the room; be empty, so he can act more fairly.

M: He does not need your material things.

V: No, what he needs is you, to contribute your power, and to make yourself available to him. If you can do that you will multiply the benefits.

Writing a book about him is a very good project for you, and his power is now spreading. This book is going to snowball going down the hill. It has to be written because what he does has to reach people.

M: Yes, it should reach more people. One day he said, "You should interview Vicky, she is now in Toronto, and she will have something to say about me."

V: It is important that his effect spreads worldwide. Right now, the population of this continent is sick. Fifty percent are overweight; fifty percent are obese people. This is very serious. We are gluttons, and we are dying for certain from one of the seven deadly sins. In North America, we eat too much, we have too much stuff. We are dying of sexual diseases. We are dying because of our own desires. We are greedy, and these desires are inappropriate for our health. We are ruining ourselves by denying the virtues of the ethics which made us strong. It appears to me that we are so far off the path that in the next ten years, there will be numerous deaths as people die as a result of this greed, which is gluttony. The lack of regard and faith in God, like the fear of God, is also a problem. We know it is too late to stop it now. Some people have said that by being in the presence of types of people like Raju, you can choose an alternative. You will be able to influence others and you can spread it to the world. That in itself is good. Because we killed, we feared, we craved, we take, and we don't give anything back to God. We give nothing back to the plants.

M: We give nothing back to nature, we are just taking.

V: Yes, we are not learning from history. This is very serious. We are on this planet but we don't have any regard for our bodies or the right to say thanks to others. We have no fear of God because we are so far away from the spiritual culture. This is putting pressure down, and we are brought down by our own nature and the path we have taken. If you don't feel it, then you are among those who will die and will die horribly.

M: So, those who are aware of that, have to do something about it, starting from themselves.

V: There are a very few Godly people like that available to us. And Raju is one of them. He has to be brought to more people.

M: I thought in the beginning I was doing that for myself, to know more about him, and to enhance my gratitude towards him. But now it's not just for me to know him, it is to bring the light that he is to more people.

V: This is very important.

M: This is the way to bring the light to a larger group of people.

V: Because once you do your work, you will have to realize this: In other words in the Tao Te Ching, the wise sage, the wise woman do their work and then let it go quickly. This is what you have to do. So do your work and let it go quickly.

Bethina, Professional Engineer (Chicago)

M: Bethina, how did you get to know Raju?

B: We were working together, but I didn't really know who he was. I have been working for this company for about six years or maybe more. I had seen him, and did not know him. But I remember the impression that I have of him. He just looks like a boy; he has something that the children have. He is one of these people you won't know. He can be thirty or fifty years old. Then after I joined "the healthy living club" that had been initiated in the company, we were meeting at lunch time, and we talked about all those healthy subjects. People were giving presentations on different topics, and one time I mentioned meditation. I thought maybe we should talk about meditation because it's something I would like to talk with people, but you can't really share it with anybody. So I asked that question. He looked around to see if anybody were listening, then he said to me, "We have been meeting for quite a year and a half already, we are meditating together, and maybe you should join us."

M: There was already a group in the company who were meditating together and you didn't know about it.

B: Yes, I didn't know. It was a little bit surprising to see that I was looking for something that was right there. I think it came to me when it was time to.

M: This is how you came to know and started attending his sessions at lunch time once a week.

B: Oh yes! Every Tuesday, and I know this. If I have to miss it, I must be away or something very important might hold me.

M: What would you say about the kind of relationship you have with him, as a colleague or at the spiritual level?

B: It's like he said today at the class. For me he is like a teacher, but he is really not. I don't see him like a teacher. You feel like you are blending with him. He is one of us, very humble. He is very subtle but he is sort of pulling you in.

M: Since how long have you joined the meditation sessions?

B: I had been going for almost a year now.

M: What did you learn that you are applying in your daily living?

B: Before I started the courses, I was not meditating every day. Since then, I do it every day. You know, I noticed a complete change in my personality. In our company, I used to go out in the hall and would be shy. I was a bit afraid approaching people. Now I walk down the hall, I smile, and say hello to everybody. I almost know everyone. I am not afraid of people anymore because I do accept them as they are part of me. It's just amazing! I think it's only the result of meditation and everything he had taught us. I am a person who does think a lot. Like when I first joined the class, I was thinking "I wish you know how much I understand what you are talking about!" And later on when I started taking class notes for each session and send them to him so he can pass them to everyone, I realized that was his way to make me know that he knew my thought. Because I know now that he sees when he talks to us and write it down, that's how he looks to us. I then realized that he knows what's going on. It's very nice and reassuring.

M: If you meet some people who don't know him, what would you tell them to inspire them and make them benefit of what you had got from him?

B: I think there was a person in this company who was interested to meditate, and I mentioned Raju to him. I did not force it. Raju said, "It has to come from inside," and I believe in that, and for someone who is ready, he will help him.

M: I think it's the way he operates. He needs no publicity. When somebody is ready, he just pulls the person towards him.

B: I think what you can say to people that might awaken their interest is maybe to say, "Raju is a very nice man and has a lot to say." Then they might ask. "What has he to say? I want to go and find out!"

M: What do you know about him as a colleague or as an ordinary individual?

B: Before I met him on the Tuesday class, I remember seeing him in one meeting where people started arguing about something. Then he just jumped in, and with a very strong voice he puts things in order. I was surprised. I mean he is a nice person and has a good sense of humor. He must be very intelligent to understand all these aspects of life.

M: Do you have anything else to say?

B: Raju is unconventional. I had been in his home for the classes. I noticed he has no dining table. I am thinking "It's because he does not need it!" He is living according to his own standard.

M: I have completed my questions, unless you want to have more to express about him.

B: It is his sense of humor that I really like. I don't know, maybe it's the Indian way of joking or his way of being?

M: That's his special way of being.

B: I am lucky. I have said that already to a few people. I love my job. But, if one day I don't love my job anymore, the reason why I would stay in this company is the Tuesday meeting with Raju. So in case, I do not like my job anymore, I will tell him, "Let me know how long you are staying in the company so I can plan my life around it." (Laughs)

M: That's great! Thank you!

Laura, Secretary (Chicago)

M: Tell me about you and Raju.

L: I've known Raju for about five years now. I met him through my job. We started talking and we ended up making a deeper connection. What particularly attracted me to Raju is his knowledge about spirituality. I consider myself to be a spiritual person, and that was the connection between us. I became more curious about him when I started attending his meditation classes.

M: How did you find out about the classes?

L: It was through another friend of mine who also is a colleague. When I met Raju, my friend had already initiated what we call "the healthy living club" in the company. We invited Raju to join the meeting of the club. Eventually, my friend talked to Raju about having a spiritual class once a week. It was how we started going to his home at lunch time to meditate since 2002. Sometimes we were seven to eight people every Tuesday. The number decreased when some people moved to different companies. Anyhow, we continued to enjoy the weekly meditation sessions with Raju.

What I like about Raju is his humbleness. Before attending his class, I remember being a little bit stressed. Going there at lunch time, to meditate with him for fifteen or twenty minutes and doing some breathing exercises, just made me feel so much better. In his class, I learned about yoga, meditation, and spirituality. He told us about the breathing and its connection with God. It was a new concept for me and it made a lot of sense.

Besides being humble, Raju has no problem getting along with anybody. He is kind and is always willing to share. I actually work with him in the same group, and anytime I need help for the job or about spirituality, I feel very comfortable to ask him for it. I also never heard anyone saying anything bad about Raju. He is very respectful and genuine. He is a great man. Raju is so authentic and so willing to share his knowledge, and that generates in you the feeling of security. Many years ago, I didn't have any idea about the Indian culture. I knew nothing about it because we tend to stay among our own community, I am Mexican. Today, I thank my friend and Raju for the wonderful sessions. Through him I became more open to the world and I met many wonderful people. It is really enriching to open yourself to others. I enjoy Raju's company because of his spirituality. After all, this is the only thing which will give peace in life. The rest is all temporary. Physical beauty will fade away, but the beauty in your heart will stay and it is how people will remember you.

It is very nice of you to do this book. It's such a great idea, and I am sure that Raju will be happy to know what people think of him and how he has transformed their lives. I can't wait to read it.

Adam and Grace, Scientists (California)

Mercy: Adam, tell me how you came to know Master Raju?

A: Ten years ago, I went to some Indian program in Montreal Canada and I met a friend who told me about a yoga course. Then I forgot about it. When the time was near, they called me to remind me the forthcoming course.

I went to the first meeting. We were half an hour late and I missed the introduction. I think he talked about commitment, but I missed all of that. (Laughs). Anyway, that was the first time I had ever seen him. I don't think I had ever experienced this kind of course or discourse before. I knew I was attending something called yoga, and I was waiting for him to tell me about yoga. I was waiting and waiting for a long time!

M: Previously, Grace talked about who he is. Do you have any specific idea of what or who he is?

A: He is enigmatic. Sometimes he will be a normal person, a normal friend. At other times, he is just like anybody else. He will be childlike, and then suddenly he is what really matters and he will change into the Master. He leads an easy going life, but sometimes he becomes serious in the drama of life. When such seriousness or difficult situations come to us, we are alone to handle them. Those who are near and dear to us cannot absorb the seriousness. They will deny that is serious. They will not allow you to express anything. But Master Raju is able to take the force of the seriousness to himself, and that's what I call magic. He sometimes creates a material change. Sometimes he will change an attitude towards an event. So it will be your experience of a material event versus the material event itself. Sometimes he will change it. He can do that at will. So who is he? He cannot be a normal ordinary human being like a thousand of other people that I have met. He has abilities that you can only call powers. But he does not use or misuse them for any reason other than love for the other person. He never interferes in anybody's life. He is always very respectful of others and very considerate. If I am too shy to ask him something, he will know that and he will give it to me even without my asking.

M: It's like he can read your mind!

A: Oh! Yes! Yes for sure. But he can read your mind, although it's not reading the mind for the sake of mind reading. He only cares about what is happening to you. I have also met others who can read your mind and understands what is really good for you. But with him, what is different is that, compared to any other person who can read minds, he also knows the answers. So if you read my mind, you will come to the same question that I have in my mind, and you will either judge me for having such a question or you will be puzzled by the same question yourself. But Master Raju has an ability to look at that question, to look at me, and separate the two. It is extremely rare that I think that someone like that really exists. So I would say he is from some other planet. He is not from the planet Earth. He is someone from some other place.

M: Some people see him as a prophet. Could he be an avatar? What do you think?

A: For a while I had a lot of duality, a lot of conflicts with that. Swamiji Satchitananda Ganapathi, Sai Baba, Sri Ravi Shankar, Master Raju, Ammachi, and all others. Too many to name. This complicates the situation. Do I believe in all of them? Who is the biggest one? Who is the most popular? I struggled with this for a while, and it was difficult to try to live with that. But I realized it is all mind play where the mind is trying to evaluate. To compare is the mind's job. I realized with all of them, I don't relate to any of them from the mind. I relate to them from the heart. The mind's voice is beyond what I can understand. The heart speaks other words, in the same language as me. That's the only way I know them all. Maybe in the last few months with him here, my perceptions have changed. It has become different.

M: What has happened now?

A: Before, it looked like they are all different points made of one cloth. You pull the cloth from here, from there, and they all look different. Right now, if I look at Master Raju, normally God is outside of our master, and all of them are God like. Now I don't have this God/Master problem. Everything that I know has been taught. I learned by observing and watching people. How they feel, how they express themselves. If somebody comes with something new, it can only be understood by itself, not in a language that I already know. It is like I know seven colors. And there are more colors which do not fit into any of the colors and cannot be classified. Then you have to start thinking of another way of looking at the world using not only seven colors, but something else too. Maybe sounds are also there and could be used as filters. In conclusion, this is what he is to me: someone I can't fit in any category.

M: Did you ever asked him a question like that or heard him saying something about himself in the same context?

A: No, you know Master Raju. I have not actually asked him such question. He teaches about the world and about you. He always stays hidden, you never think of him when you are in front of him. He makes himself invisible. But I have to say that "Who is he to me?" is a question from a mind point of view. And I understand also that from the world or mind point of view, I cannot measure him. I cannot gauge him. If I stick to this point, then who I am to him becomes apparent. That only I can understand it's not possible to look from his side and understand who he is.

M: Right! What kind of impact has he made in your life?

A: Before I met him, I was chasing things. I was chasing something material and it was very much in turn to increase my material possessions. I was a good guy I think, but I was unaware of the real thing. I can say that my mind was the only thing that I was engaged in life. I had the desire to get to the truth but I did not have the means to get there. Whatever I knew was whatever I did, and it was going along like that. At the emotional level, my emotions were almost impossible to deal with. I have been, in some ways, like an iceberg, but Master Raju touches a few knobs here and there and makes sure that emotions are being unlocked. During all the years before, my emotions used to be destructive, and life was always an emotional struggle. I would say I was like an airplane which was grounded, and he pushes so that it flies. You know when you are on the ground you are afraid to fall once again. He takes care of that. He knows you were about to fall down, and he holds you. The specific impact I would say, is that I have more awareness of choice in everything that I do now. So I am much more aware of what I am up to, what is going on, what is going to happen.

M: You mean he had helped you by increasing your awareness!

A: Currently, I am only focusing on self-awareness, and I am not yet entering any other kind of awareness. Before, it was not complete self-awareness; it was something else more or less.

M: Earlier on you were talking about another planet. I think he was joking when he says he is from Mercury! Now I am asking you from which planet is he from?

A: He is the kind of person that does not want to overwhelm you. He does not want to scare the core of you. To me, he first appeared like the sun. Secondly, he has a lot of wisdom like the sun, which is very strong, producing hot energy, warmer than other planets. The sun is the only shining object. The moon shines too but it's only a reflection. The sun is the source, not a reflection. But I know that the sun is a small body compared to the galaxy of universe. And I think he is this way because he does not want to blind you. If he did more than that, I would have more difficulty too. I would probably have gone nuts. When I will rise up and become closer to the brightness of the sun, then he will show me more of the galaxy.

M: Now tell me what specific ally you got from his being, his teachings that you are applying in your daily living. You said you have increased awareness, is there anything else?

A: The thing is, as you watch him and are with him, you take on some of his qualities without trying to do so. You are not trying to become like him, but something is happening and you start looking from the same point of view as he does. I think of him as he is looking at the world in some particular way. When I am with him, I realize that I am starting to look at the world the same way. Even though my way of looking used to be different, now there is only one way of looking. My way of relating to people is also becoming less reactive and more observing. I am now looking at all things just the way he would look at them. I can't be like him. I cannot talk like him, but I can look like him. I can observe the way he would observe, and this is what I am doing now. I am not there yet when it comes to thoughts, actions, and words. I can give an analogy. It is like a piece of charcoal. It is sitting there dead and cold. But when fire accesses it, the charcoal brings light and heat. So the charcoal itself was not generating the light, but after being in contact with the source of fire it does. He has the property of the light itself; it

223

warms other people and finally it burns by itself when no one is there. If someone looks through a telescope, he would say, "Hey! I see a new sun over there."

M: I think this is what all those people we call avatars are doing. I think this is the purpose of them being among us. It is to transform all charcoals, which are ready to let themselves be transformed!

G: We were talking about relationships. We were saying how sometimes it's difficult to stay in a certain relationship or to be with certain people, and I asked Master Raju about that. He told me, "The way is that you should be able to live life in such a way that you don't say I cannot live without this person, and at the same time, you should not say I can live only with this person. You live your life with or without this person. The person being lovable or not, you live in the middle way, the perfect way."

A: If you look at what is most important in your life, and leave him out of it, you will forget for years what is really the most important for you. His presence will make you remember again what is most important in your life. Then you will work to realize what the most important thing is for you in your life. And it appears that he is the best person I have ever met. For you he may be kindness, to another person love or compassion.

G: We started the question sometime back and I have not completed it yet. Let's say the way he would talk about the Ashtavakra-Gita, and it supposed to be very deep and high philosophical teachings. But he makes it coming in a way like he is infusing it into you. I remember that after a week I was walking around, with those ideas in my head, and could not figure out the application of it in my day to day life. Then it came back like a witness, like flashes, and I just felt it. It is like you were saying, you are everything, the universe is you and you are also the whole universe. So what is bad, what is good in it? There is no difference. Anything is everything; it is the way you see it and relate to it which makes it appear different.

M: It's like fire, is it good or is it bad? It's what you do with it that makes it good or bad, the fire itself remains the same form of energy. Now tell me what did you get from his being, his teachings that made a difference in your life?

A: You know, when I was a young child, I had a very secure family so I lived deeply within the family bounds. That made it difficult for me to integrate with other people. I always felt other people were far away from me. So after staying with Master Raju for the last few months, the one thing I learned is not to be so afraid of other people. I was afraid of being hurt, because in a family that you trust nobody will really hurt you. Even if they do, their intentions are always good. But with other people, I assume that if you say harsh words, your intentions might not be good and they will manipulate you without love. You know, when a mother is telling her child "don't do something," if she is manipulating, it's always out of love. Other people may not have that love. So I have big barriers about getting close to others. It is very difficult, and it has been getting worse. However, the more you stay away from people, the less you are going to integrate. If you meet forty people and you don't become friendly with anybody, it becomes tougher and tougher to take that step. So, after being with Master Raju for a few months, I stopped distrusting people. I started to allow them to be just the way they are naturally. This makes it easier to be with people and also easier for people to be with you.

M: How do you explain the way he brought these changes in you? Did he say something or did he do something in particular?

A: In the beginning I was not even aware that I was unable to relate to people. After some time I started to understand that I have a problem. He asked me to take some courses like "landmark forum." I was thinking, "Why has he asked me to do this course? But doing this course helped me to realize that maybe I was not relating to people hopefully.

M: Were these courses given by him?

A: No, by other people he had been in contact with the technology field. He introduced us to them.

M: Was it a class on communication or what was it about?

A: Yes, you can say something like that "personal levels of communication." That course made me aware that I don't let people get close to me. Realizing that, and not being able to do anything about it, is very frustrating. I felt I don't want to continue living like this. I was not happy with myself knowing I had this difficulty and basically I wanted to hide away. In the beginning I didn't have the skills, or practice communicating, and that made it difficult. After staying with Master Raju for a few months, things changed for me. He understands exactly how I feel. He had empathized, and bit by bit he made me drop my concerns. So now I don't feel so isolated. I feel somebody understands me and it does matter to me. He is okay with the way I am and he does not judge me. He has ways of listening, which makes you feel you are really heard. You can express any kind of so-called emotions. The way he eases it is by taking away the energy of that emotion until it becomes like a flat vehicle which makes you feel okay and completely free from it. When that emotion vanishes, the next moment some other emotions come. So he is able to completely still the emotion so it does not return like an itch. If you keep scratching it, it becomes more and more apparent. So he does the opposite. He just soothes it, like putting a lotion on it just by listening to you. You feel you are totally understood. You feel you trust him so much there is nothing to hide, there is nothing to feel ashamed of, and there is nothing to worry about. You can also feel angry and can just show it. He has a way to relieve everything. It can be anger; it can be sadness or anything else. He can eliminate it as though as he has gone through all of those emotions in a previous life. He knows exactly what you are going through, and he will support you. The beautiful thing about communicating with Master Raju is even if I am not expressing myself clearly he will catch exactly what I mean.

M: Uhu, uhu

A: When you are talking to him, without him saying anything, you will know that he understands. Even though your words would say one thing, he would hear what was really behind them. He would be able to let you know, without showing off, that he catches what is really inside you. Intuitively, silently, he will let you know. That has happened often, but I have been noticing it more in the last few months after the past four to five years.

Let me give you an example. It is a different subject. I was struggling because I did not know what to do with my emotions. By listening to me so well he alleviated the situation. I had suppressed emotions from the time I was a teenager. It was mostly anger and I was unable to control or do anything about it. I would be quiet and then suddenly, "boom," starts acting towards violence. Now those emotions are becoming very peaceful. The water is becoming calmer. This has happened during the last few months he has been with us. The calmness started when Chandrika came in October 2000. She made me aware of what I am like, and who and what I really stand for in life. After that, I stopped pushing Master Raju so far, treating him like a friend. She made me see why I treat him like a friend, although he is more than a friend and she helps me understand that. When my baby was born, I stopped putting distance and barriers between us. Only when I got upset about something would I start treating him as a friend. Even when I am treating him as a friend he will be so humble and so perfect. So even if I say he is a friend, he will be like my best friend.

M: There is nothing wrong in being a friend. The only thing is to keep your reverence for him.

A: That's what I mean, but it won't be there when I have anger. It's unintentional, your ego wants to run and it's not thinking of reverence. So at that time, walls will be put up temporarily. Even then, he will not cross that wall. He will be just on the other side of it and still be there. He will be very helpful. He will let you control yourself, at your pace. He won't force you to do anything. He will just let you understand that and be with it. It's very effective in how quickly you will learn and realize that anger is unproductive. When you are around Master Raju, he is the part of you that is aware of what is going on. In the beginning you don't notice that. For example, when you first meet Master Raju, you experience new things and nice things. It's pleasant, you feel happy, and you feel joyous and feel freedom. Then you realize that life is easier when you are around him. I noticed that whenever he is around. If I grieve, I automatically notice that other people also have grief in their existence. In other words, I am more aware of my emotions and other's emotions. It is a witnessing effect. One part of you is watching and the other part is experiencing what is happening on the inside and what is external to me. What is really happening is that observing yourself is being established, and the experience itself of letting go is starting to take place. You are becoming the observer. So you are aware of what is being experienced without losing the awareness. I mean, if you get too much into experiences, you can forget who is experiencing itself. If you are tired of being ruled by emotions, then all that really helps. Thoughts are okay, you are not ruled by them so much. They are more or less empty all the time. If I keep quiet nothing would be running in my head. There would be only small things. On the other hand, emotions would be going on and on and on, creating lots of struggles on the line. When you dream at sleep, it would be struggling. When I meditate, it's a pause, a break. Otherwise, I am caught all the time and it might even show outside in my behaviors. So staying with him helps me watch it and it takes me back to my knowing. It helps me switch off. Now I find it amusing when I look back to what's happening at work. Before, I used to postpone and avoid certain tasks, which I didn't like. After a certain time, I realized I had been doing that and it felt uncomfortable. Now the delay has been shortened from six months to only four days.

M: So the time between the delay and the time completing the project had decreased.

A: Yes, it is decreasing and with it, the stress decreases too.

M: The fact is you have noticed such positive changes in yourself just by being in contact with him.

A: Yes. Definitely, and more than that, I am not bothered about judging myself so much. Usually people keep themselves perfect in one or two areas of their lives and ignore other aspects. I can't do that. For me everything is the same. If my work sucks, my family life would feel that same. Anytime if I am struggling at work, I know that I am also struggling at home. Perhaps that sounds funny.

M: No, it's not so funny because we are not divided. We are one unique entity. If one aspect is not functioning properly, the other aspect gets the negative impact too.

A: But actually, what to say is that many people are divided and are living unconsciously. One aspect of them is high functioning and the others are weak. I used to be like that. One aspect of me would be very strong, like being very good at my studies, and another being very weak in relating to other people.

M: Yes, because it's easier to manifest our stronger abilities and to ignore our weaknesses. And because the aspects of us which are weaker are more difficult to deal with; it's easier to go slowly or ignore altogether. We pretend they are not there, but deep inside we know they are.

A: It's interesting that you say that as this is the real problem. You find one easy and the other one difficult, so you keep choosing the easy one and leaving the difficult one out. Then overtime, you tend to develop some fears about the difficulty, and it gets harder and harder to do it.

M: You said all these transformations happened since he began living with you. How long had he been with you?

A: Eight months. During this period of time, I realized I needed to grow. I was like an immature kid. I was stuck emotionally.

M: It's great that you can be aware of it now. Some people are past fifty to sixty years old and are still not aware where they are leading to.

A: I was aware of it, but I did not know what to do with it. I did not know how to get out of it. But it's a skill, which can be learned. It cannot be taught in a course. You can only observe and understand.

M: How does Master Raju do that?

A: Most of the time he shows us by the way he communicates. Let's say I had a question about something, a second later I will have learned what he said. I have understood what he said inside my head but without going through the logic. He simply puts the understanding there. So I would just say, "Oh yeah, I got it." It's really amazing.

M: How do you explain that?

A: Oh! It's a powerful communication.

M: I agree with you it's powerful, but how do you explain the process?

A: You know, he comes and gets you just like that! It's like "wow!" You feel like something suddenly happened.

M: Like a flash?

A: He can give you all of it without you noticing it.

M: You see, in my case, I cannot say that Master Raju told me many things. Most of what I have learned from him has been through silence, very subtly. It is as he gets into me like magic and he infuses ideas to me in an intangible way.

A: For about five years I did not know about what you are saying. I thought I was getting it myself. I had noticed it two or three times. He said something, and a second later I became aware of it. I realized then my own model did not match, so he changed the model just for me. He is able to communicate at mind to mind level.

M: Sure.

A: And the kinds of things that he communicates this way are not trivial things like "I want ice cream." He won't communicate that kind of thing this way.

M: He is not there for that. He has not taken body and life for trivialities. Playing in trivialities with us is only the first step to reach us. His purpose is not only to play the game. His real purpose is to take you beyond it, to yourself.

A: The way in which he works is very simple. He first puts forward the knowledge knowing who you are. He makes a thirst inside you to make sure that you are able to be receptive without any struggles. He eases some of the frustrations and makes you realize in which direction to actually go. He is always there to support you.

M: Now, what can you tell people about him to inspire them?

A: To inspire them?

M: Yes. I mean something like; I invited a friend of my group to meet him. I told her he is very special. You just have to go there and be in his presence. You don't have to ask for anything if you don't want to, just be in his presence. That is how I inspired her to meet him. I was convinced that even if you are not aware of it, you are still receiving a lot from him by being in his presence.

A: That's true.

M: I remember, in my case, in the beginning I was not aware that anything was happening. At first, I did not know who he was and what I was doing around him. I went to his course like I would have gone to a Spanish class. After the class, you take your notes and leave. I was not aware that something was happening between him and me. With regular teachers, you get the information. You understand them and then it's over. Even if you are not aware of it, he is getting into you. It is one aspect that could inspire somebody. You can tell someone, "If it happens he is there, never miss his presence."

A: Yes! I see but I know there are people who will resist. They won't come and you cannot do more. You know some people will come to the introduction of a course and never come back.

M: He will wait for you, later in this life or the next one. I always say that God is not in a hurry; he has eternity and he is very patient.

A: What he has explained is that you have to be really patient. And the patience can sometimes be a lifetime.

M: Exactly! Sometimes I say, if it's not in this lifetime, it will be in the next life or the next one. He has already waited for us so long!

A: He never refuses anybody. People are usually afraid of change. Change means giving up the things that you have collected, and you have to throw away lots of junk. That can be scary. You can think, "Maybe I'll change. I might become someone who doesn't care enough about money. Or will it make me someone who will start paying more attention to staying away from people?" These kinds of thoughts can prevent you from becoming close to him. That's okay, but the thing is, to know where to go when you become sick and tired of money, when you know it does not help you. So he never forces anyone.

M: I know, and I also know that he is very patient with each soul. He will wait until you are ready to make the move. Do you have anything more to add?

A: The first thing to benefit others is to get your own peace inside.

M: How do you get the peace you are talking about?

A: The most important thing is to be aware. He is generating this awareness in you. It is more obvious when you are around him.

M: Now, what do you know about him as an ordinary person?

A: I know that he had a very difficult childhood. He grew up with his grandparents, so he had a difficult start in life by not being with his parents like any child would want it to be. As a result of this experience, he is able to be more compassionate. He faced difficulties himself so he can understand how it can be for others. Anyway, it's always a handicap having a difficult childhood. I have not experienced that. It is the opposite for me. I had an extremely good and safe childhood.

M: An easy childhood?

A: I would not say easy, just very solid and safe. You can have it easy by having all the toys but no love. Then it's not a big deal.

M: No, what I mean by easy is the love. Kids invent their own toys; they don't need "Fisher Price." It's not the toy they play with, and it's whatever is there. What kids need is love. And sometimes when love is lacking, this is the real poverty. This is what I think. You said he had a difficult childhood?

A: Yes. He had to resolve all of those things. He had a great relationship with his parents. A lot of people would never forgive their parents for leaving him with his grandparents. They would not forgive, but he did! So how he did that, I don't know. This is the kind of thing, when you think about it, which can be inspiring for you. It is not like he is some kind of angel who came from somewhere and had it all easy. He knows how all these things work. He went through all these difficulties and also figured out away to overcome them.

M: This evening I was thinking t he is working so far away from home and I know it is a burden on his body and I said, "Master, you don't have to put up with all these miseries!" It bothers me; seeing him going through all these things. But in another way, I knew he was going through the same kind of miseries as the rest of the world. And by going through these difficulties, he is teaching us by experiencing the same things, yet managing to stay joyful and peaceful. I realized that might be the reason why he is going through all of that. I believe that in the same way as he can create magic in your life, if he wanted to, he could have made it different in his own life. But that might not be very helpful and supportive for people who are facing difficulties and struggles. I think he is preaching by his way of handling life's difficulties.

Do you know anything about the impact he could have at the level of the community, national or international?

A: You saw him giving his programs such as when he does "energy ecstasy." Those programs are all hobbies for him. They are not the real thing. Even work is not the real thing. The real thing is that he is working on something. What I am saying is, even when he is helping one person, he is not only helping that person, he is solving such problems for all mankind. He is bringing a new light on how people are able to solve such problems. I will give you an example. Hundreds of years ago, people had difficulties about resources. Even today there are many people who are thinking that the world is full of hatred and full of such things as shortages, etc. But there are also lots of people who think that the world is a beautiful place. Slowly the human mind is not thinking of it as if it is bad or horrible all around.

M: You mean that the level of consciousness of people is raised up.

A: Yes. What he is doing is applicable to all mankind. So as I make a progress it's contributing to the entire human consciousness or becoming a pool of hope for you and others. This way, he is healing hatred and other fears that have existed over the years. Eventually this healing will reach the other side of the world directly. It's difficult to understand and to explain, but you know how he intuitively gives you that knowledge.

M: Yes, I know. I have experienced that.

A: So, what he is doing is at the level of consciousness which is not known to us right now.

M: I know. We cannot catch his every way of operating.

A: The same as he did for you, giving the knowledge without you thinking of it. He doesn't have to talk. He will make it accessible to your heart directly. By working this way through people, he will make them move from mind to heart. They will get some balance between mind and heart. This is his gift to the world that he has been working on all these years. He is creating a different kind of human beings.

Romeo, Scientist, Engineer (Toronto)

I worked with Raju in a company called Rockwell International, located in Toronto. He was in the laboratory and I was in the manufacturing department. We had been there for almost twenty-two years.

Raju is a very peaceful person. I have attended a number of meetings with him. I could never see any concern in him. When he talks in a group, everybody listens and nobody questions him. At lunch time, I used to spend lots of time with him. This is how I came to think, "How can a man always be so peaceful?" I enjoyed being with him at lunch time every day. Once, I was ready for lunch, and as usual, I went to the spot under the tree where we used to sit for lunch, and I could not find him. So I went back to the secretary and asked about him. She told me Raju had already gone for lunch sometime ago. I went back to the same spot and looked again. He was there and I asked, "Raju where were you? I came here and you were not here." Then he said, "I was here, I was in Samadhi." At that time, I thought that this man must be a very great soul. He can do many miracles and always lets the credit go. He never shows or claims anything.

He became my spiritual Master. In the beginning, I used to call him Rajuji, and slowly I figured out that he is not an ordinary person, and that he deserved special respect.

In 1984, a program has been organized in Toronto. Raju told me. "I want you to take this program." I did and I encouraged my wife to do it too. We went for a retreat and since then we got into the spiritual practice.

In conversation, he never cuts people off. He always listens. He never contradicts whatever I share with him. He would acknowledge me, but at the same time tell me what is wrong. I think different ways can help you. Whatever I do in my life is fine with him. The fact that he is not cutting me off really helps me to understand life. After the retreat training, my vision changed for the better. He was very patient with me. He gave me a few key words, which really work for me.

He had a major impact on my relationship with my wife. I used to argue with my wife all the time. Whenever we had to go for a party for example, I used to ask my wife to buy something nice even if it was too expensive according to our resources. I used to insist, and my wife would say, "No, no, we will give this!" So conflicts were always there. I shared that with Raju. He said, "Do one thing in your life. Always say yes to your wife, it will change your life." I started doing that, and believe it or not, my wife paid better attention to what I would say. I told him what happened and he said, "You see the difference!"

One day, my wife and I went to visit him and his wife in Scarborough. He was in the basement cleaning the fish tank. It was almost 4:00p.m., and I said "Raju did you have lunch?" He said, "What time is it right now?" I replied "4:00 o'clock," then he said, "Chandrika had not called me." It was said with no anger. That was very inspiring to see. My wife and my three children are also closer to him than to any other person from outside. Even if they are busy in their schedule, when Raju is here, they will find time to be with him. The whole family is connected to him.

There is something that I would like to share. We were all going to a Pooja function. Raju was with us and had planned to go to another program. In the morning, he changed his mind and said, "I am going to the Pooja with you." While going there, Raju suggested that we get some fruits for the Pooja. On the way, I went to the E.D.market, and got two bunches of bananas. The kids wanted some bananas. Raju said, "The bananas are for the Pooja, we will have bananas there." The bananas were behind his back. He put his right hand under the seat and pulled out two bananas and gave them to the kids. Shauna, my daughter was behind his back, and then he pulled out another banana from under his seat and gave it to Shauna. That was special. After the Pooja, when we came back home, the kids asked him, "Uncle, where did you get the bananas? We want to see!" He answered, "I did not get any bananas." The kids continued, "Where did you get those bananas?" He said, "I bought them. I don't do magic." But the kids knew there were no bananas under the seat. So they knew that Raju had made those bananas for them.

In 1986, our younger son was born. Raju came to know out of the blue that he was going to suffer. Those days, he used to fly from Montreal to Toronto just for us. He did that for a few months. One day, Karla was crying because our son was very sick. He had a kind of infection in the internal pipe of the liver that was changing the color of his stool from brown to white. So he needed a new liver. It was a birth defect; there is one in a thousand births. But Raju knew as usual, without us telling him, that our son had a birth defect. One day, Karla was crying a lot. Raju told her, "As long as I will live; your son will live too." His first transplant happened on the 9th of May, 1987. That was the beginning of transplants then, so the news had been in the Toronto Sun, the Toronto Star, and the Globe & Mail newspapers. When we got the liver the day before, I called up Raju, but he already knew before I told him. The first liver transplant did not work. The second transplant was on September 1, 1987. I remember I had a call from my brother in India to say our mother had passed away. I called Raju saying there is a cancellation. And he knew that also. So he knows what is happening via internal connection. Of course, when I don't call Raju for months, he is always with me. He guides me from within. When I need him, he always helps me. He is in my heart all the time.

He also knows about past lives. He told my wife and my sister-in-law that I was a king, and he was a poet at that time. He used to come to my kingdom to share the poems with me. He said that's why I am connected to him in this life. Every time he comes to Toronto he stays with us. He knows everything. He is what I call a living God.

He had blessed me and my whole family. He took a weekend to give us teachings on how we should meditate. He came and did the Pooja in my home. Whatever he gave us were great blessings. He has really helped each and every one in my family to grow spiritually. So I wish that everyone who crosses his path gets his blessings for their spiritual growth. Raju said, "When we don't accept the truth we suffer." The amount of stress and depression people face is a function of their acceptation of the truth. For example, raising children and giving them freedom is difficult to accept in regard to the way we were brought up. But since times have changed, we have to face the dilemma. This might lead you into depression, and Raju said, "If you accept the truth, you will be able to handle the situation. By you accepting the truth it will help the children also live this truth." Every time we meet Raju and every time my son sees him help him, you can see the light radiate in him.

Every time Raju comes to the town Papaji, Mataji, everybody touches his feet. Raju always touches their feet back. Everybody meets him as if he is the Father. We all feel great reverence for him.

I remember he shared with me that, as young boy, he used to gather people together and tell them some spiritual stories. The whole village knew him as being a very special person. Later on, he married Chandrika because of some past life connection. Chandrika's great grandfather was Subramania Bharati. And that's the time Raju had also the connection with me. Raju was a poet and was very poor because at that time, people could not understand the poems and he could not make a living out of it. Chandrika was also his wife at that time, and she wanted money to run the family. After two lives with her, he found the same woman and he recognized her again. In this life, he can give her all the money she needs. It is a past life connection he can remember of course, but I cannot remember. You see, we are beginners and he is at the highest step.

When he was living here in Toronto, he was writing a palmistry book for a publisher.

He is a great astrologer. And he could see your life without even looking at your palm. He could tell you about your life. He does not want people to know that he can do that. He wrote that book, and it was almost complete and still half to be done. Even for his brother in law, he wrote things that happened as predicted. The publisher wanted him to complete the book but somehow, Raju got a book written by Acharya Rajneesh, and after reading it, he destroyed the astrology book he was working on. He decided to stop writing it and the book remains incomplete. Even today, the publisher is still anxious for him to complete it. He felt that reading people's palms and telling them their future might stop their spiritual growth. That's why he stopped this kind of activities.

There is another incident I want to relate to you. When my son was really sick, there was a Japanese technique being taught in a Japanese temple in Montreal. Raju suggested to Karla to come to Montreal and learn that technique. Without the chanting of mantras, you can produce radiation rays from your palm and that can help a sick person to heal. Karla went to Montreal with the baby and her father. Raju came to receive them. As soon as the train stopped, Papaji saw Raju standing at the station waiting for them. Papaji asked him, "Raju, how did you know we would arrive now?" Raju said, "Papaji, I know." Karla learned the technique and it helped our son to heal faster. Before Raju convinced Karla to learn the technique, he came to Toronto and in everybody's presence, he said, "I am going to help you understand the technique." While Morris, my son, was sleeping, he made the radiation flow from Morris's heart and we could witness it happening. That was an amazing experience.

When he moved to Montreal, I used to keep his son to help him organize the courses. I was quite involved in those activities. Ten years ago, we were engaged in some charity activity that we called "Seva Canada" or "Service Canada." We applied for a license and we got a charity status. We organized a big dinner to sponsor the activity. Raju was supposed to be there, but he was in China on a business trip. He said, he remembered the activity even though he was far away that day. There were 1,000 people in attendance. I told Raju, "I feel you are doing this." He said, "I am really doing it. It was always my desire to help the poor children in India, and to bring them education." Being the president of Seva Canada, I always feel that it is not me who is doing it, but Raju doing it through me. He was very happy when I shared with him that we collected $20,000. Sometimes we don't ask people, we don't invite people, but they just feel like giving to help the children in India. As you can see, Raju is always the instrument to put me on the right path. He had written the following article for the Seva magazine when we started the project. It's a pleasure to share it with the world as homage to Swami Raju Bharati, as he was known at that time.

Love all and serve all

"Service is an expression of a basic orientation in life where your focus is more on giving than on receiving. Learning the joy of giving is one of the ultimate lessons you will learn in your life, apart from learning how good it is to give, and what to give. However, you cannot do service or give so that it will lead you to heaven. Then the real joy is not learned. That's why the Bible says: "Let not your left hand know what your right hand has given." The real you, who you really are, is all about giving, and knowing. This is the only sign of maturity. One is immature until this lesson is learned, regardless of how old one is.

Service also means feeling one with the other. In Sanskrit, the word 'seva' really means he/she is also included in my being. It means the point when I and thou disappear, when you as an ego are no longer there; then God can start functioning through you. Mother Teresa said that when she served the lepers, she never saw a leper there. She saw Jesus in the form of a leper. The Hindu Puranas say that it is Narayana (God) hiding in the form of the one being served.

Sai Baba also said, "Love all, and serve all." He added, "Service to men is service to God." Service to God is nothing but a way of prayer and it is a very potent way of prayer. If you serve, you are praying. If you serve without prayer, then service remains at the periphery. If you pray without service, your prayer becomes isolated from life. You become like an island. When you pray and serve, you remain on the inner center and yet at one with God, you are not on the periphery or isolated."

Victoria and Bernard, Accountants (Montreal)

V: I had seen Master Raju in the beginning at Khalil's bhajans. But I did not know anything about him in those days. During the bhajans, he used to sit upstairs in the living room. He would not come down where the gathering was. He used to come down only at the end when we reached the last song addressed to Lord Subramanya. That is how I first met him. He did not talk to anyone and nobody would talk to him either. He was a very quiet person, just sitting by himself in the living room. He only talked to my father. I am so grateful to father that he went to Master Raju and asked him questions like "Who are you?" "What's your name?" "What was your great parents' name?" After meeting with Master Raju, my father used to come and say, "Oh, that man sitting alone on the couch does not talk to anybody, but I spoke to him. I found out who he is, where he is living, and all those things you know!" I said "Father, he doesn't talk to anyone, why did you go to him, why did you bother him?" Father said, "That's the way I am, that's the way I will know more about him." Mercy, this is basically how I came to know about Master Raju, through what father told me. Then quite often, we used to see him from a distance. One day, when I was doing the Goddess Lakshmi Pooja, we invited him. I also invited Paula and she brought him with her. She had known him for a long time. While doing the Pooja, Master Raju was chanting the mantras. I was very happy. Later on, I got sick, suffering from a pinched nerve which was very painful. My friend asked me, "Why don't you talk to Master Raju about this, he can give you healing light. You know he is really a good person. You will come to know him." Then I called Master Raju at the office and said, "I wish you could come and give me some healing light because I have a lot of pain." He came that evening to give me the healing light. I was very much impressed by that and by the relief that I got from the treatment. That was the first time he came to our home.

B: Before that, it was for our son's thread ceremony, and we wanted a Brahmin to bless him according to our traditions. We asked him and he came willingly and participated in the three-day function. So Albert has been blessed not only by father but also by Master Raju.

When my wife had the pinched nerve problem, I saw him giving healing sessions to help her, and I thought to myself, "He is not an ordinary person." I felt that he was something beyond everybody's knowledge." They say "A Master will come and look for you, rather than you go looking for him." He came and knocked at our door and said, "I am your Master!" That's how he came to us in 1993. Then in 1994, we came to know him better. That year, we started hosting the personal development program which went on in Montreal until he moved to Chicago.

V: We were fortunate to have him Mercy. Having him visit regularly to give me the healing light made him spend more time with us. I remember I was crawling like a baby because the pain was so strong. But after receiving this light, I started moving more. I will never forget the help he gave me during such a difficult time in my life.

B: He had lived with us when we were organizing the classes here in Montreal. We used to talk until very late at night with him. When these classes came into discussion, we were already thinking to start something similar in our home. Our father asked him, "Why don't you start Gita classes here? Master Raju never says "no" to father. So he said, "We will start." Then we fixed the date for the following Saturday. Since that time, he used to come every Saturday for one and half hour class. He went through the Gita chapter by chapter and discussed it. The first day I decided to tape it on video. But I was so engrossed in his talk that I forgot to record it. I asked him, "What is this? "He said, "That's it, it was not meant to be recorded."

About his life, Master Raju told us that he was very spiritual from a very young age and was brought up by his grandparents and his father's sister. They were themselves very spiritual people. We met his aunt when we went to India. We have her on video also, which we recorded during our visit. She told us that Master Raju used to talk a lot about God. She is the one who brought him up and took care of him.

V: Somehow, father found Master Raju's birth place, Krishnapuram. Then he found who his father and mother were. Through his village's people, father found many people who were connected to Master Raju's family.

M: It is just too bad that your father is already gone. He would have told me more about him!

V: Yes. We always think of him, and it is because of him that we became so close to Master Raju. We miss that wonderful time when Master Raju was coming here giving Gita's classes.

Now I will tell you how he started the personal development sessions. When I started recuperating from the pinched nerve condition, Master Raju told us that he was going to teach us natural breathing exercises. So we gathered about fifteen people together and had the first class here in our living room in June 1994. It was a very pleasant time. We taped all the classes on video covering the whole sessions. We were so fortunate to learn all those new concepts and those exercises which are so beneficial for our health and the bodies. We were very blessed. When the first group was over, we started organizing the next one. We had five to six groups here. More than 200 people learned the program with Master Raju. Through this program, we got to meet so many nice people who learned to meditate from Master Raju. Finally at the age of eighty, my father also took the class. In that group the age range was eight to eighty years old.

My father has never had a Master in all his life, but at the age of eighty-five, he accepted him as his Master. Father called him "Sukha Brahma!" Master Raju will explain the meaning to you. He never calls him Raju, always "Sukha Brahma." Master Raju was very special to him.

Master Raju had brought changes to our lives. He brought material and spiritual changes. From the spiritual side, we learned a lot from him. He showed me how to bring spirituality to my daily life. I learned acceptance, and it is from him that I learned that true happiness in life comes when we accept situations as they come.

We found it so important to have his kind of teachings that I suggested to Master Raju that it should be open to all, whether they could pay for it or not. Money should not matter, as spiritual knowledge has to be spread to all people. That's why I tried my best to get as many people as possible to come to the classes.

We enjoyed those moments when he was sharing his experiences with us. He would come over straight from work and would stay with us from 5:30 p.m. to 9:30 or 10:00 p.m. He would talk about his family, his work, etc. He is very close to my children, and they are very attached to him. Both children are so special to him, and he also is very special to our family.

Anyone who meets with Master Raju is very blessed and very fortunate. And this is my personal experience. Anytime I think of Master Raju, something particular happens to me. I always felt him, felt his blessings with me. It is very comforting and satisfying for me. Sometimes I wish that something would happen and I think of him and that thing always comes to me; exactly what I wished and just the way I wanted it. I am confident that this is the way he manifests his blessing in my life. Even in difficult times, as well in happiness, I always feel him there for me. So, one is very fortunate to meet him and to listen to his lectures.

B: When Victoria's father was sick, Master Raju was in Chicago. He came all the way exactly one week before his death, and talked to him for a long period of time. Normally when he left, papa used to say his goodbyes standing from afar. But, that day, papa went all the way to the door and said goodbye to Master Raju just as he was leaving. Later, after papa passed away, Master Raju mentioned that to us; that it was a last goodbye from papa. Master Raju said that papa had felt it at that time that day when he left him. So when papa died on December 5, 1996, Master Raju felt something had happened. While he was watching a movie about Shankaracharya, where Shankaracharya's father passed away, he suddenly got the feeling that something had happened to papa too.

We had called Master Raju's wife to pass the news on to him of papa's death. But Master Raju never got the message. Master Raju arrived at our home the night of the day of the funeral ceremony. We asked him, "You got the message?" He replied, "I did not get any message. I was watching a movie and I just felt that something happened, so I took a plane and came." So, this is the way he got the intuition about papa and came to our place. That incident showed us too how much he was connected to papa. You can also see how much he can foresee things that have not happened as yet.

V: Master Raju was so close to papa that he could feel his death.

M: Some people see him as a prophet, what do you think?

B: It's true! Why not! Who is a prophet? We call him a prophet, a Master in English, but a prophet is nothing but a Guru! That's all. He is the one who can foresee what to preach.

I remember that one day he shared with us this anecdote. He said that when he was a child and wanted something and he could get it, he would be overjoyed. It so happens that at one time, he wanted a bicycle, and in those days not all parents could afford to give that to their children. So whenever Master Raju could help his friends with something, they would let him borrow one wheel of the bicycle with which to play. Whenever that happened it was like he got something he did not expect to get in life. He said that he used to be so overjoyed, so happy! One could feel his joy and happiness as he talked about it, it's like he was still enjoying it all over again.

M: (Laughs). That shows that you can be happy with very little things. It is the enjoyment that you get, which is more important than the thing itself. It is the ability to be happy. He did not need the whole bicycle to be happy. Just a wheel was enough for him to enjoy, be fulfilled, and be thankful.

V: He is always happy. I have never seen Master Raju looking sad. He never showed his troubles or difficulties on his face. He is happy all the time, and spreads happiness to all the people around him.

B: For him, everybody is the same. He is the person of the future! Listen to him and you will know more about him and about yourself.

V: Master Raju told us one day, "I am already living in the Satya Yuga." He never tells lies.

B: Satya Yuga does not mean just truth. It means that people will live in a straightforward way. People will love each other. It is being in a state of bliss. It is a kingdom where people will walk freely, with no animosity between them. People will live together as a family, feeling love for each other. Master Raju is already living in that Yuga.

V: Once, Ted asked Master Raju's age. He replied, "For me, no birth, and no death." Master Raju can read our minds. It's happened to me so many times. After father's death, I was thinking of him all the time. I don't know how Master Raju found out. We were on retreat and doing some exercises, writing about our loved ones. Everyone was writing about their husbands, children, etc., when came my turn. He already knew that I wrote about papa before I shared it with everybody. He is a very special man. He is a superman for me.

M: Thank you very much to both of you for sharing this with me and the world. God bless you and your family.

References

· · · · · · · · · · · · · · · · ·

Miller, Ronald S., and Editors of New Age Journal. 1992. *As Above So Below: Paths to Spiritual Renewal in Daily Life*. Los Angeles: Jeremy P. Tarcher, Inc.

The Holy Bible: The New King James Version. 1982. Nashville: Thomas Nelson.

Yogananda, Paramahamsa. 1946. *The Autobiography of a Yogi*. Los Angeles: Self-Realization Fellowship.

Prabhupada, A.C Bhaktivedanta Swami. 1968. *Bhagavad Gita As It Is*. London: Macmillan Publishers.

Judith, Anodea. 1999. *Wheels of Life: A User's Guide to the Chakra System*. Woodbury: Llewelyn Publications.

Brennan, Barbara. 1988. *Hands of Light: A Guide to Healing Through the Human Energy Field*. New York: Bantam.

Myss, Carolyn. 1996. *Anatomy of the Spirit: The Seven Stages of Power and Healing*. New York: Three Rivers Press.

Horsley, Mary. 2006. *Chakra Workout: Balancing the Chakras with Yoga*. London: Gaia Books.

Pfender, April. 2018. *Chakra Balance: The Beginner's Guide to Healing Body and Mind*. Althea Press.

Wills, Pauline. 2002. *Chakra Workbook: Rebalance Your Body's Vital Energies*. Boston: Journey Editions.

Fox, Emmet. 1996. *The Sermon on the Mount: The Key to Success in Life*. New York: Harper & Row.

Maclaine, Shirley. 1989. *Going Within: A Guide for Inner Transformation*. New York: Bantam.

Online Resources

· · · · · · · · · · · · · · · · ·

To listen to the author speaking on Yoga or Chakras, go to You tube and search for *Is Yoga for Everyone?* by Datta Yogi Raja.

To access guided meditation, search for *Be Still and Know* by Datta Yogi Raja.

You could also purchase copies of the same through the secure website of www.aksharayoga.com

To get more information on the activities of Raju Ramanathan go to www.rajuramanathan.com or www.gloryofyoga.com

To purchase copies of Music concerts entitled *Music for Meditation and Healing* by Dr. Ganapathy Sacchidananda, go to www.yogasangeeta.org and look for *Chakras and Music.*

CPSIA information can be obtained
at www.ICGtesting.com
Printed in the USA
LVHW110208280819
629212LV00001B/18/P

9 781643 145952